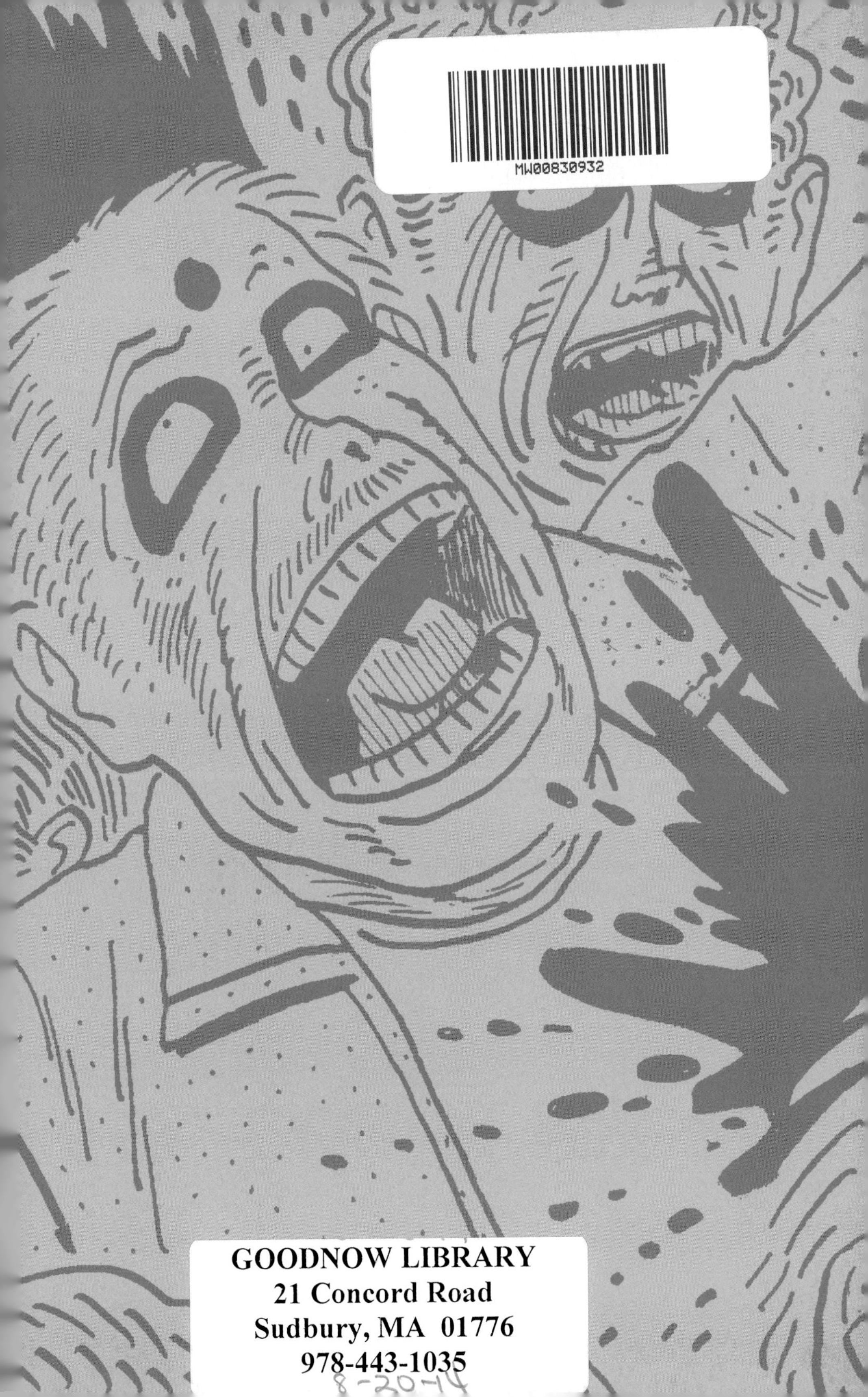

FATIMA™

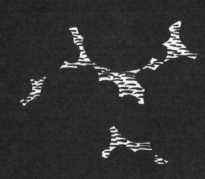

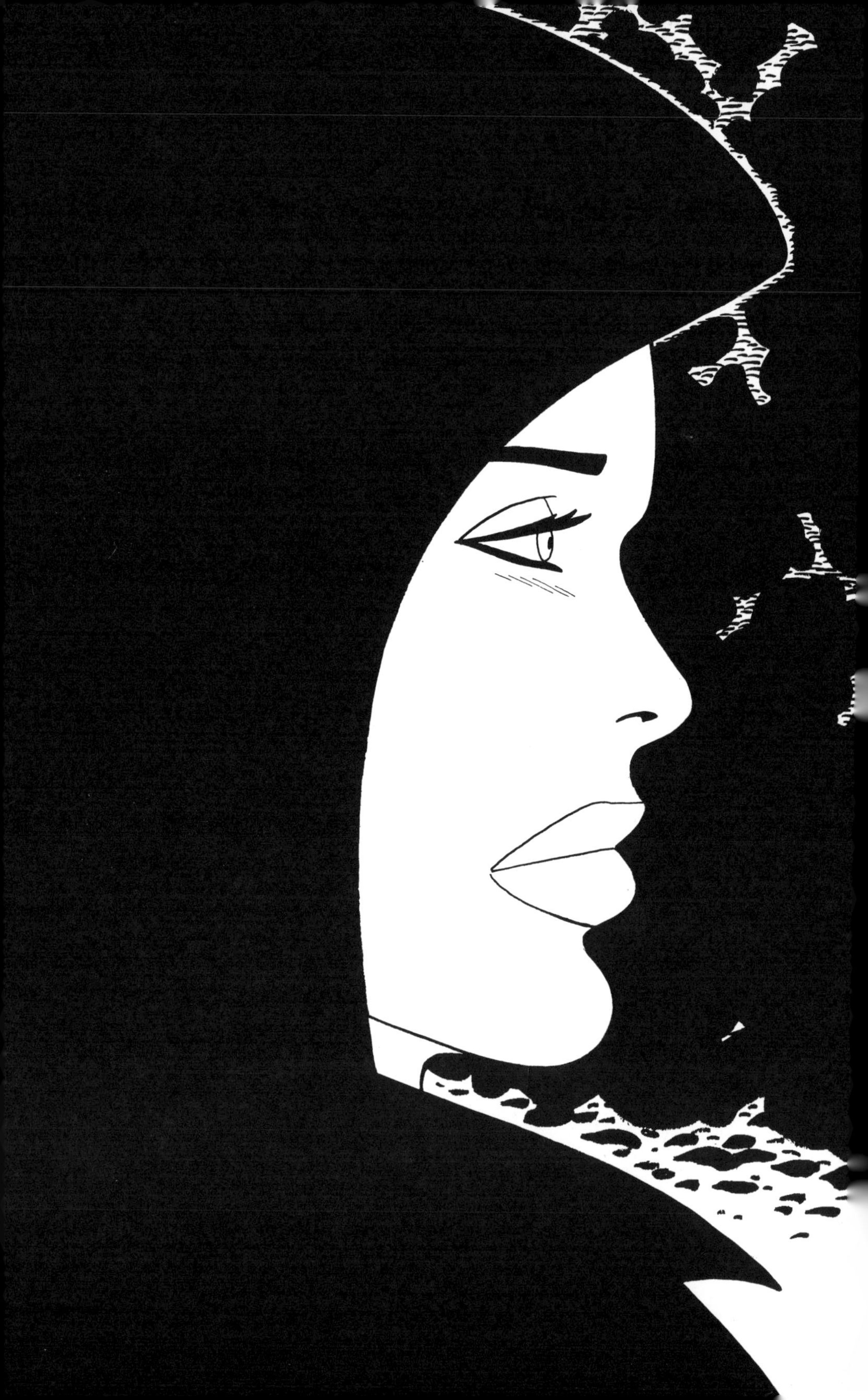

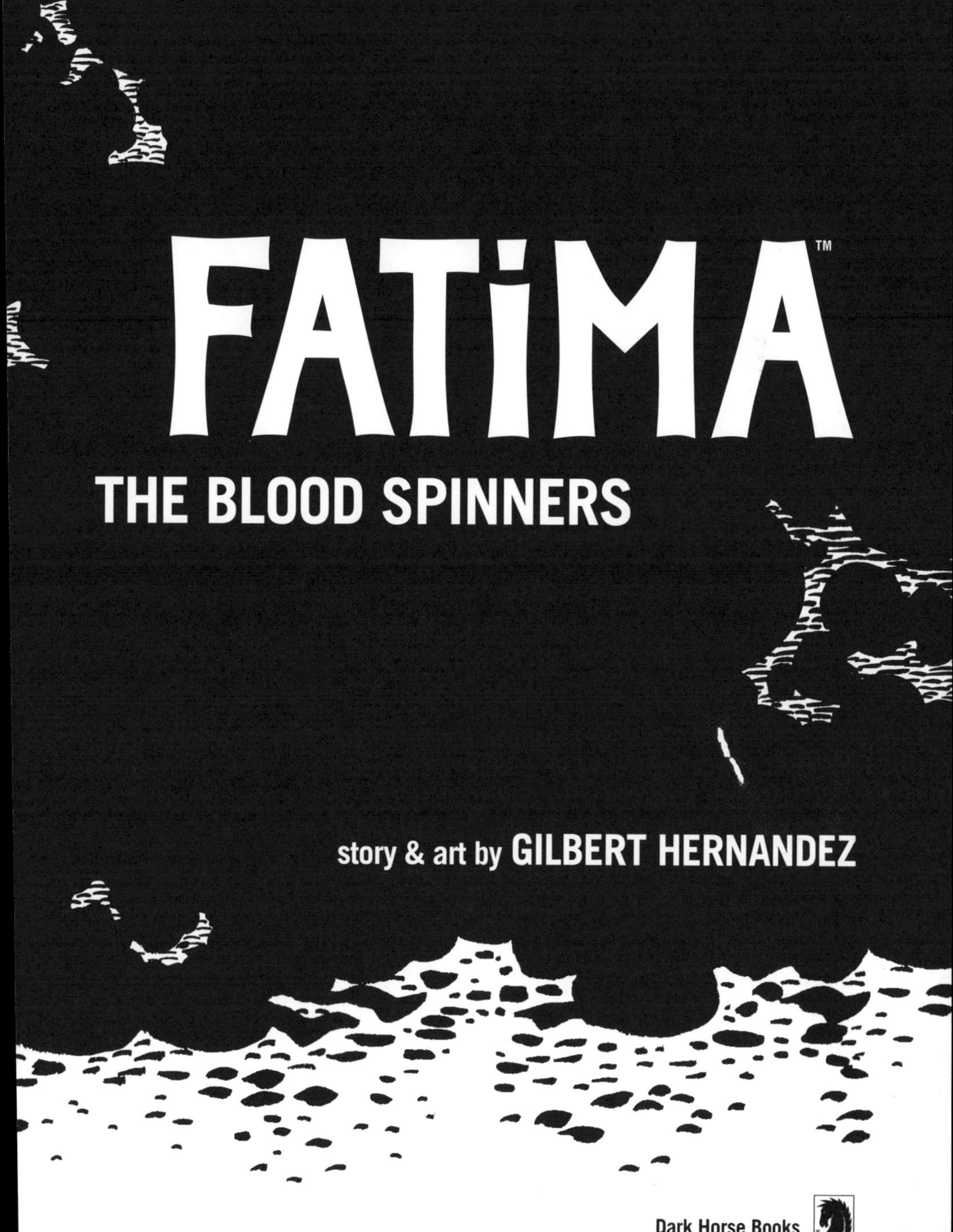

FATIMA™

THE BLOOD SPINNERS

story & art by GILBERT HERNANDEZ

Dark Horse Books

editor DIANA SCHUTZ

associate editor BRENDAN WRIGHT

assistant editor AARON WALKER

book design AMY ARENDTS

digital production RYAN JORGENSON

publisher MIKE RICHARDSON

FATIMA: THE BLOOD SPINNERS

© 2012, 2014 Gilbert Hernandez. All rights reserved. Fatima™ and all prominently featured characters are trademarks of Gilbert Hernandez. Dark Horse Books® and the Dark Horse logo are registered trademarks of Dark Horse Comics, Inc. All rights reserved. No portion of this publication may be reproduced or transmitted, in any form or by any means, without the express written permission of Dark Horse Comics, Inc. Names, characters, places, and incidents featured in this publication either are the product of the author's imagination or are used fictitiously. Any resemblance to actual persons (living or dead), events, institutions, or locales, without satiric intent, is coincidental.

This book collects issues one through four of the Dark Horse comic book series *Fatima: The Blood Spinners*, originally published June through September 2012.

Published by Dark Horse Books
A division of Dark Horse Comics, Inc.
10956 SE Main Street
Milwaukie, Oregon 97222

DarkHorse.com

First edition: April 2014
ISBN 978-1-61655-340-1

10 9 8 7 6 5 4 3 2 1
Printed in China

Mike Richardson-President and Publisher · Neil Hankerson-Executive Vice President · Tom Weddle-Chief Financial Officer · Randy Stradley-Vice President of Publishing · Michael Martens-Vice President of Book Trade Sales · Anita Nelson-Vice President of Business Affairs · Scott Allie-Editor in Chief · Matt Parkinson-Vice President of Marketing · David Scroggy-Vice President of Product Development · Dale LaFountain-Vice President of Information Technology · Darlene Vogel-Senior Director of Print, Design, and Production · Ken Lizzi-General Counsel · Davey Estrada-Editorial Director · Chris Warner-Senior Books Editor · Diana Schutz-Executive Editor · Cary Grazzini-Director of Print and Development · Lia Ribacchi Art Director · Cara Niece-Director of Scheduling · Tim Wiesch-Director of International Licensing · Mark Bernardi-Director of Digital Publishing

FATIMA

BETO 2011

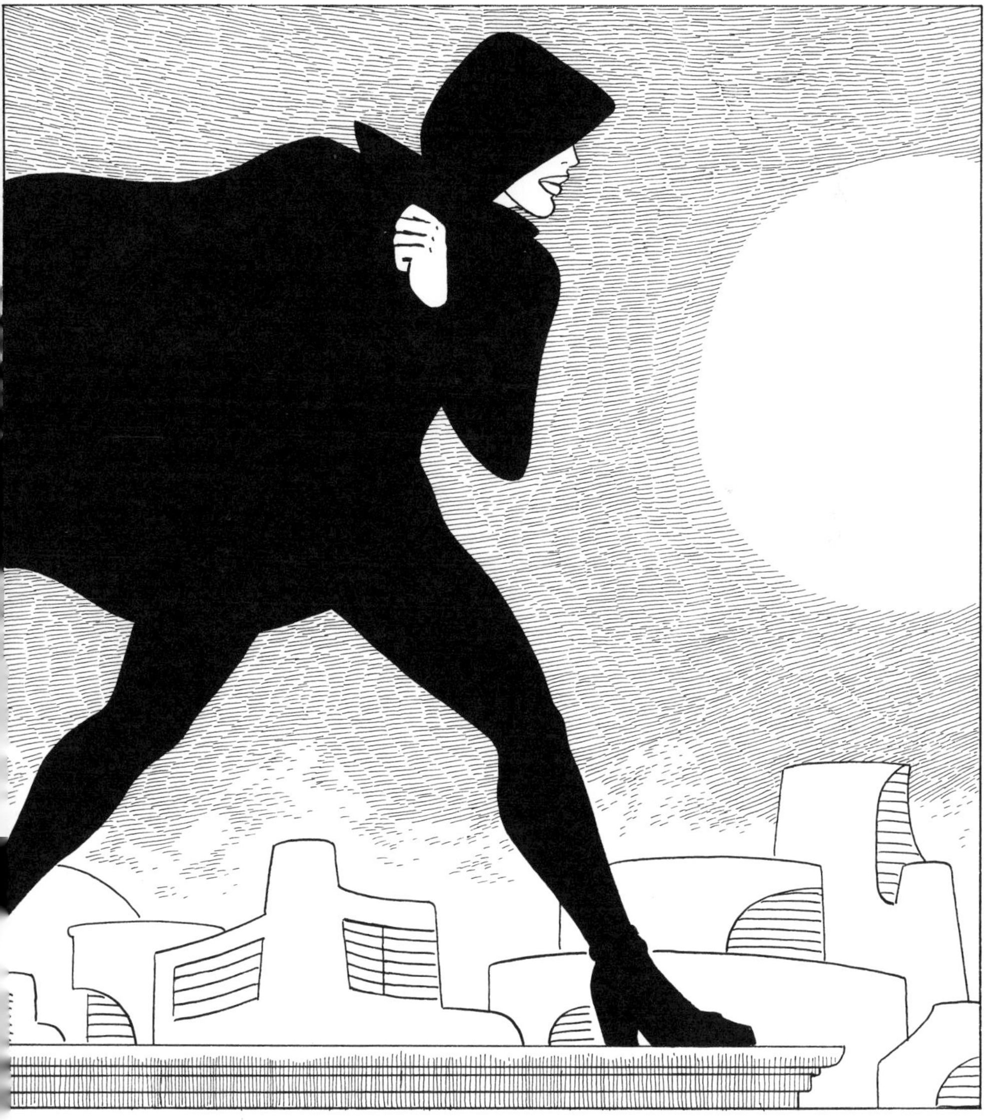

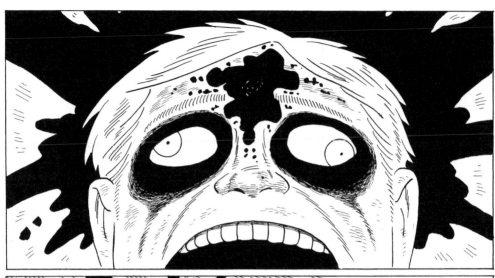

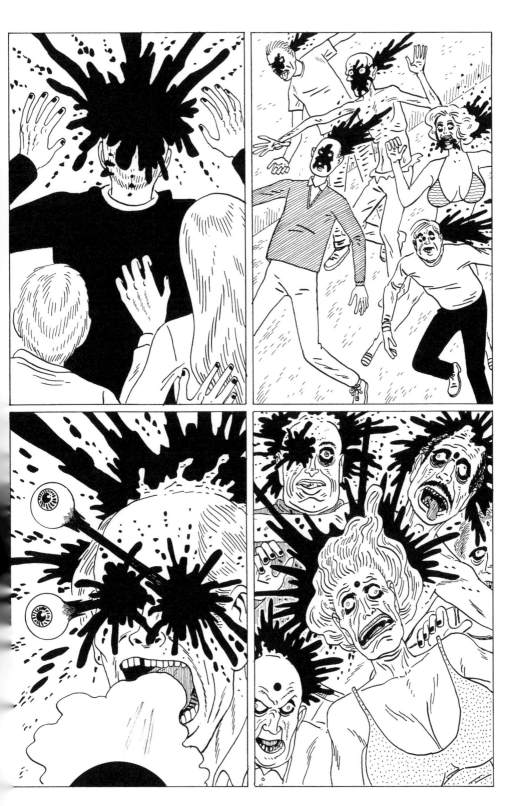

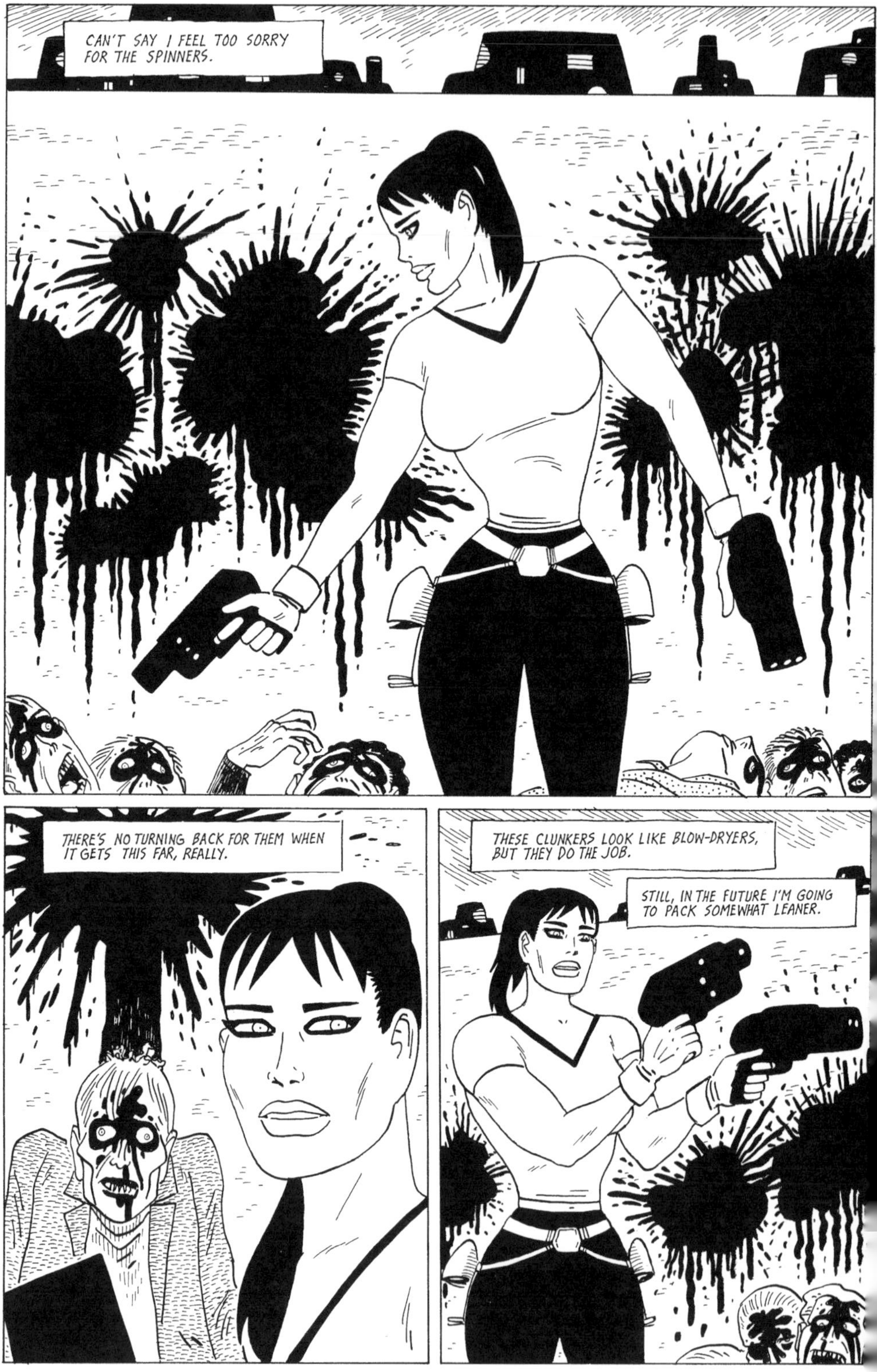
CAN'T SAY I FEEL TOO SORRY FOR THE SPINNERS.
THERE'S NO TURNING BACK FOR THEM WHEN IT GETS THIS FAR, REALLY.
THESE CLUNKERS LOOK LIKE BLOW-DRYERS, BUT THEY DO THE JOB.
STILL, IN THE FUTURE I'M GOING TO PACK SOMEWHAT LEANER.

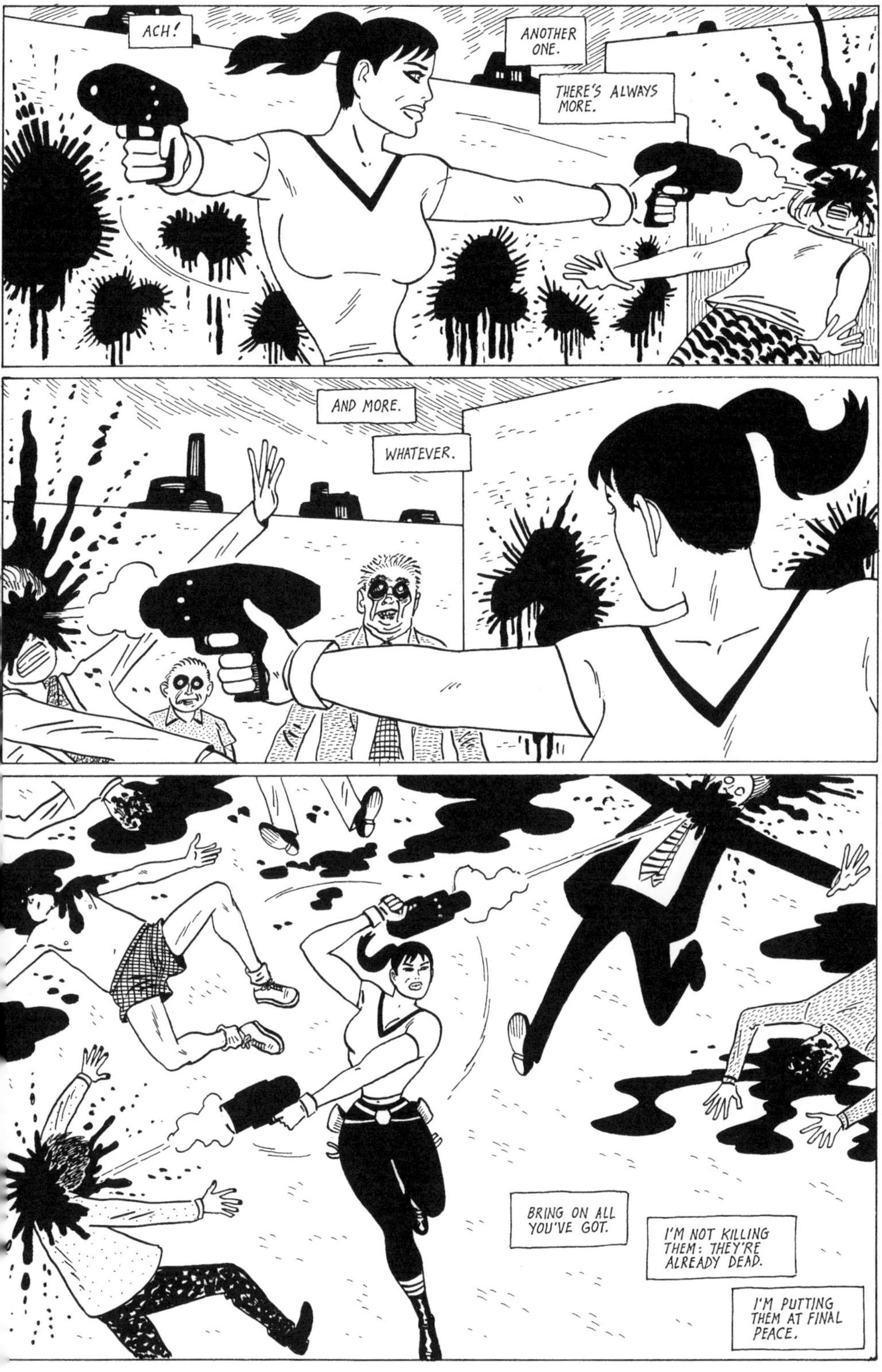
ACH!
ANOTHER ONE.
THERE'S ALWAYS MORE.
AND MORE.
WHATEVER.
BRING ON ALL YOU'VE GOT.
I'M NOT KILLING THEM: THEY'RE ALREADY DEAD.
I'M PUTTING THEM AT FINAL PEACE.

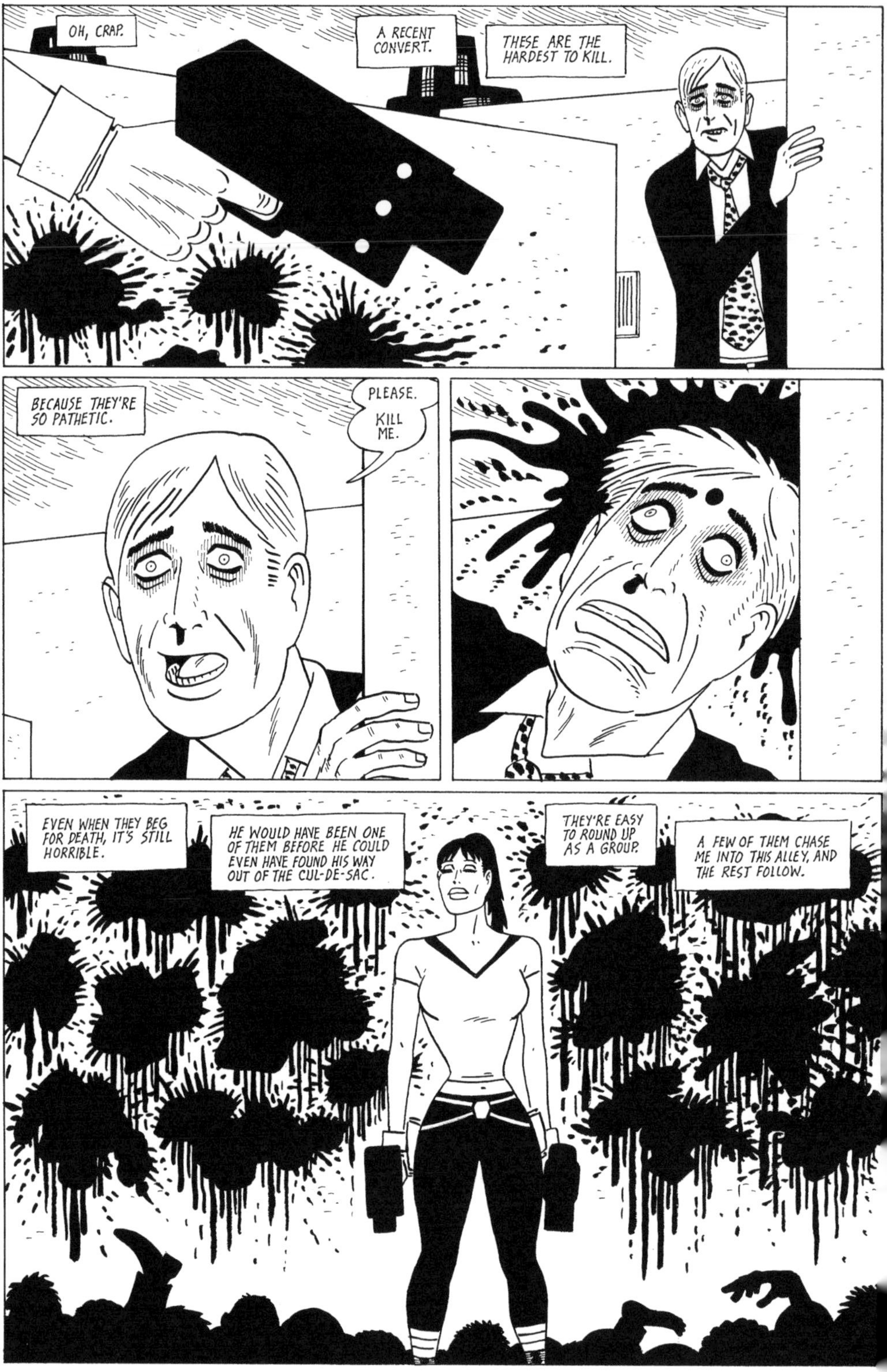
OH, CRAP.
A RECENT CONVERT.
THESE ARE THE HARDEST TO KILL.
BECAUSE THEY'RE SO PATHETIC.
PLEASE. KILL ME.
EVEN WHEN THEY BEG FOR DEATH, IT'S STILL HORRIBLE.
HE WOULD HAVE BEEN ONE OF THEM BEFORE HE COULD EVEN HAVE FOUND HIS WAY OUT OF THE CUL-DE-SAC.
THEY'RE EASY TO ROUND UP AS A GROUP.
A FEW OF THEM CHASE ME INTO THIS ALLEY, AND THE REST FOLLOW.

SPIN.

PRETTY LIGHTWEIGHT NAME FOR THE WORST, MOST ADDICTIVE DRUG EVER CONCEIVED.

IT'S PUBLIC KNOWLEDGE THAT WITH ONLY ONE DOSE, SPIN WILL GIVE YOU WHAT YOU'RE LOOKING FOR, BUT IN A MATTER OF HOURS IT'S ZOMBIETIME.

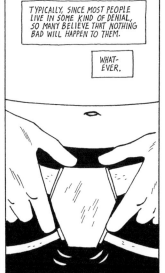

TYPICALLY, SINCE MOST PEOPLE LIVE IN SOME KIND OF DENIAL, SO MANY BELIEVE THAT NOTHING BAD WILL HAPPEN TO THEM.

WHAT-EVER.

I GUESS THE RUMOR OF A CURE IS WHAT GIVES THEM THE GO-AHEAD, THAT LITTLE PLACEBO OF HOPE.

WHATEVER.

THEY'RE GOING TO DO WHAT THEY'RE GOING TO DO, AND I'M GOING TO DO MY JOB.

The BLOOD SPINNERS

BETO
2011

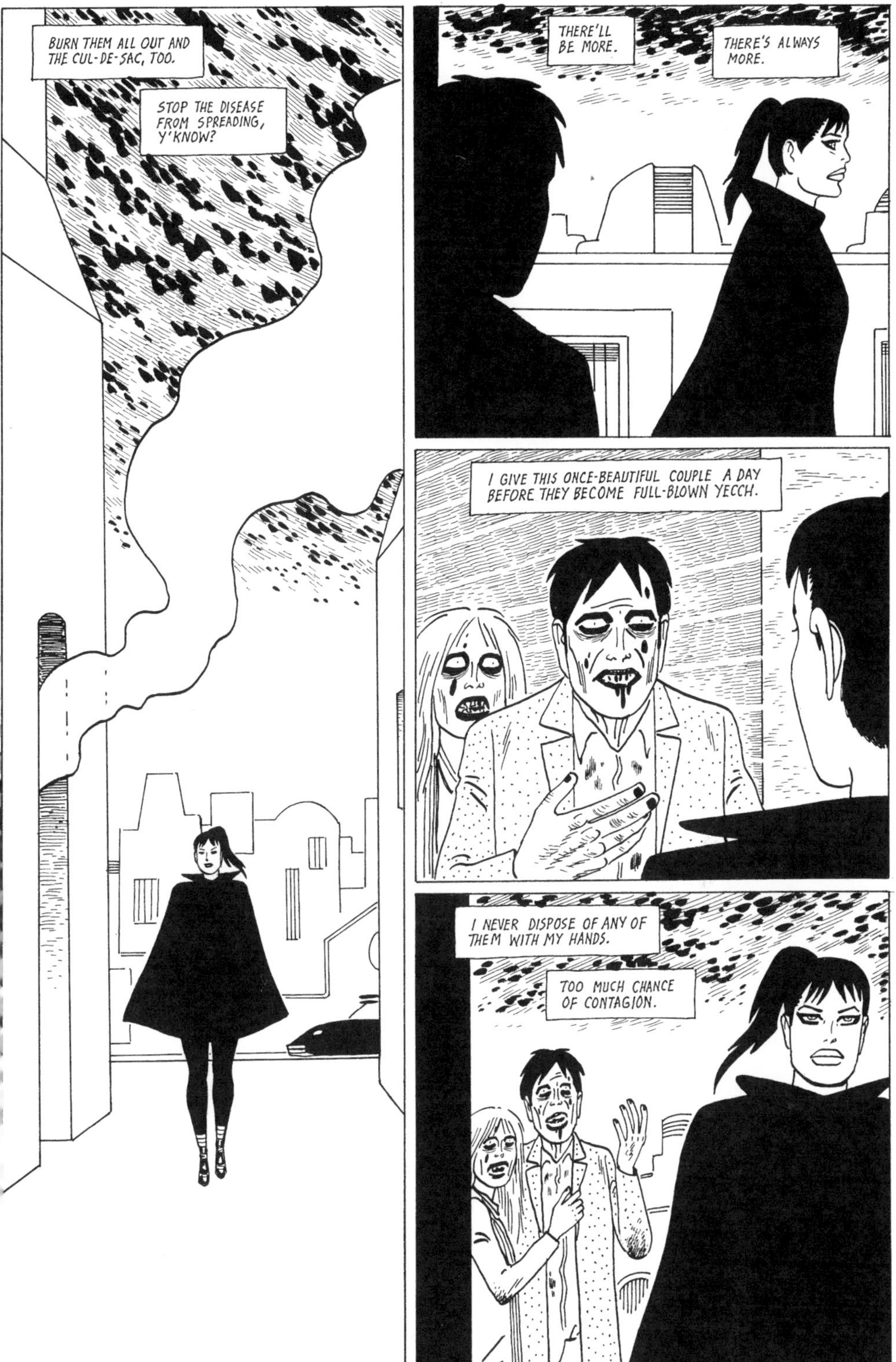
BURN THEM ALL OUT AND THE CUL-DE-SAC, TOO.
STOP THE DISEASE FROM SPREADING, Y'KNOW?
THERE'LL BE MORE.
THERE'S ALWAYS MORE.
I GIVE THIS ONCE-BEAUTIFUL COUPLE A DAY BEFORE THEY BECOME FULL-BLOWN YECCH.
I NEVER DISPOSE OF ANY OF THEM WITH MY HANDS.
TOO MUCH CHANCE OF CONTAGION.

THE NEIGHBORHOOD WELCOMING COMMITTEE.

IS IT A NEW CONVERT?

A FULL-BLOWN?

OR JUST A SAD, BEAT-TO-HELL-LOOKING HOMELESS PERSON THAT THIS CROWD'S NOT TAKING ANY CHANCES WITH?

TOO LATE TO MAKE ANY SUCH DISTINCTIONS NOW.

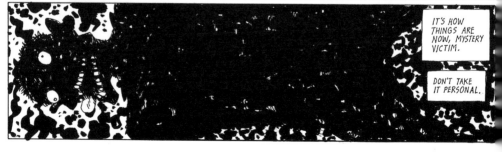

IT'S HOW THINGS ARE NOW, MYSTERY VICTIM.

DON'T TAKE IT PERSONAL.

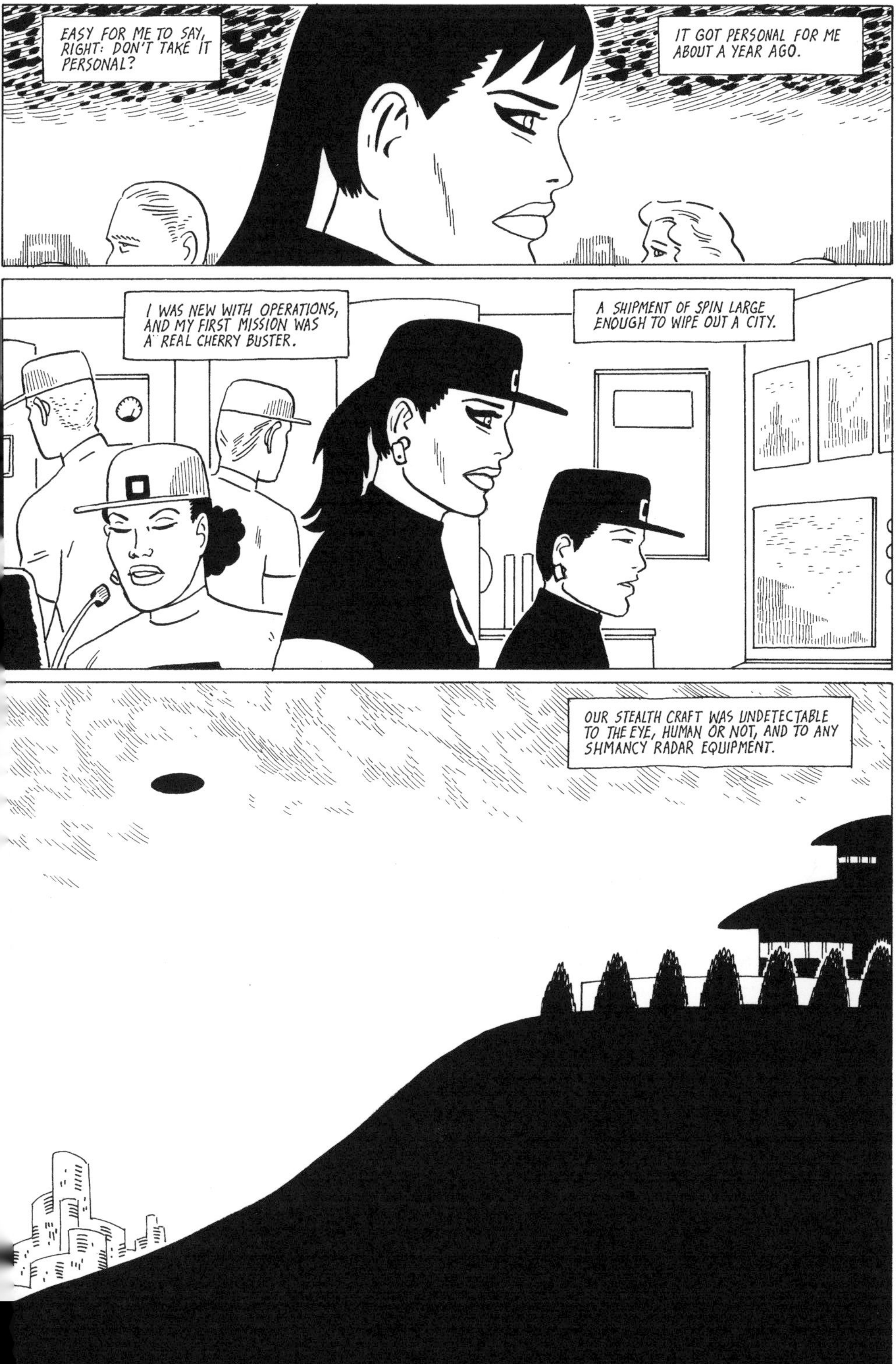
EASY FOR ME TO SAY, RIGHT: DON'T TAKE IT PERSONAL?
IT GOT PERSONAL FOR ME ABOUT A YEAR AGO.
I WAS NEW WITH OPERATIONS, AND MY FIRST MISSION WAS A REAL CHERRY BUSTER.
A SHIPMENT OF SPIN LARGE ENOUGH TO WIPE OUT A CITY.
OUR STEALTH CRAFT WAS UNDETECTABLE TO THE EYE, HUMAN OR NOT, AND TO ANY SHMANCY RADAR EQUIPMENT.

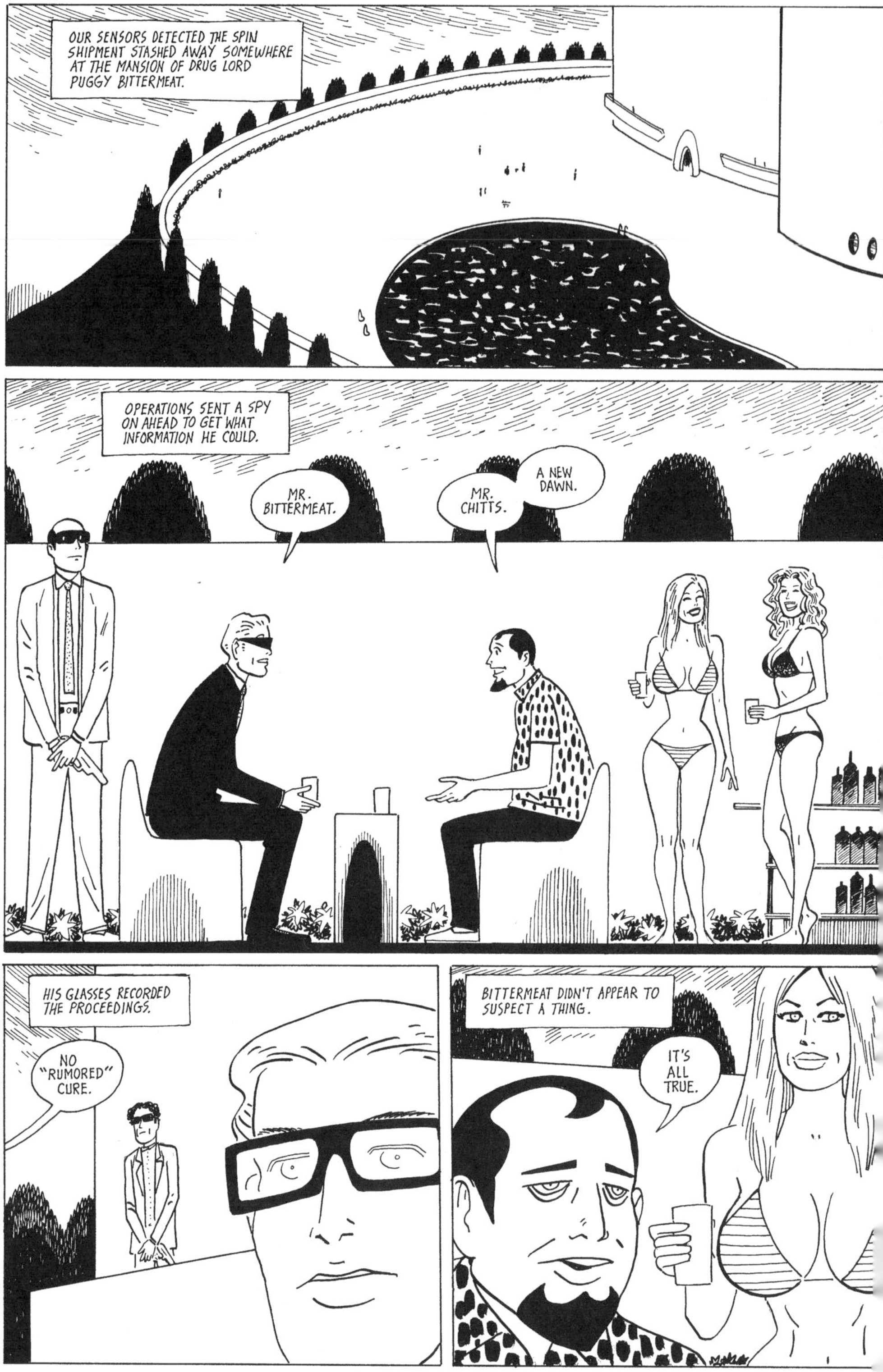
OUR SENSORS DETECTED THE SPIN SHIPMENT STASHED AWAY SOMEWHERE AT THE MANSION OF DRUG LORD PUGGY BITTERMEAT.
OPERATIONS SENT A SPY ON AHEAD TO GET WHAT INFORMATION HE COULD.
MR. BITTERMEAT.
MR. CHITTS.
A NEW DAWN.
HIS GLASSES RECORDED THE PROCEEDINGS.
NO "RUMORED" CURE.
BITTERMEAT DIDN'T APPEAR TO SUSPECT A THING.
IT'S ALL TRUE.

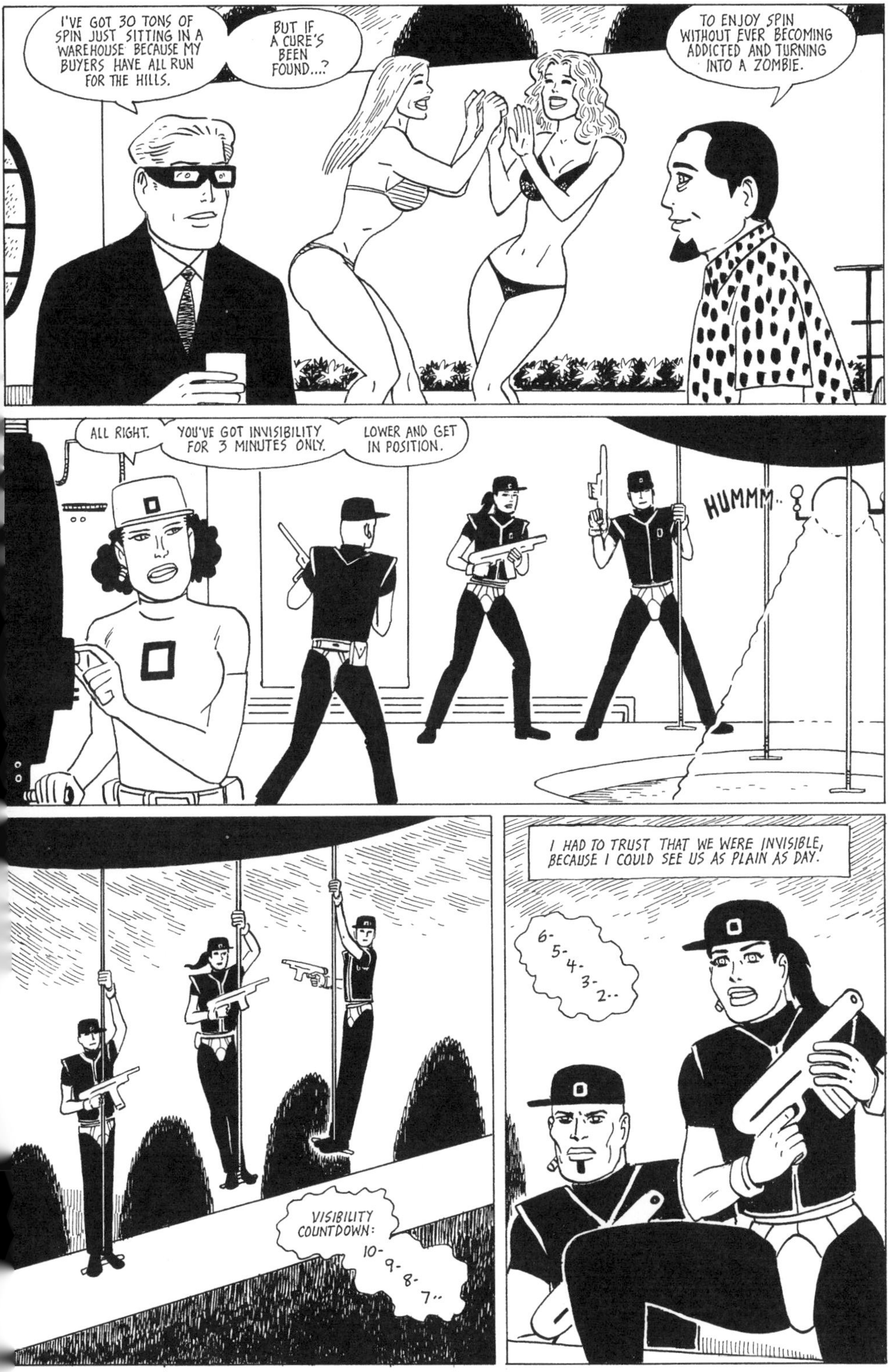
I'VE GOT 30 TONS OF SPIN JUST SITTING IN A WAREHOUSE BECAUSE MY BUYERS HAVE ALL RUN FOR THE HILLS.
BUT IF A CURE'S BEEN FOUND...?
TO ENJOY SPIN WITHOUT EVER BECOMING ADDICTED AND TURNING INTO A ZOMBIE.
ALL RIGHT.
YOU'VE GOT INVISIBILITY FOR 3 MINUTES ONLY.
LOWER AND GET IN POSITION.
HUMMM..
VISIBILITY COUNTDOWN:
10- 9- 8- 7..
I HAD TO TRUST THAT WE WERE INVISIBLE, BECAUSE I COULD SEE US AS PLAIN AS DAY.
6- 5- 4- 3- 2-.

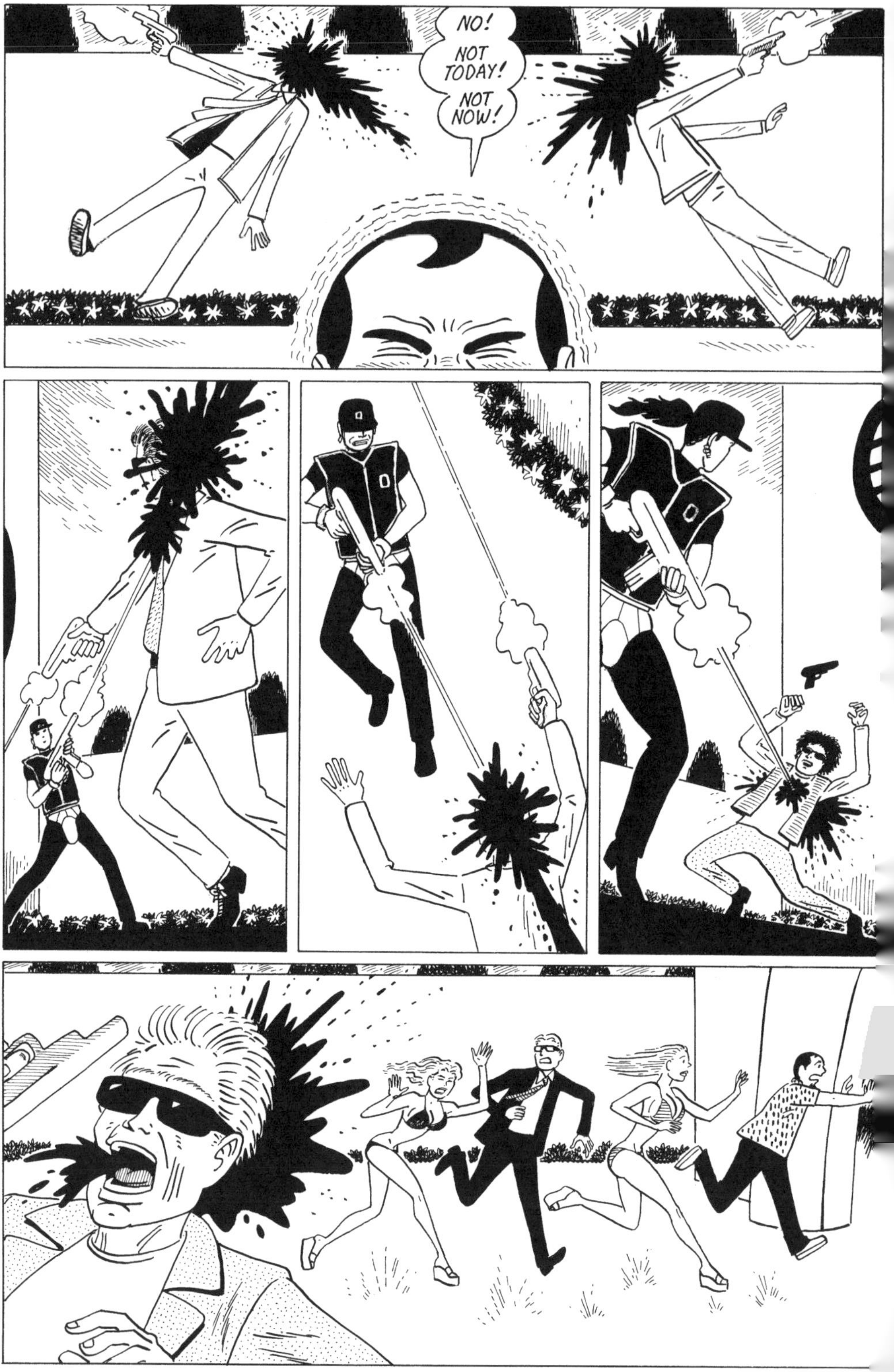
NO!
NOT TODAY!
NOT NOW!

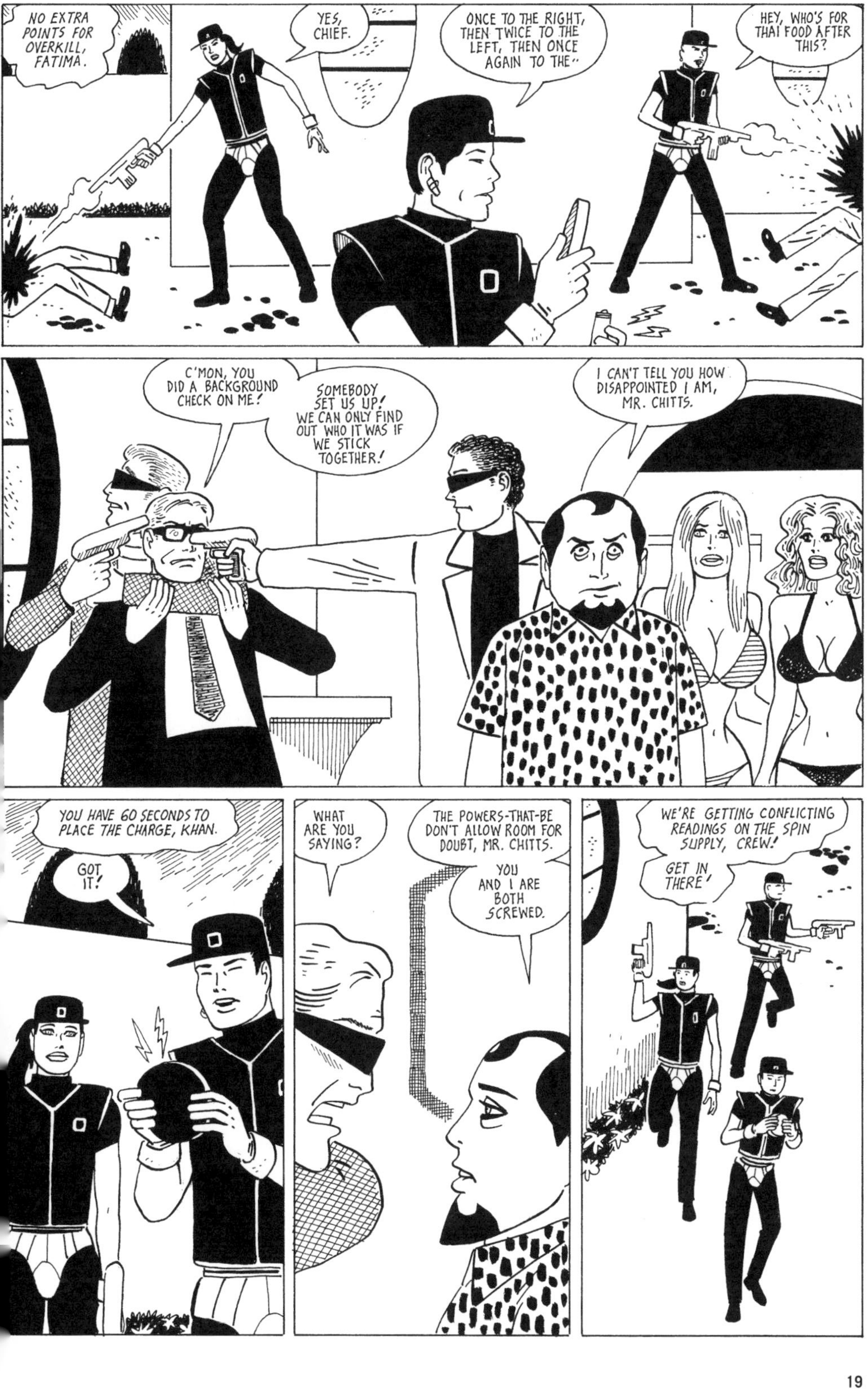
NO EXTRA POINTS FOR OVERKILL, FATIMA.
YES, CHIEF.
ONCE TO THE RIGHT, THEN TWICE TO THE LEFT, THEN ONCE AGAIN TO THE--
HEY, WHO'S FOR THAI FOOD AFTER THIS?
C'MON, YOU DID A BACKGROUND CHECK ON ME!
SOMEBODY SET US UP! WE CAN ONLY FIND OUT WHO IT WAS IF WE STICK TOGETHER!
I CAN'T TELL YOU HOW DISAPPOINTED I AM, MR. CHITTS.
YOU HAVE 60 SECONDS TO PLACE THE CHARGE, KHAN.
GOT IT!
WHAT ARE YOU SAYING?
THE POWERS-THAT-BE DON'T ALLOW ROOM FOR DOUBT, MR. CHITTS.
YOU AND I ARE BOTH SCREWED.
WE'RE GETTING CONFLICTING READINGS ON THE SPIN SUPPLY, CREW!
GET IN THERE!

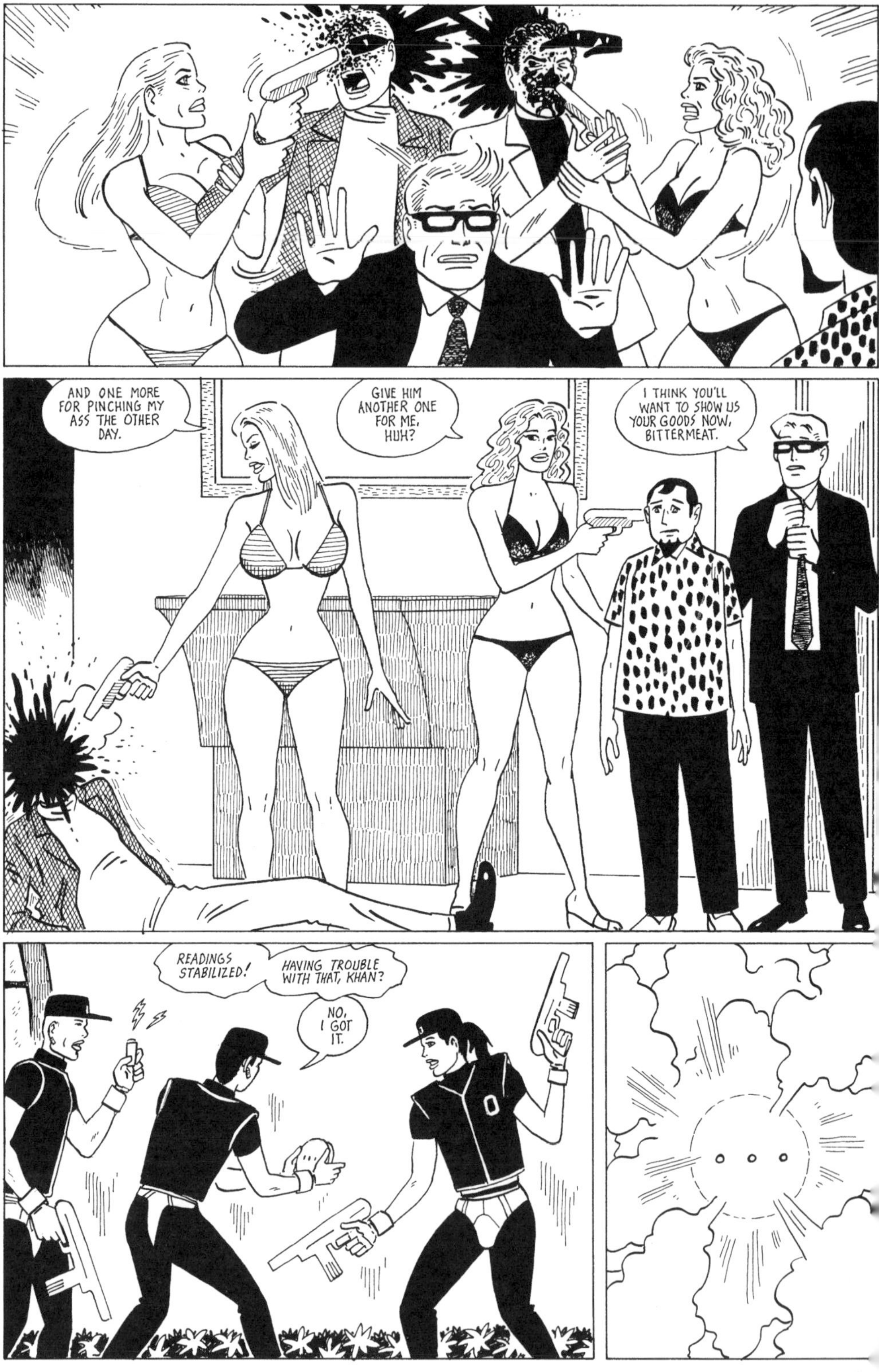

AND ONE MORE FOR PINCHING MY ASS THE OTHER DAY.
GIVE HIM ANOTHER ONE FOR ME, HUH?
I THINK YOU'LL WANT TO SHOW US YOUR GOODS NOW, BITTERMEAT.
READINGS STABILIZED!
HAVING TROUBLE WITH THAT, KHAN?
NO, I GOT IT.

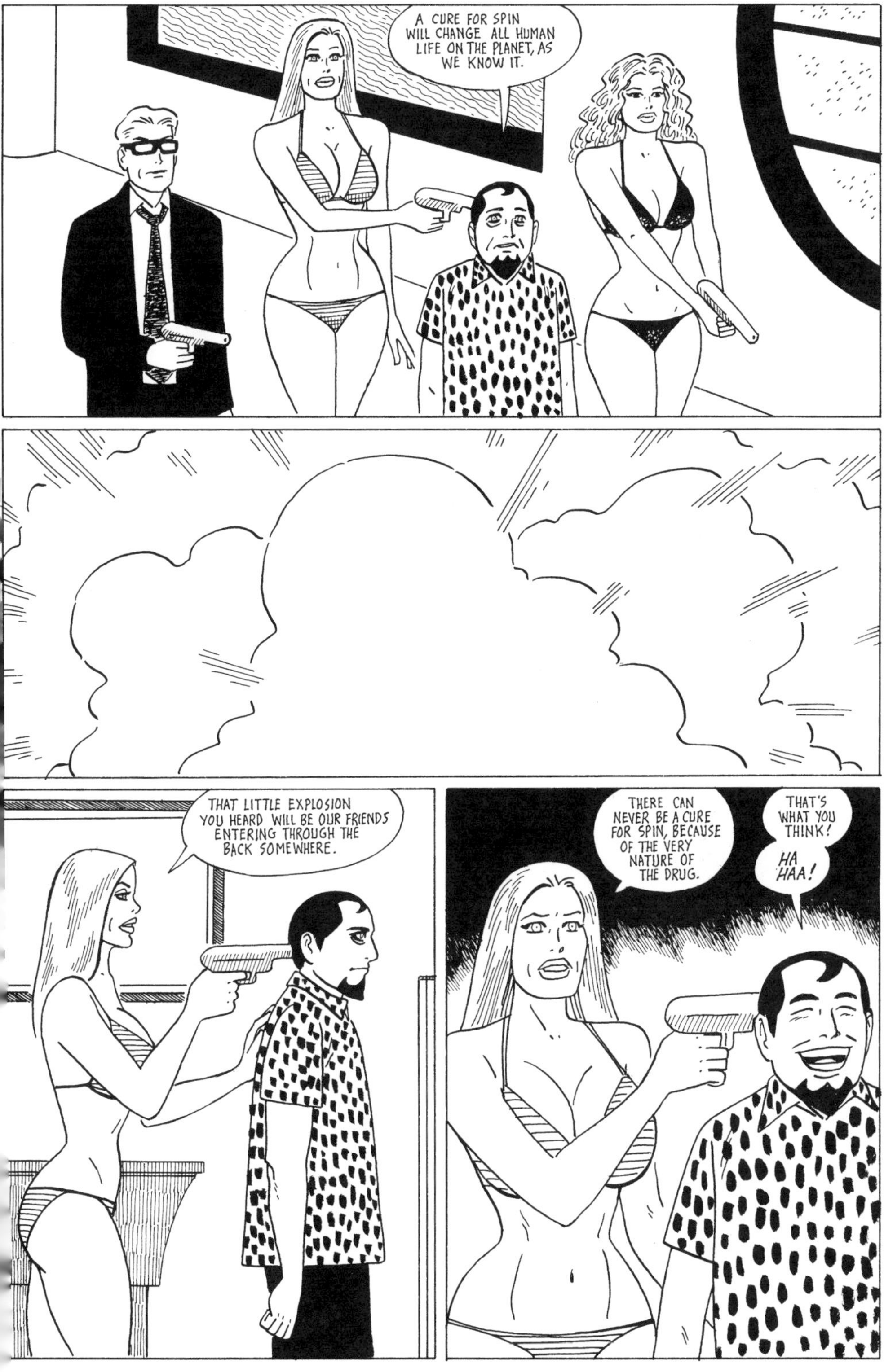
A CURE FOR SPIN WILL CHANGE ALL HUMAN LIFE ON THE PLANET, AS WE KNOW IT.
THAT LITTLE EXPLOSION YOU HEARD WILL BE OUR FRIENDS ENTERING THROUGH THE BACK SOMEWHERE.
THERE CAN NEVER BE A CURE FOR SPIN, BECAUSE OF THE VERY NATURE OF THE DRUG.
THAT'S WHAT YOU THINK!
HA HAA!

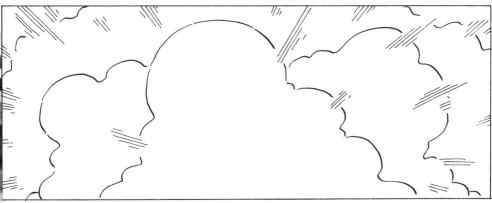

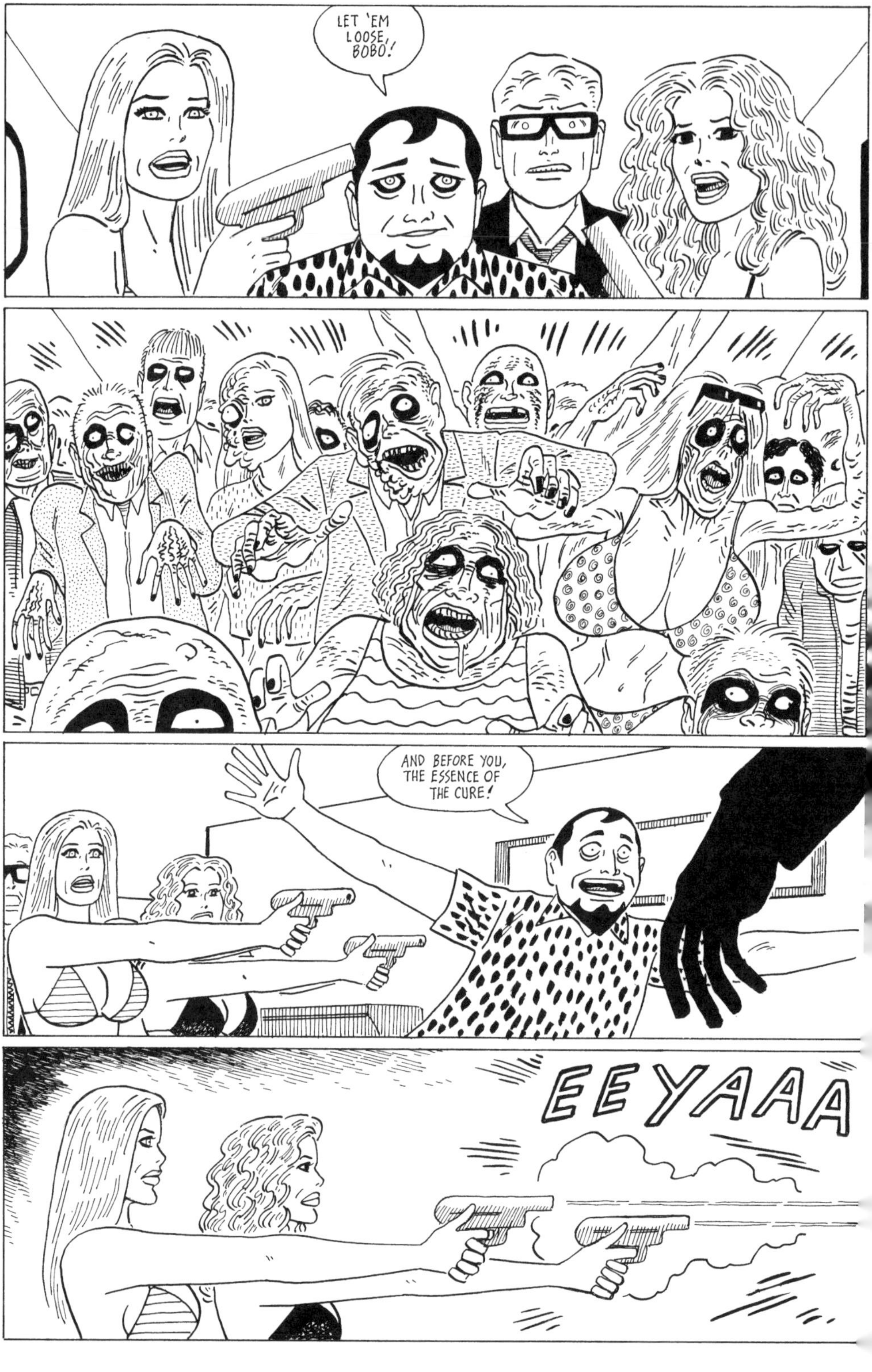
LET 'EM LOOSE, BOBO!
AND BEFORE YOU, THE ESSENCE OF THE CURE!
EEYAAA

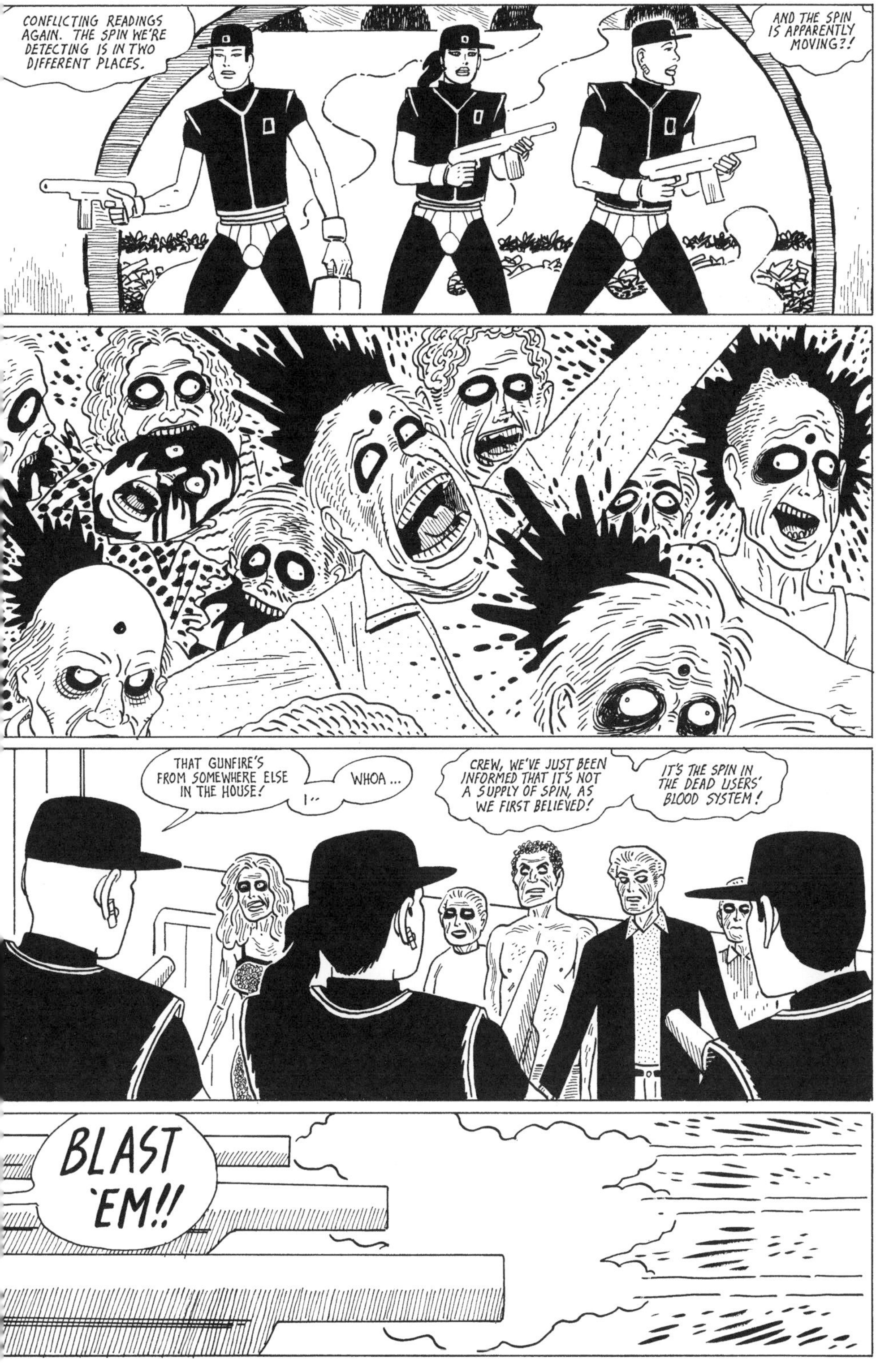
CONFLICTING READINGS AGAIN. THE SPIN WE'RE DETECTING IS IN TWO DIFFERENT PLACES.
AND THE SPIN IS APPARENTLY MOVING?!
THAT GUNFIRE'S FROM SOMEWHERE ELSE IN THE HOUSE!
WHOA...
CREW, WE'VE JUST BEEN INFORMED THAT IT'S NOT A SUPPLY OF SPIN, AS WE FIRST BELIEVED!
IT'S THE SPIN IN THE DEAD USERS' BLOOD SYSTEM!
BLAST 'EM!!

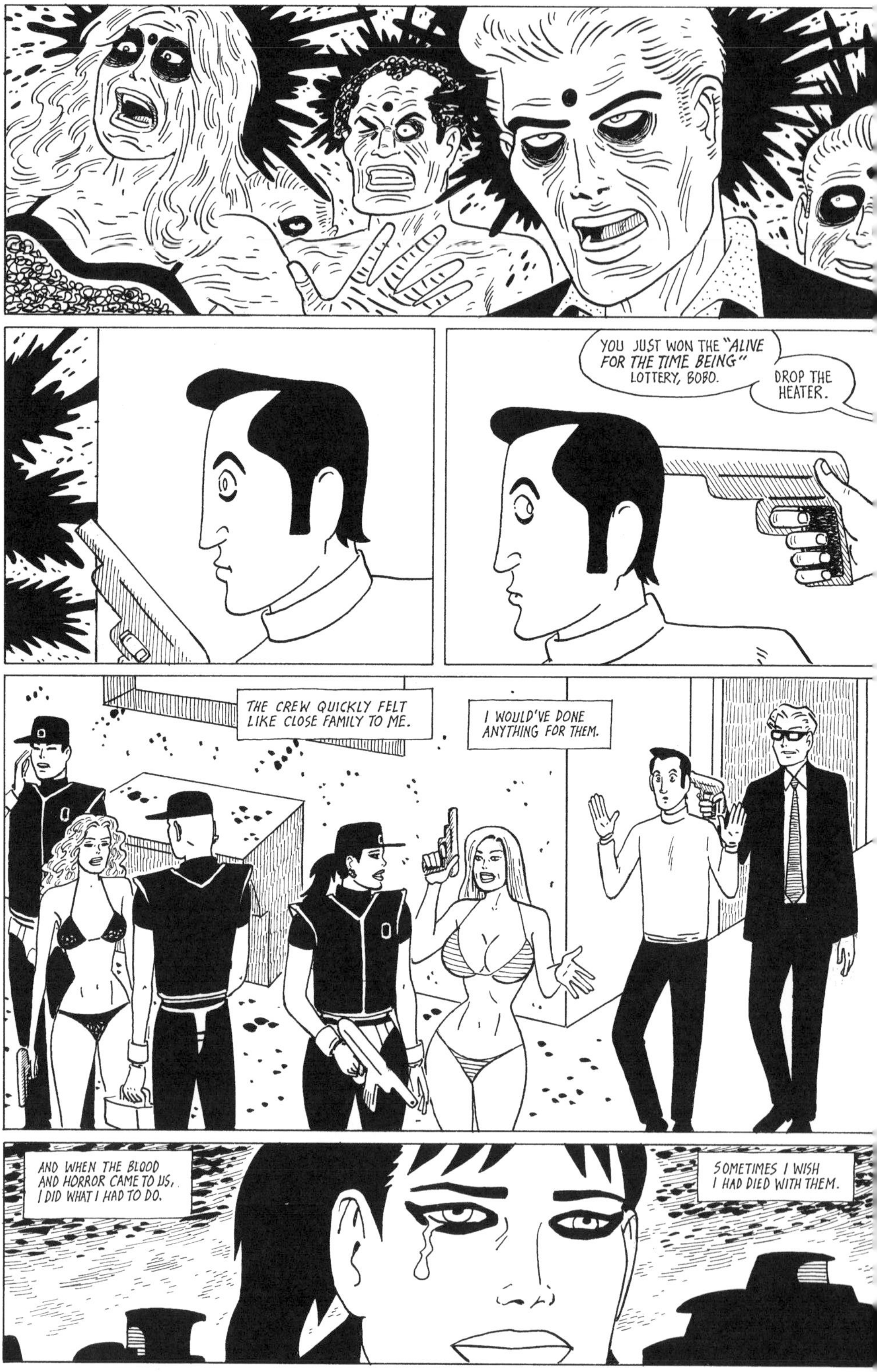
YOU JUST WON THE "ALIVE FOR THE TIME BEING" LOTTERY, BOBO.
DROP THE HEATER.
THE CREW QUICKLY FELT LIKE CLOSE FAMILY TO ME.
I WOULD'VE DONE ANYTHING FOR THEM.
AND WHEN THE BLOOD AND HORROR CAME TO US, I DID WHAT I HAD TO DO.
SOMETIMES I WISH I HAD DIED WITH THEM.

Fatima: the BLOOD SPINNERS 2

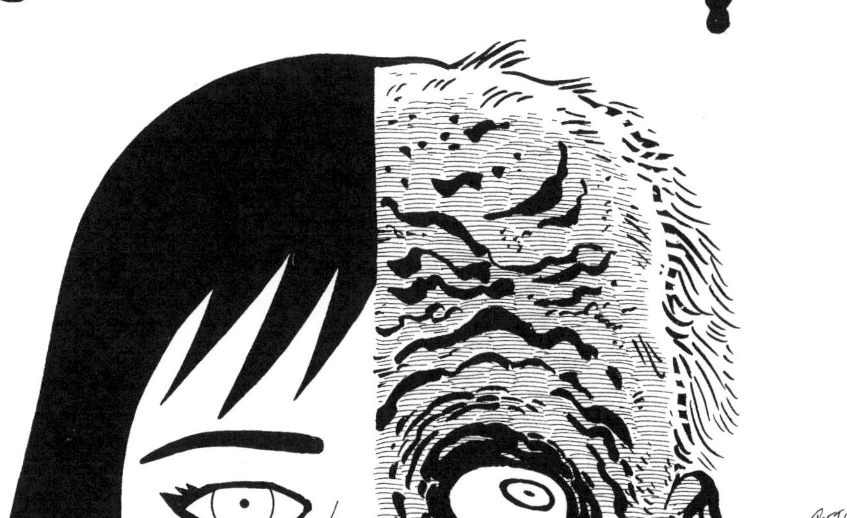
BETO-
2011

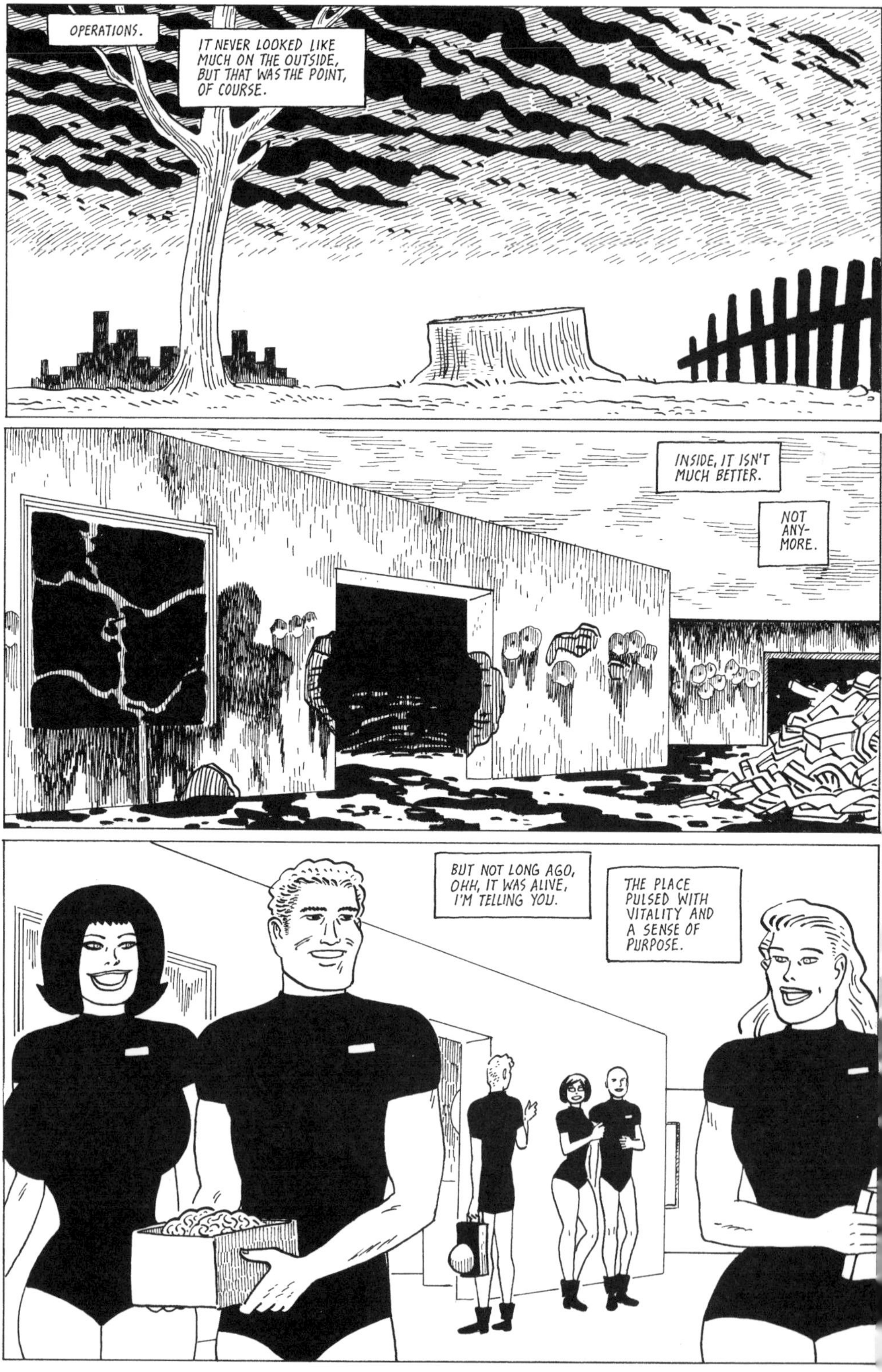
OPERATIONS.
IT NEVER LOOKED LIKE MUCH ON THE OUTSIDE, BUT THAT WAS THE POINT, OF COURSE.
INSIDE, IT ISN'T MUCH BETTER.
NOT ANY-MORE.
BUT NOT LONG AGO, OHH, IT WAS ALIVE, I'M TELLING YOU.
THE PLACE PULSED WITH VITALITY AND A SENSE OF PURPOSE.

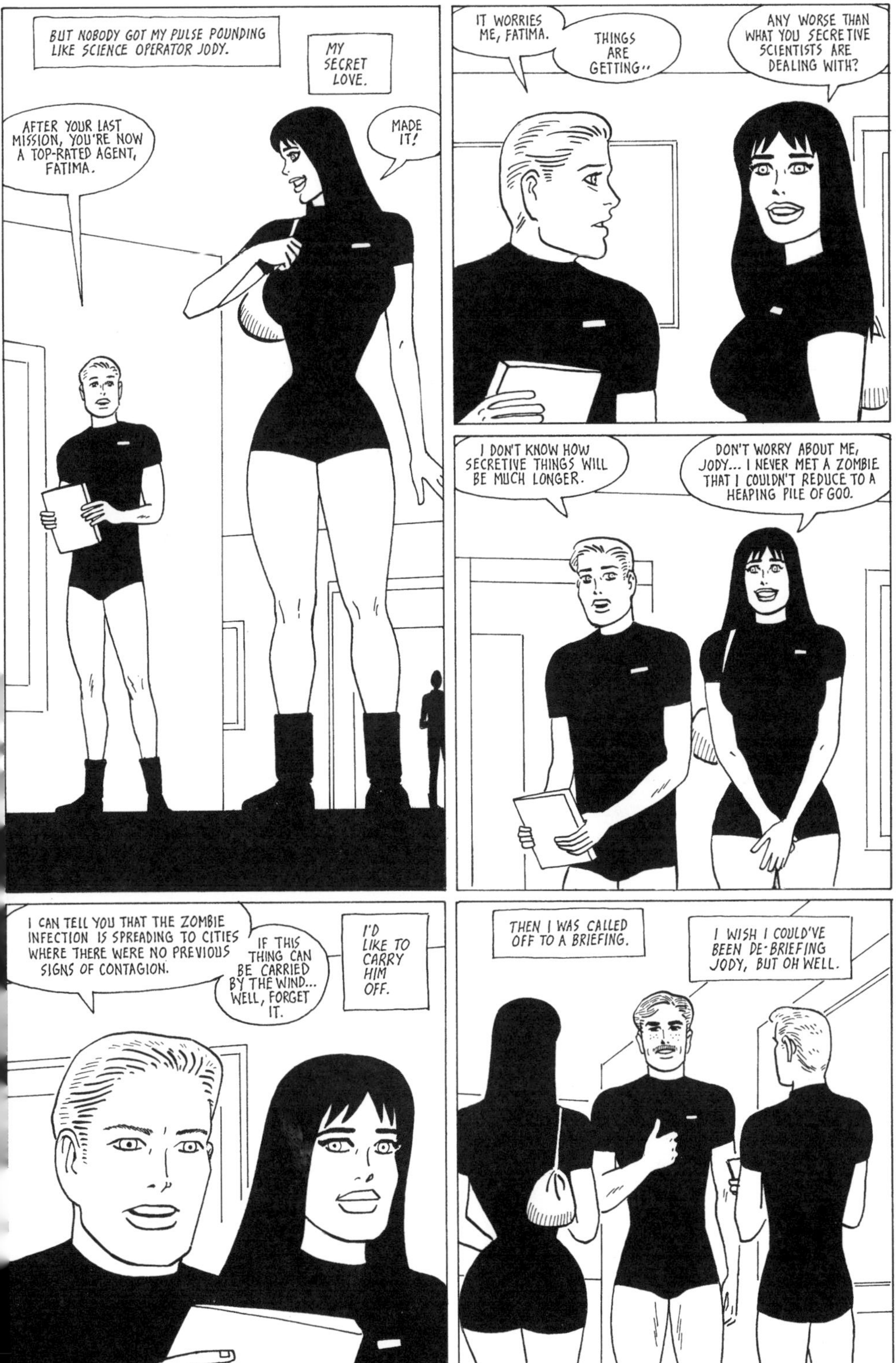
BUT NOBODY GOT MY PULSE POUNDING LIKE SCIENCE OPERATOR JODY.
MY SECRET LOVE.
AFTER YOUR LAST MISSION, YOU'RE NOW A TOP-RATED AGENT, FATIMA.
MADE IT!
IT WORRIES ME, FATIMA.
THINGS ARE GETTING..
ANY WORSE THAN WHAT YOU SECRETIVE SCIENTISTS ARE DEALING WITH?
I DON'T KNOW HOW SECRETIVE THINGS WILL BE MUCH LONGER.
DON'T WORRY ABOUT ME, JODY... I NEVER MET A ZOMBIE THAT I COULDN'T REDUCE TO A HEAPING PILE OF GOO.
I CAN TELL YOU THAT THE ZOMBIE INFECTION IS SPREADING TO CITIES WHERE THERE WERE NO PREVIOUS SIGNS OF CONTAGION.
IF THIS THING CAN BE CARRIED BY THE WIND... WELL, FORGET IT.
I'D LIKE TO CARRY HIM OFF.
THEN I WAS CALLED OFF TO A BRIEFING.
I WISH I COULD'VE BEEN DE-BRIEFING JODY, BUT OH WELL.

WHAT IS SPIN?

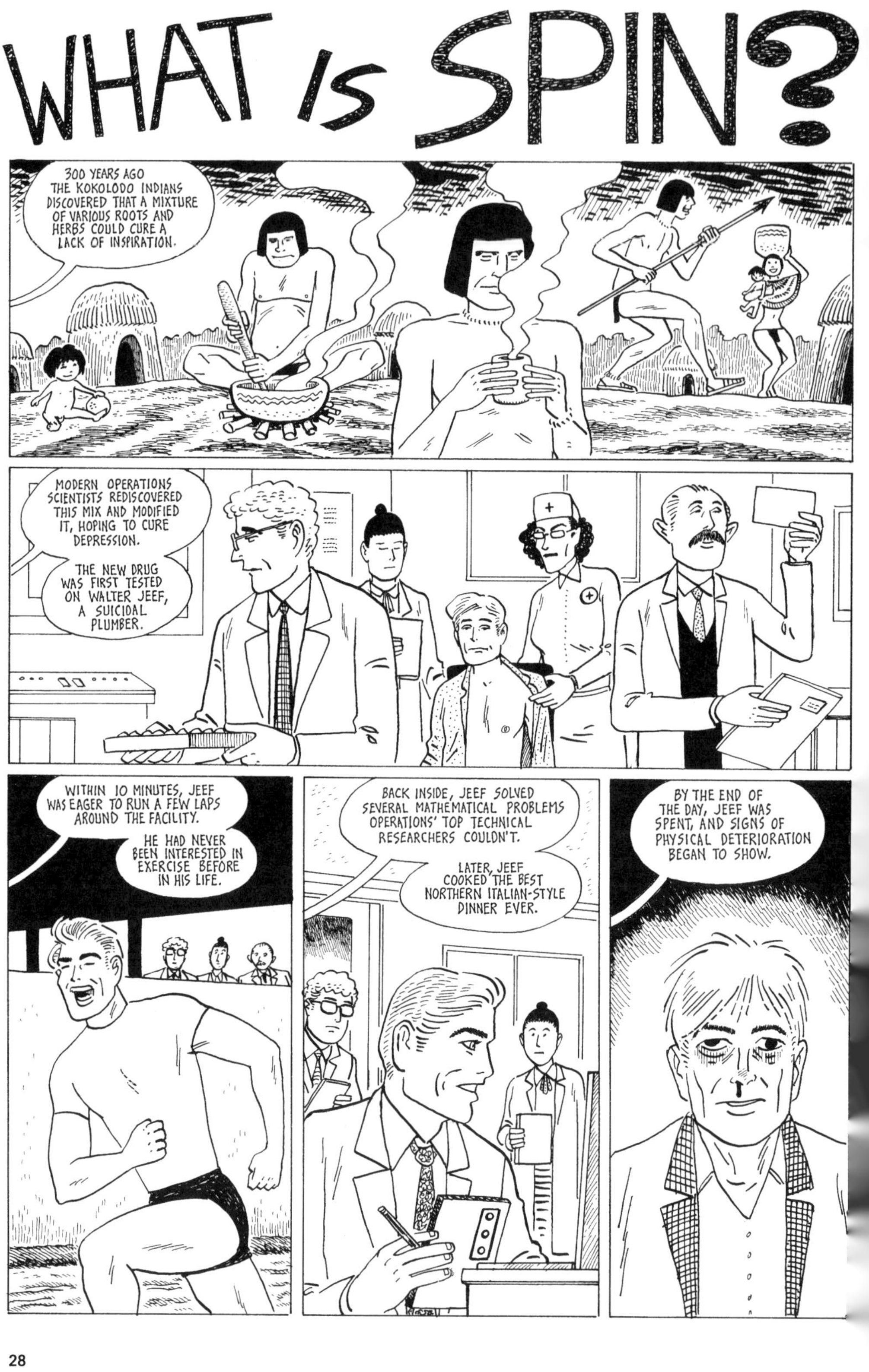
300 YEARS AGO THE KOKOLODO INDIANS DISCOVERED THAT A MIXTURE OF VARIOUS ROOTS AND HERBS COULD CURE A LACK OF INSPIRATION.
MODERN OPERATIONS SCIENTISTS REDISCOVERED THIS MIX AND MODIFIED IT, HOPING TO CURE DEPRESSION.
THE NEW DRUG WAS FIRST TESTED ON WALTER JEEF, A SUICIDAL PLUMBER.
WITHIN 10 MINUTES, JEEF WAS EAGER TO RUN A FEW LAPS AROUND THE FACILITY.
HE HAD NEVER BEEN INTERESTED IN EXERCISE BEFORE IN HIS LIFE.
BACK INSIDE, JEEF SOLVED SEVERAL MATHEMATICAL PROBLEMS OPERATIONS' TOP TECHNICAL RESEARCHERS COULDN'T.
LATER, JEEF COOKED THE BEST NORTHERN ITALIAN-STYLE DINNER EVER.
BY THE END OF THE DAY, JEEF WAS SPENT, AND SIGNS OF PHYSICAL DETERIORATION BEGAN TO SHOW.

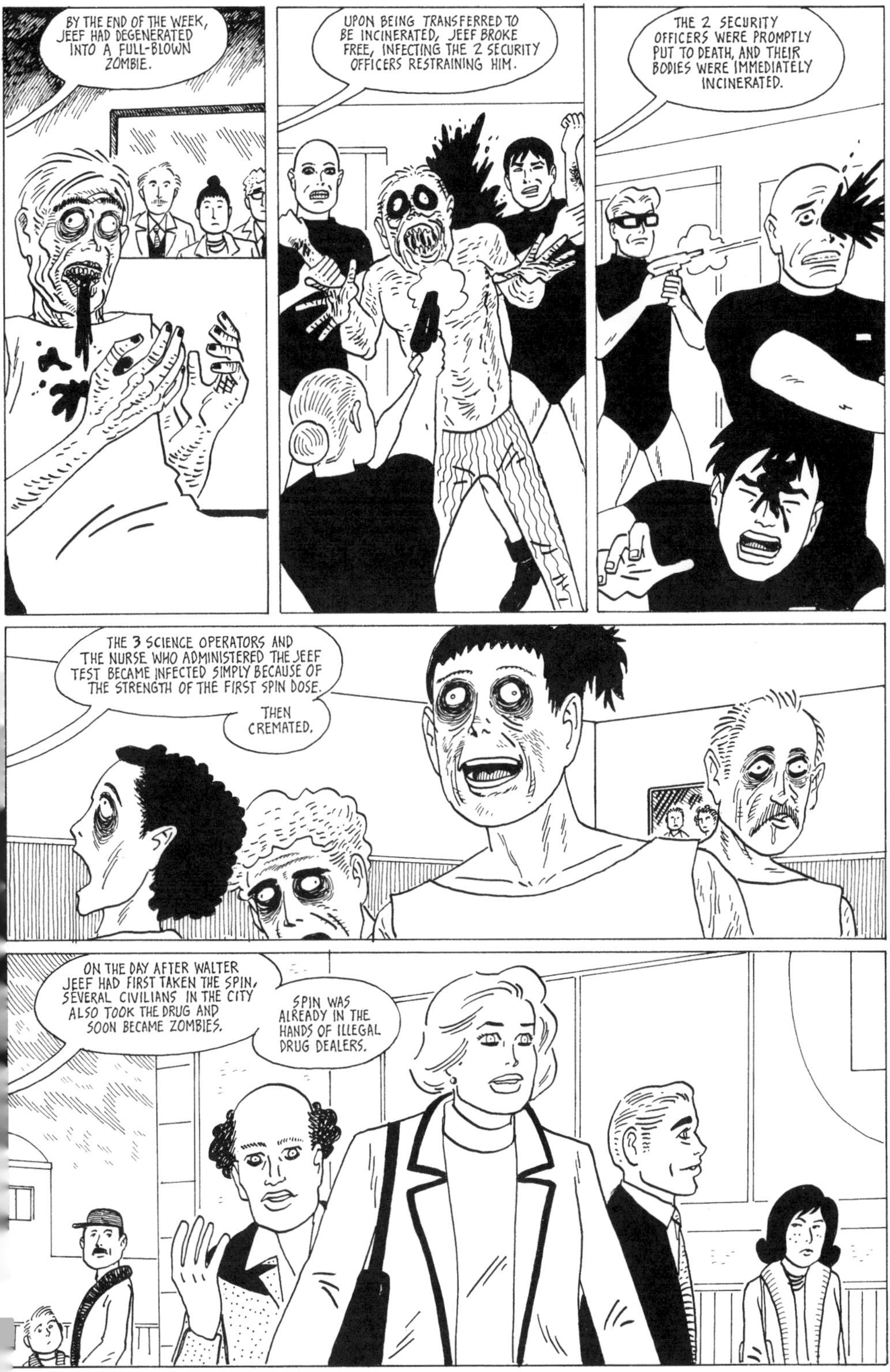
BY THE END OF THE WEEK, JEEF HAD DEGENERATED INTO A FULL-BLOWN ZOMBIE.
UPON BEING TRANSFERRED TO BE INCINERATED, JEEF BROKE FREE, INFECTING THE 2 SECURITY OFFICERS RESTRAINING HIM.
THE 2 SECURITY OFFICERS WERE PROMPTLY PUT TO DEATH, AND THEIR BODIES WERE IMMEDIATELY INCINERATED.
THE 3 SCIENCE OPERATORS AND THE NURSE WHO ADMINISTERED THE JEEF TEST BECAME INFECTED SIMPLY BECAUSE OF THE STRENGTH OF THE FIRST SPIN DOSE.
THEN CREMATED.
ON THE DAY AFTER WALTER JEEF HAD FIRST TAKEN THE SPIN, SEVERAL CIVILIANS IN THE CITY ALSO TOOK THE DRUG AND SOON BECAME ZOMBIES.
SPIN WAS ALREADY IN THE HANDS OF ILLEGAL DRUG DEALERS.

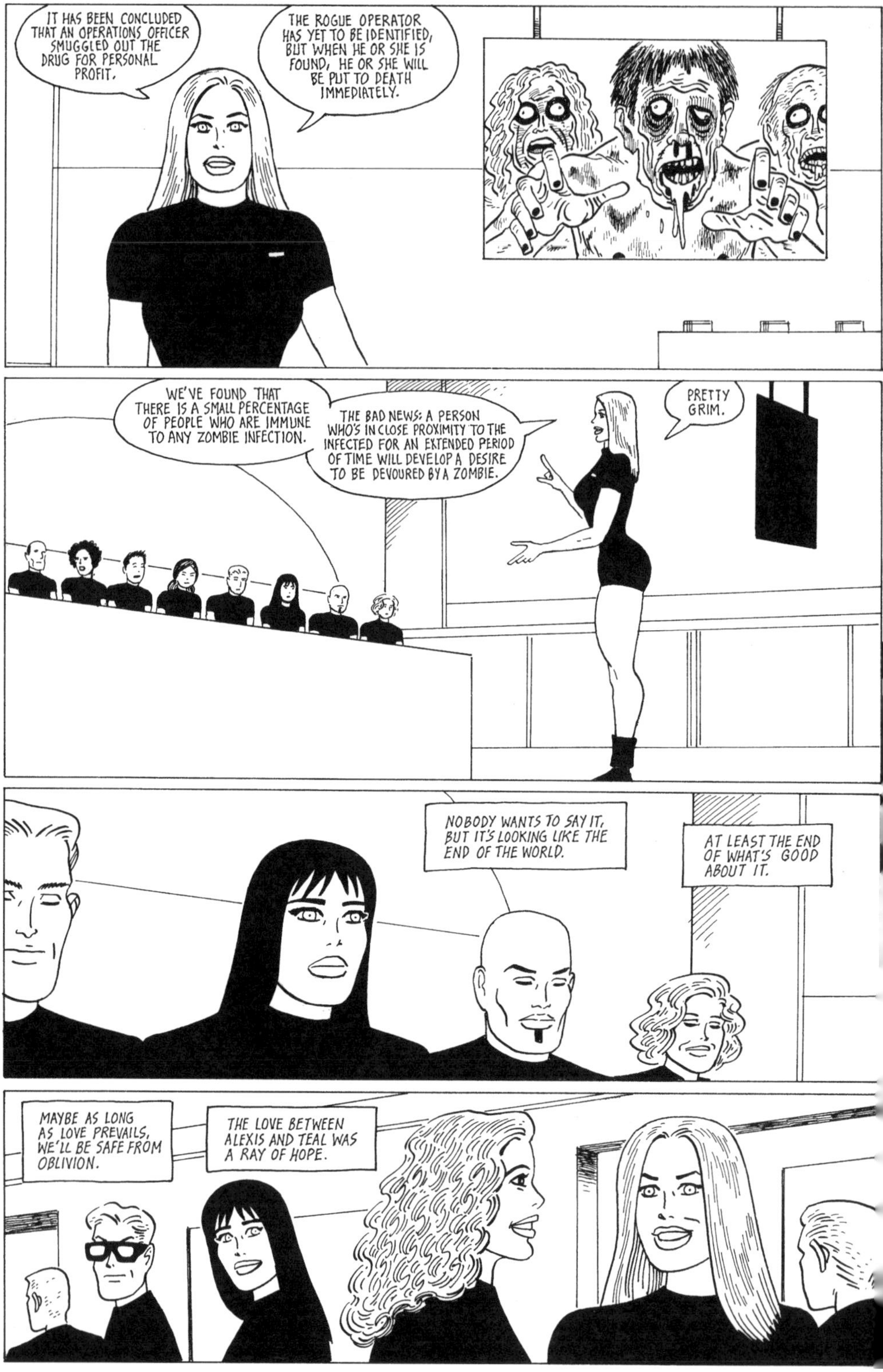
IT HAS BEEN CONCLUDED THAT AN OPERATIONS OFFICER SMUGGLED OUT THE DRUG FOR PERSONAL PROFIT.
THE ROGUE OPERATOR HAS YET TO BE IDENTIFIED, BUT WHEN HE OR SHE IS FOUND, HE OR SHE WILL BE PUT TO DEATH IMMEDIATELY.
WE'VE FOUND THAT THERE IS A SMALL PERCENTAGE OF PEOPLE WHO ARE IMMUNE TO ANY ZOMBIE INFECTION.
THE BAD NEWS: A PERSON WHO'S IN CLOSE PROXIMITY TO THE INFECTED FOR AN EXTENDED PERIOD OF TIME WILL DEVELOP A DESIRE TO BE DEVOURED BY A ZOMBIE.
PRETTY GRIM.
NOBODY WANTS TO SAY IT, BUT IT'S LOOKING LIKE THE END OF THE WORLD.
AT LEAST THE END OF WHAT'S GOOD ABOUT IT.
MAYBE AS LONG AS LOVE PREVAILS, WE'LL BE SAFE FROM OBLIVION.
THE LOVE BETWEEN ALEXIS AND TEAL WAS A RAY OF HOPE.

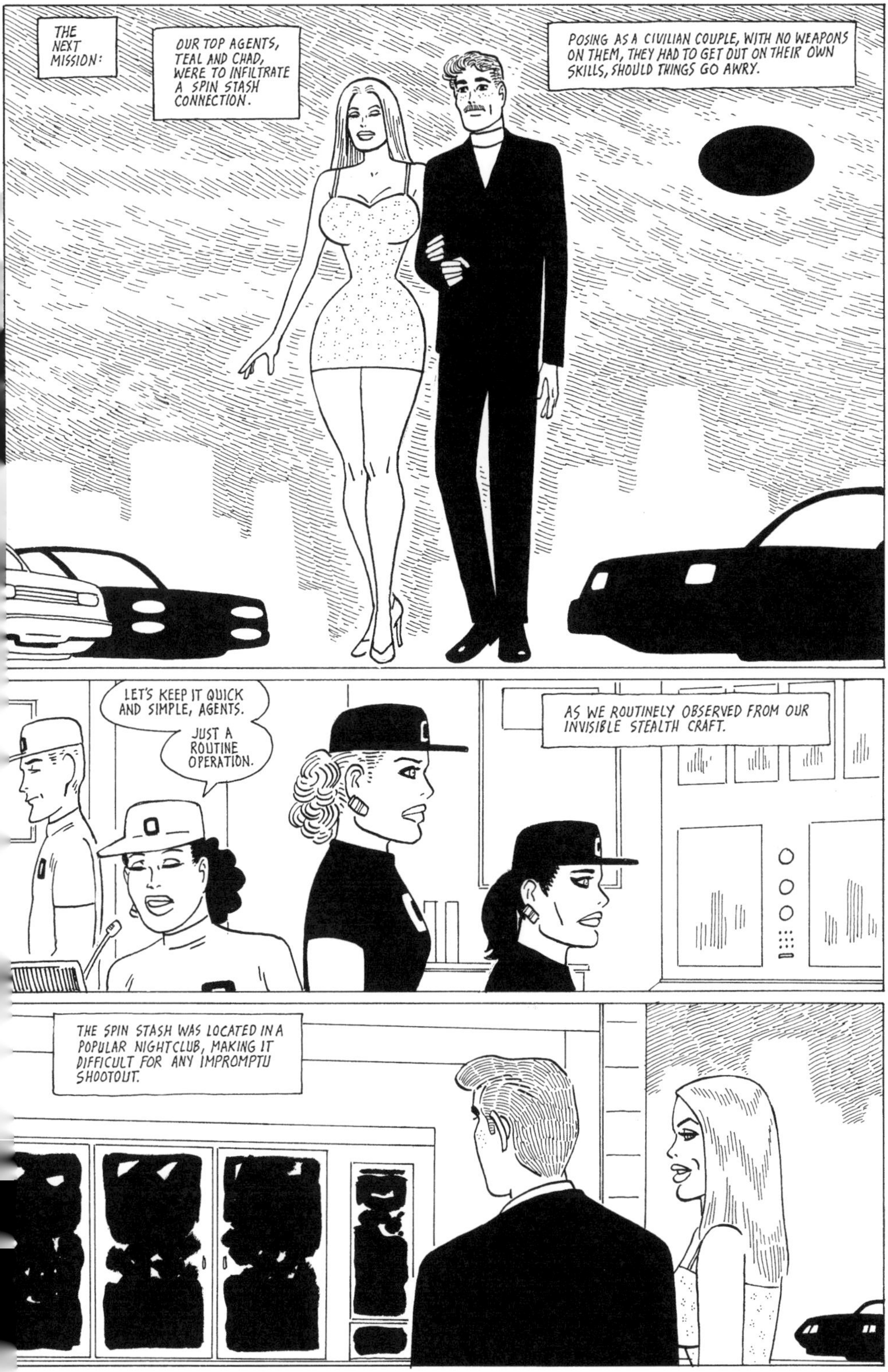
THE NEXT MISSION:
OUR TOP AGENTS, TEAL AND CHAD, WERE TO INFILTRATE A SPIN STASH CONNECTION.
POSING AS A CIVILIAN COUPLE, WITH NO WEAPONS ON THEM, THEY HAD TO GET OUT ON THEIR OWN SKILLS, SHOULD THINGS GO AWRY.
LET'S KEEP IT QUICK AND SIMPLE, AGENTS.
JUST A ROUTINE OPERATION.
AS WE ROUTINELY OBSERVED FROM OUR INVISIBLE STEALTH CRAFT.
THE SPIN STASH WAS LOCATED IN A POPULAR NIGHTCLUB, MAKING IT DIFFICULT FOR ANY IMPROMPTU SHOOTOUT.

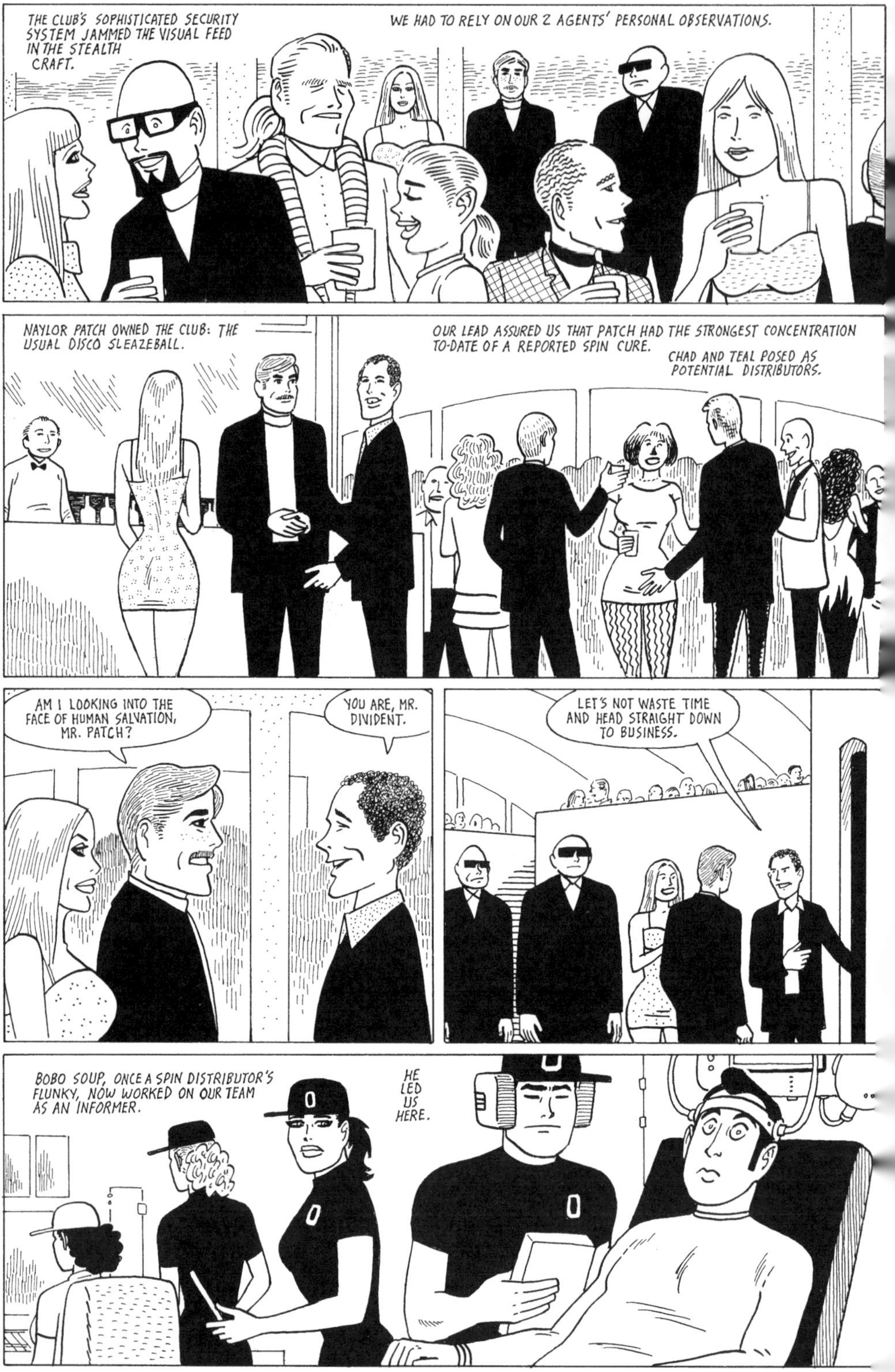
THE CLUB'S SOPHISTICATED SECURITY SYSTEM JAMMED THE VISUAL FEED IN THE STEALTH CRAFT.
WE HAD TO RELY ON OUR 2 AGENTS' PERSONAL OBSERVATIONS.
NAYLOR PATCH OWNED THE CLUB: THE USUAL DISCO SLEAZEBALL.
OUR LEAD ASSURED US THAT PATCH HAD THE STRONGEST CONCENTRATION TO-DATE OF A REPORTED SPIN CURE.
CHAD AND TEAL POSED AS POTENTIAL DISTRIBUTORS.
AM I LOOKING INTO THE FACE OF HUMAN SALVATION, MR. PATCH?
YOU ARE, MR. DIVIDENT.
LET'S NOT WASTE TIME AND HEAD STRAIGHT DOWN TO BUSINESS.
BOBO SOUP, ONCE A SPIN DISTRIBUTOR'S FLUNKY, NOW WORKED ON OUR TEAM AS AN INFORMER.
HE LED US HERE.

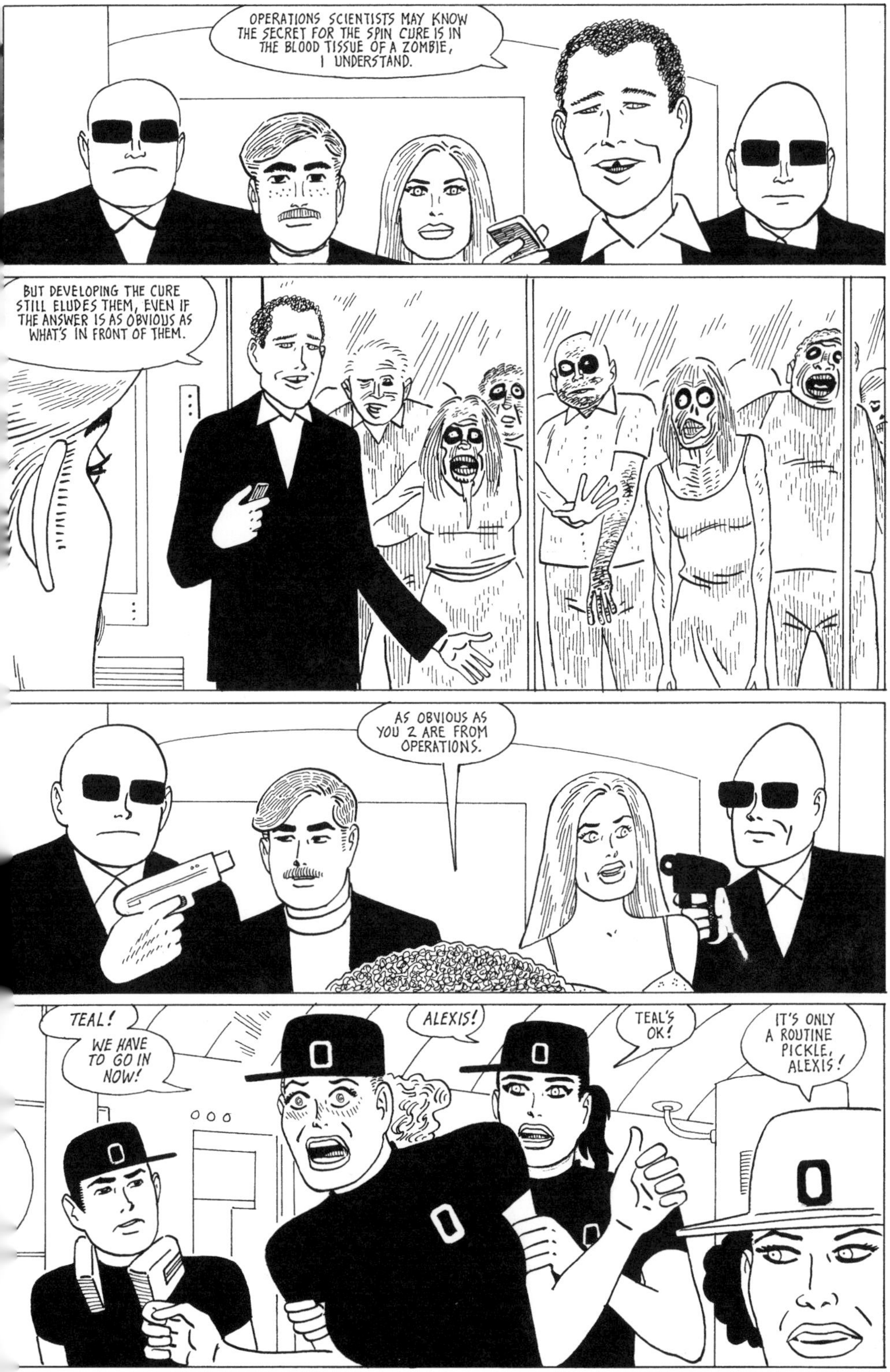
OPERATIONS SCIENTISTS MAY KNOW THE SECRET FOR THE SPIN CURE IS IN THE BLOOD TISSUE OF A ZOMBIE, I UNDERSTAND.
BUT DEVELOPING THE CURE STILL ELUDES THEM, EVEN IF THE ANSWER IS AS OBVIOUS AS WHAT'S IN FRONT OF THEM.
AS OBVIOUS AS YOU 2 ARE FROM OPERATIONS.
TEAL!
WE HAVE TO GO IN NOW!
ALEXIS!
TEAL'S OK!
IT'S ONLY A ROUTINE PICKLE, ALEXIS!

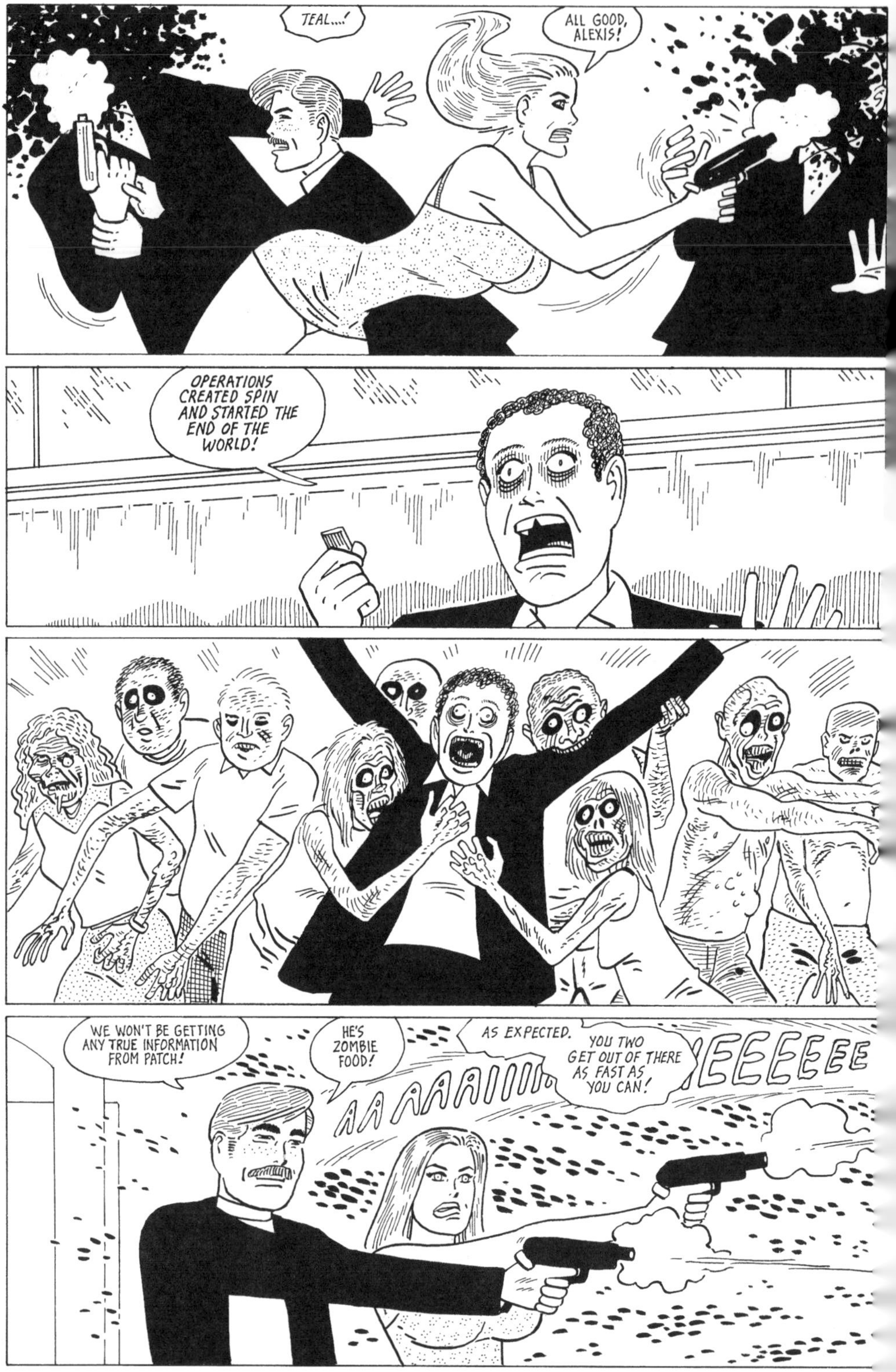
TEAL....!
ALL GOOD, ALEXIS!
OPERATIONS CREATED SPIN AND STARTED THE END OF THE WORLD!
WE WON'T BE GETTING ANY TRUE INFORMATION FROM PATCH!
HE'S ZOMBIE FOOD!
AS EXPECTED.
YOU TWO GET OUT OF THERE AS FAST AS YOU CAN!
AAAAAIIIIIEEEEEEE

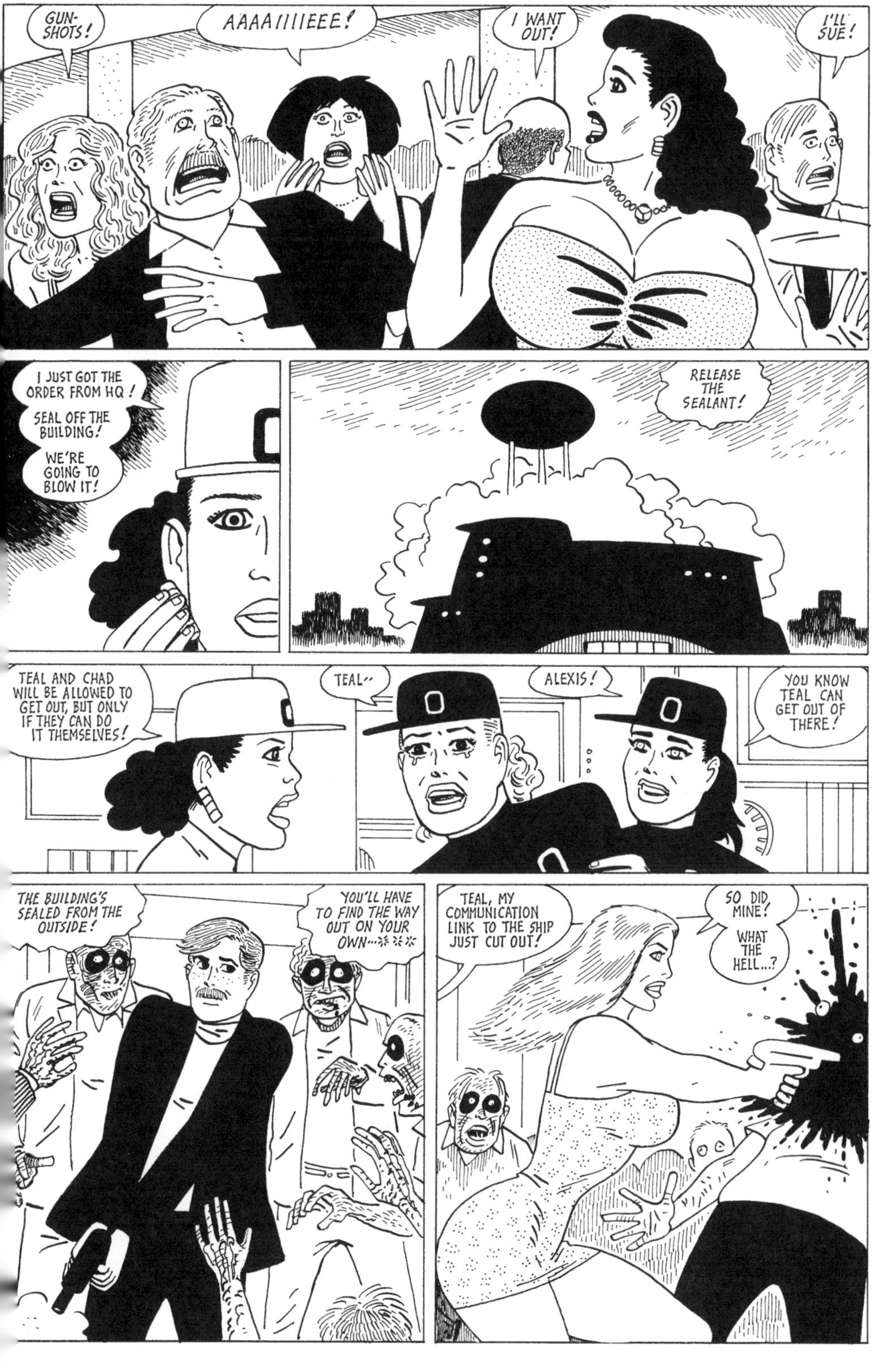
GUN-SHOTS!
AAAAIIIIEEE!
I WANT OUT!
I'LL SUE!
I JUST GOT THE ORDER FROM HQ!
SEAL OFF THE BUILDING!
WE'RE GOING TO BLOW IT!
RELEASE THE SEALANT!
TEAL AND CHAD WILL BE ALLOWED TO GET OUT, BUT ONLY IF THEY CAN DO IT THEMSELVES!
TEAL...
ALEXIS!
YOU KNOW TEAL CAN GET OUT OF THERE!
THE BUILDING'S SEALED FROM THE OUTSIDE!
YOU'LL HAVE TO FIND THE WAY OUT ON YOUR OWN...
TEAL, MY COMMUNICATION LINK TO THE SHIP JUST CUT OUT!
SO DID MINE!
WHAT THE HELL...?

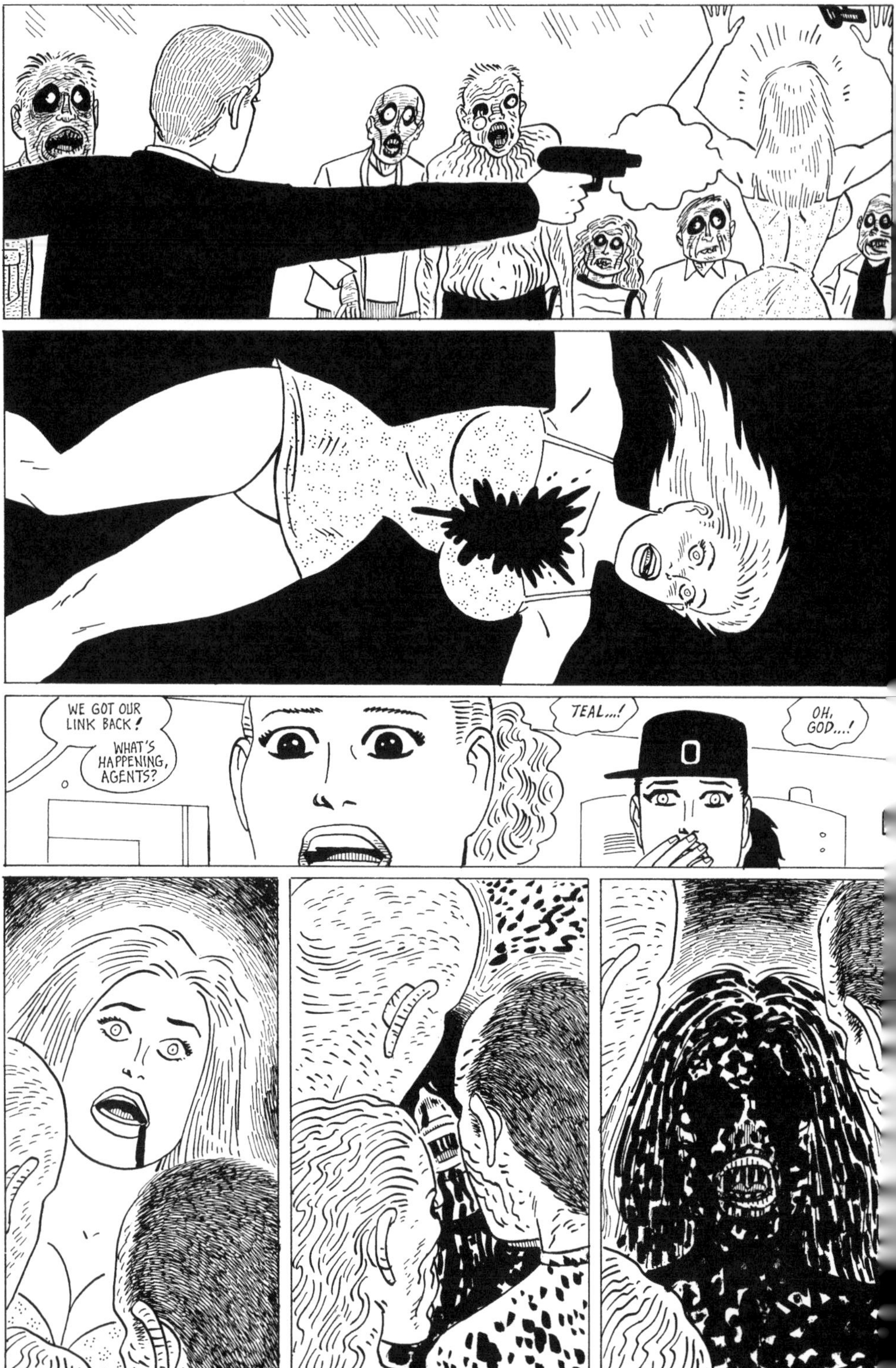
WE GOT OUR LINK BACK!
WHAT'S HAPPENING, AGENTS?
TEAL...!
OH, GOD...!

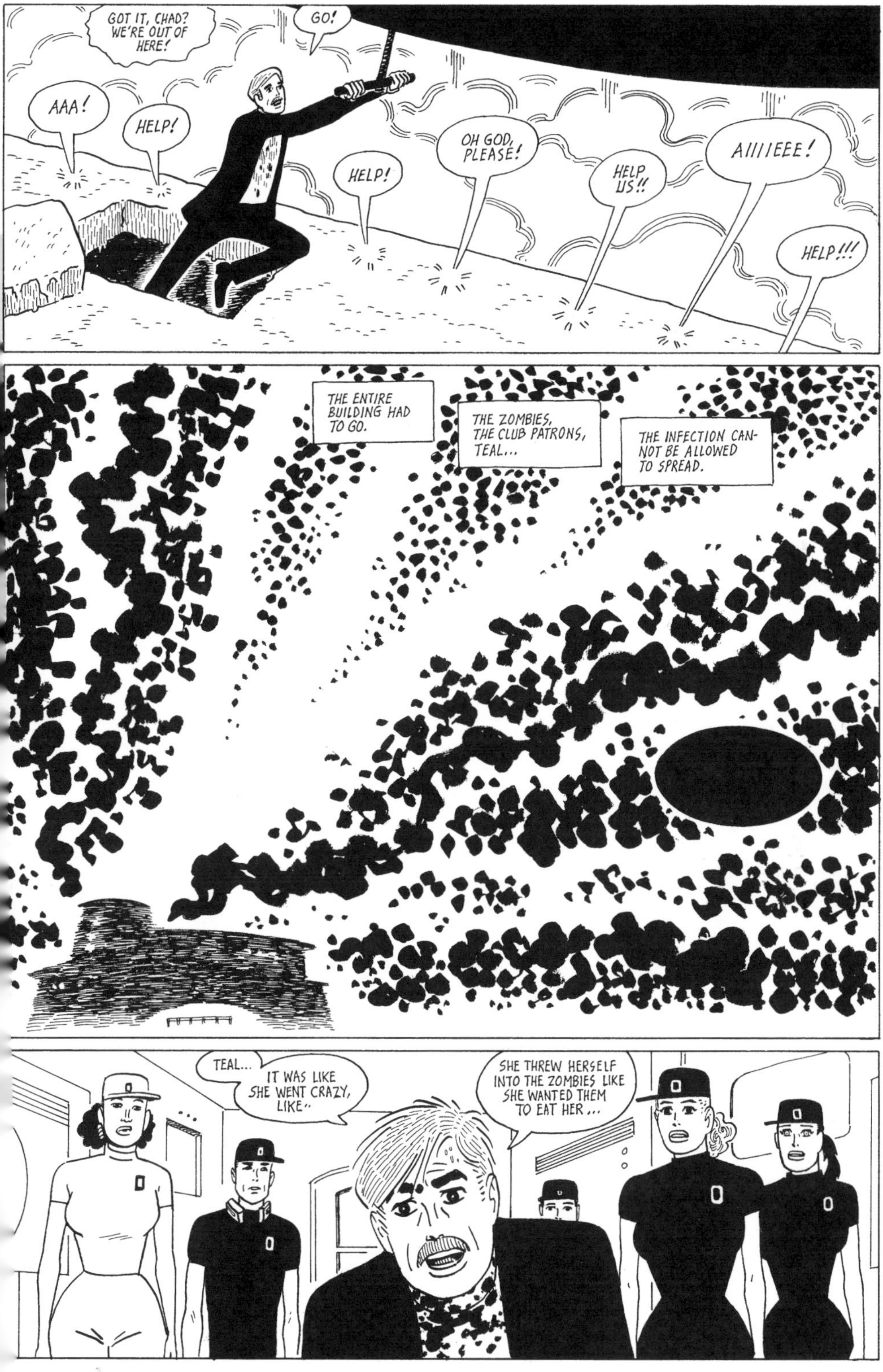
GOT IT, CHAD? WE'RE OUT OF HERE!
GO!
AAA!
HELP!
HELP!
OH GOD, PLEASE!
HELP US!!
AIIIIEEE!
HELP!!!
THE ENTIRE BUILDING HAD TO GO.
THE ZOMBIES, THE CLUB PATRONS, TEAL...
THE INFECTION CANNOT BE ALLOWED TO SPREAD.
TEAL...
IT WAS LIKE SHE WENT CRAZY, LIKE..
SHE THREW HERSELF INTO THE ZOMBIES LIKE SHE WANTED THEM TO EAT HER...

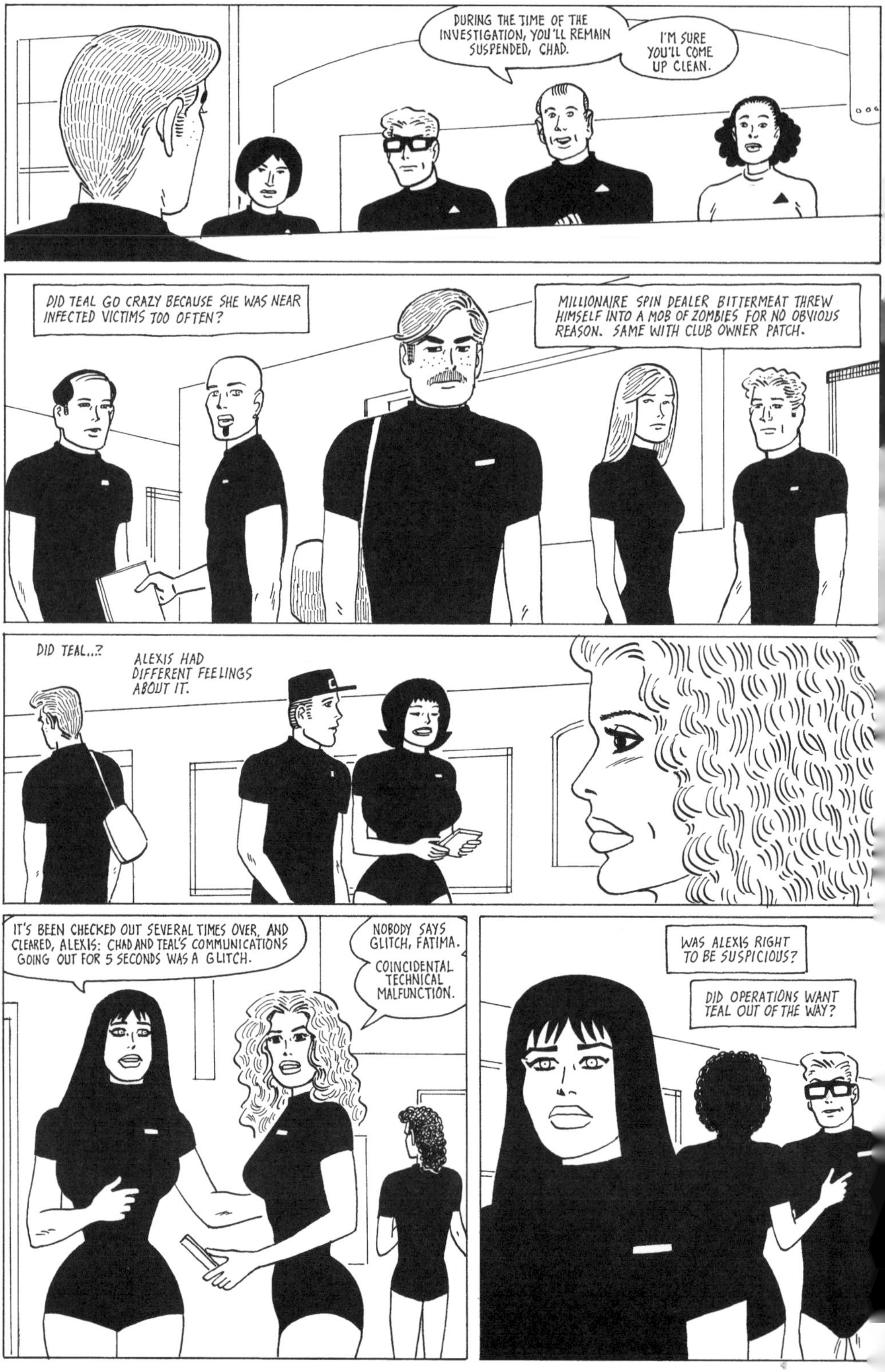
DURING THE TIME OF THE INVESTIGATION, YOU'LL REMAIN SUSPENDED, CHAD.
I'M SURE YOU'LL COME UP CLEAN.
DID TEAL GO CRAZY BECAUSE SHE WAS NEAR INFECTED VICTIMS TOO OFTEN?
MILLIONAIRE SPIN DEALER BITTERMEAT THREW HIMSELF INTO A MOB OF ZOMBIES FOR NO OBVIOUS REASON. SAME WITH CLUB OWNER PATCH.
DID TEAL...?
ALEXIS HAD DIFFERENT FEELINGS ABOUT IT.
IT'S BEEN CHECKED OUT SEVERAL TIMES OVER, AND CLEARED, ALEXIS: CHAD AND TEAL'S COMMUNICATIONS GOING OUT FOR 5 SECONDS WAS A GLITCH.
NOBODY SAYS GLITCH, FATIMA.
COINCIDENTAL TECHNICAL MALFUNCTION.
WAS ALEXIS RIGHT TO BE SUSPICIOUS?
DID OPERATIONS WANT TEAL OUT OF THE WAY?

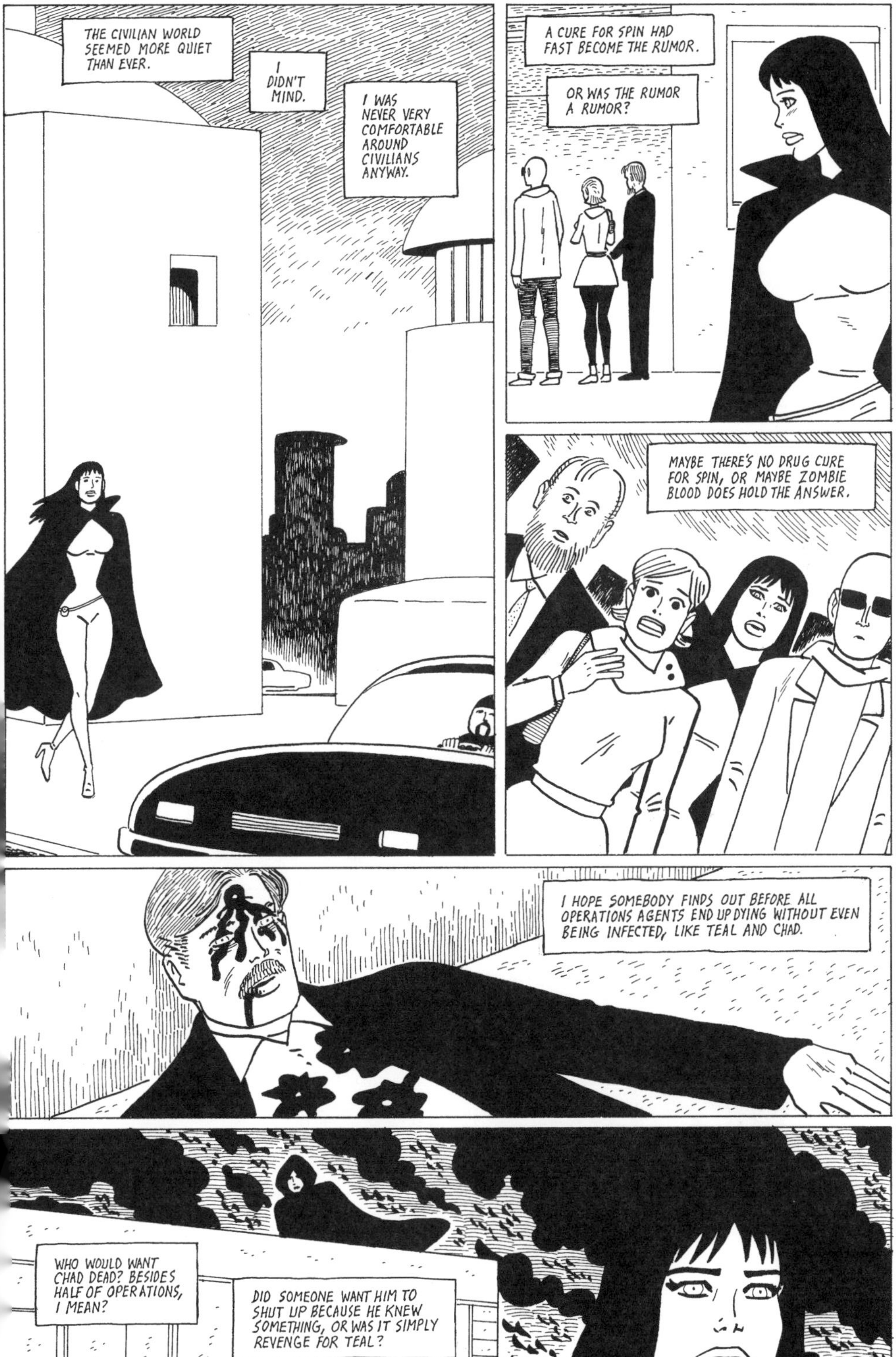
THE CIVILIAN WORLD SEEMED MORE QUIET THAN EVER.
I DIDN'T MIND.
I WAS NEVER VERY COMFORTABLE AROUND CIVILIANS ANYWAY.
A CURE FOR SPIN HAD FAST BECOME THE RUMOR.
OR WAS THE RUMOR A RUMOR?
MAYBE THERE'S NO DRUG CURE FOR SPIN, OR MAYBE ZOMBIE BLOOD DOES HOLD THE ANSWER.
I HOPE SOMEBODY FINDS OUT BEFORE ALL OPERATIONS AGENTS END UP DYING WITHOUT EVEN BEING INFECTED, LIKE TEAL AND CHAD.
WHO WOULD WANT CHAD DEAD? BESIDES HALF OF OPERATIONS, I MEAN?
DID SOMEONE WANT HIM TO SHUT UP BECAUSE HE KNEW SOMETHING, OR WAS IT SIMPLY REVENGE FOR TEAL?

AND ANOTHER DAY, ANOTHER JOB TO FINISH.

IT BECAME A TEDIOUS ROUTINE FOR ALEXIS, JODY, AND ME.

WE THREE WERE JUST ABOUT WHAT WAS LEFT OF OPERATIONS.

LEFT TO CLEAN UP WHAT USED TO BE THE GREAT HOPE FOR THE WORLD.

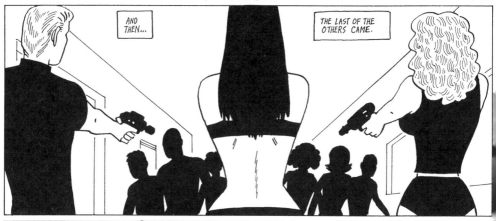

AND THEN...

THE LAST OF THE OTHERS CAME.

FRIENDS.

COLLEAGUES.

THE ONCE-BEAUTIFUL INDIVIDUALS WHO FOUGHT THE GOOD FIGHT, NOT AWARE OF OPERATIONS' CORRUPTION.

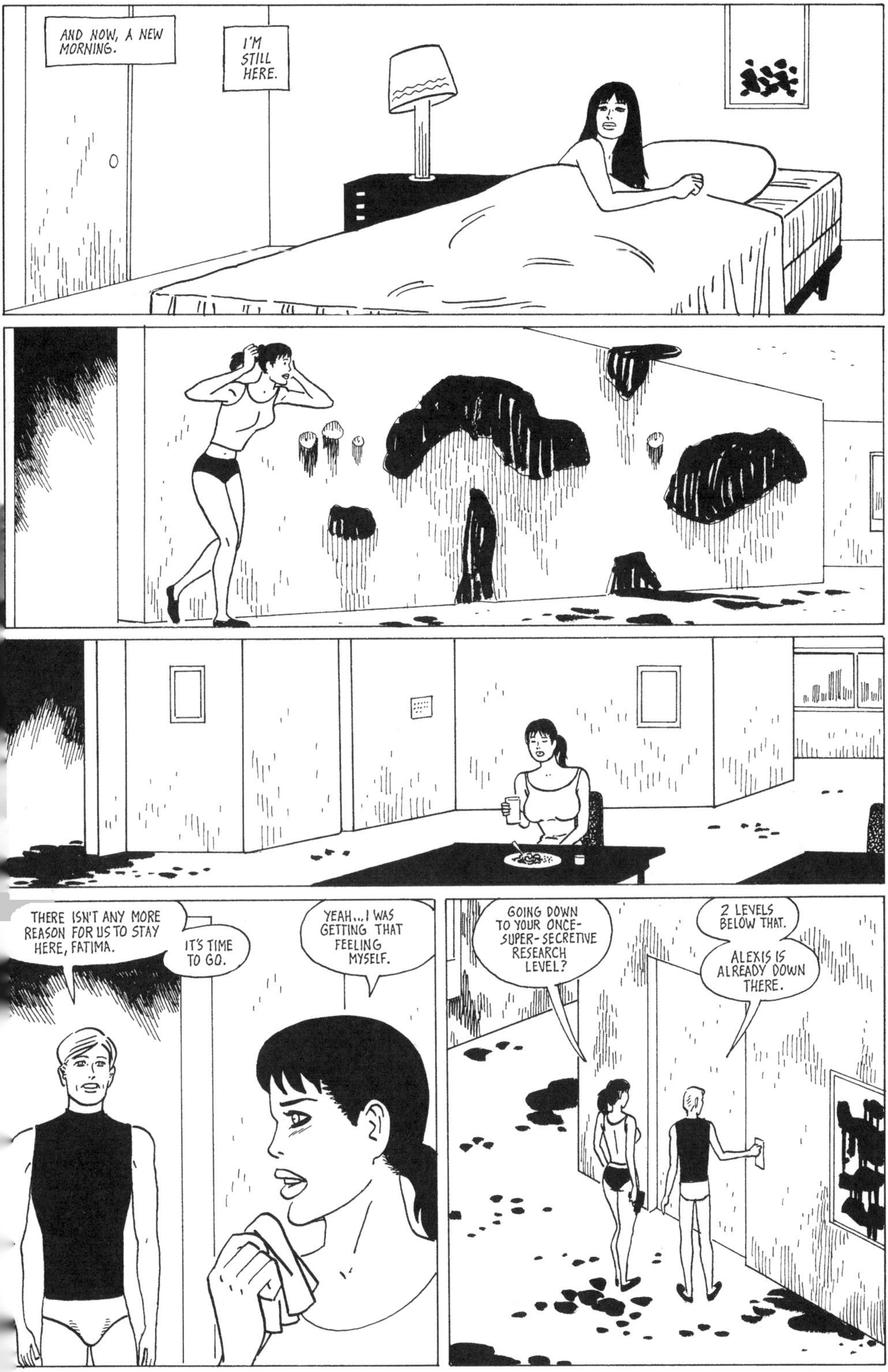
AND NOW, A NEW MORNING.
I'M STILL HERE.
THERE ISN'T ANY MORE REASON FOR US TO STAY HERE, FATIMA.
IT'S TIME TO GO.
YEAH...I WAS GETTING THAT FEELING MYSELF.
GOING DOWN TO YOUR ONCE-SUPER-SECRETIVE RESEARCH LEVEL?
2 LEVELS BELOW THAT.
ALEXIS IS ALREADY DOWN THERE.

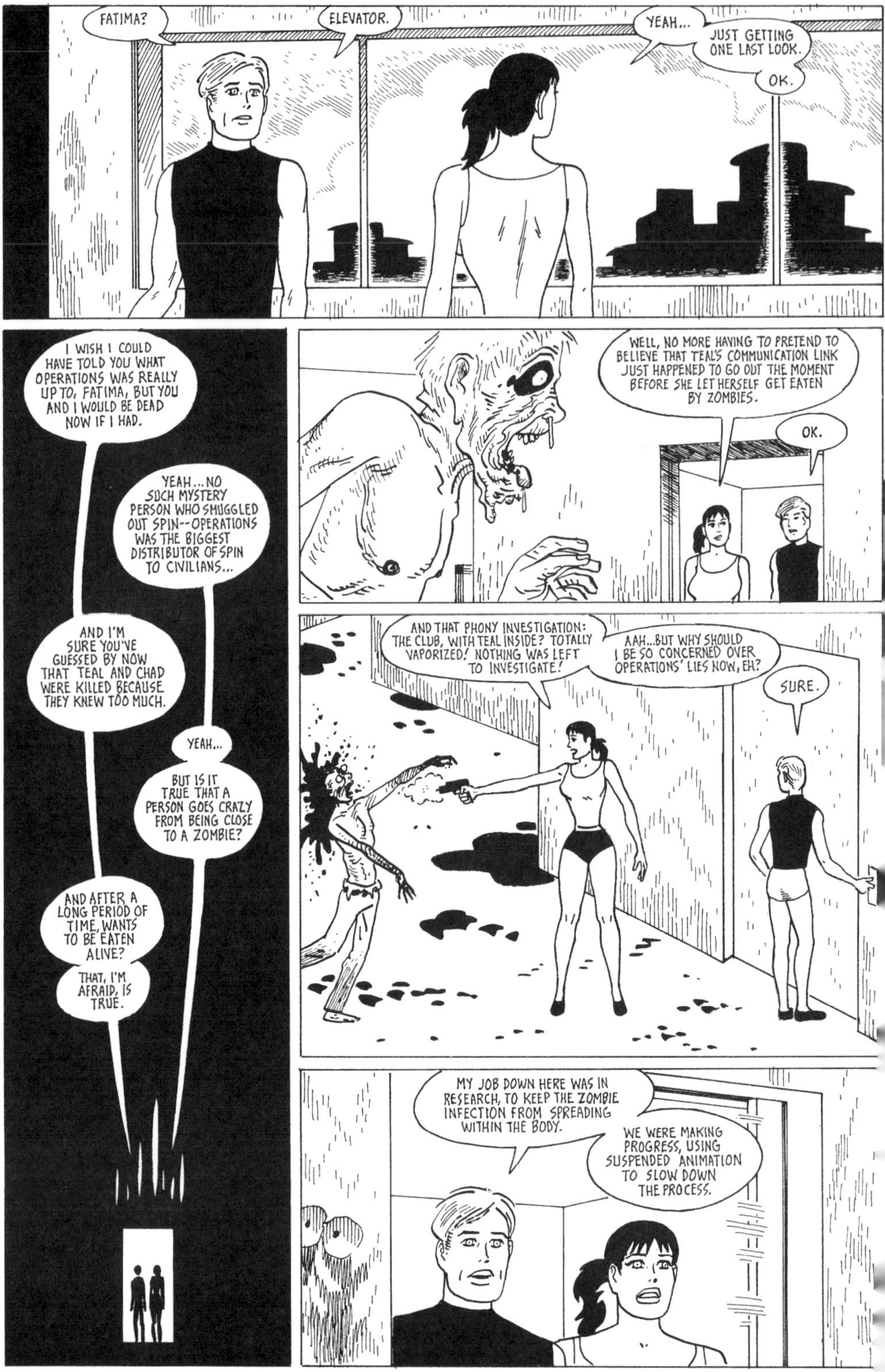
FATIMA?
ELEVATOR.
YEAH...
JUST GETTING ONE LAST LOOK.
OK.
I WISH I COULD HAVE TOLD YOU WHAT OPERATIONS WAS REALLY UP TO, FATIMA, BUT YOU AND I WOULD BE DEAD NOW IF I HAD.
YEAH...NO SUCH MYSTERY PERSON WHO SMUGGLED OUT SPIN--OPERATIONS WAS THE BIGGEST DISTRIBUTOR OF SPIN TO CIVILIANS...
AND I'M SURE YOU'VE GUESSED BY NOW THAT TEAL AND CHAD WERE KILLED BECAUSE THEY KNEW TOO MUCH.
YEAH...
BUT IS IT TRUE THAT A PERSON GOES CRAZY FROM BEING CLOSE TO A ZOMBIE?
AND AFTER A LONG PERIOD OF TIME, WANTS TO BE EATEN ALIVE?
THAT, I'M AFRAID, IS TRUE.
WELL, NO MORE HAVING TO PRETEND TO BELIEVE THAT TEAL'S COMMUNICATION LINK JUST HAPPENED TO GO OUT THE MOMENT BEFORE SHE LET HERSELF GET EATEN BY ZOMBIES.
OK.
AND THAT PHONY INVESTIGATION: THE CLUB, WITH TEAL INSIDE? TOTALLY VAPORIZED! NOTHING WAS LEFT TO INVESTIGATE!
AAH...BUT WHY SHOULD I BE SO CONCERNED OVER OPERATIONS' LIES NOW, EH?
SURE.
MY JOB DOWN HERE WAS IN RESEARCH, TO KEEP THE ZOMBIE INFECTION FROM SPREADING WITHIN THE BODY.
WE WERE MAKING PROGRESS, USING SUSPENDED ANIMATION TO SLOW DOWN THE PROCESS.

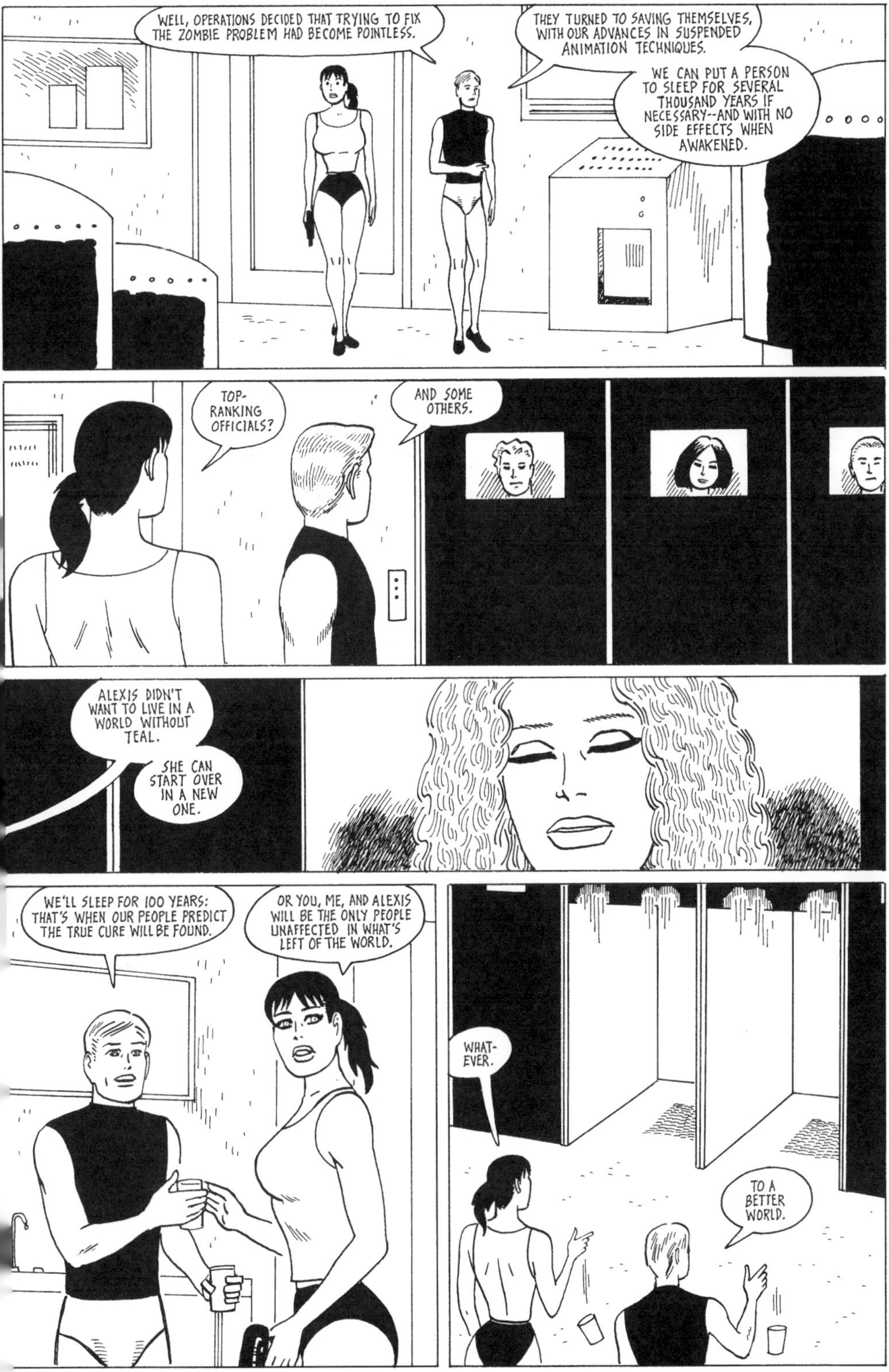
WELL, OPERATIONS DECIDED THAT TRYING TO FIX THE ZOMBIE PROBLEM HAD BECOME POINTLESS.
THEY TURNED TO SAVING THEMSELVES, WITH OUR ADVANCES IN SUSPENDED ANIMATION TECHNIQUES.
WE CAN PUT A PERSON TO SLEEP FOR SEVERAL THOUSAND YEARS IF NECESSARY--AND WITH NO SIDE EFFECTS WHEN AWAKENED.
TOP-RANKING OFFICIALS?
AND SOME OTHERS.
ALEXIS DIDN'T WANT TO LIVE IN A WORLD WITHOUT TEAL.
SHE CAN START OVER IN A NEW ONE.
WE'LL SLEEP FOR 100 YEARS: THAT'S WHEN OUR PEOPLE PREDICT THE TRUE CURE WILL BE FOUND.
OR YOU, ME, AND ALEXIS WILL BE THE ONLY PEOPLE UNAFFECTED IN WHAT'S LEFT OF THE WORLD.
WHAT-EVER.
TO A BETTER WORLD.

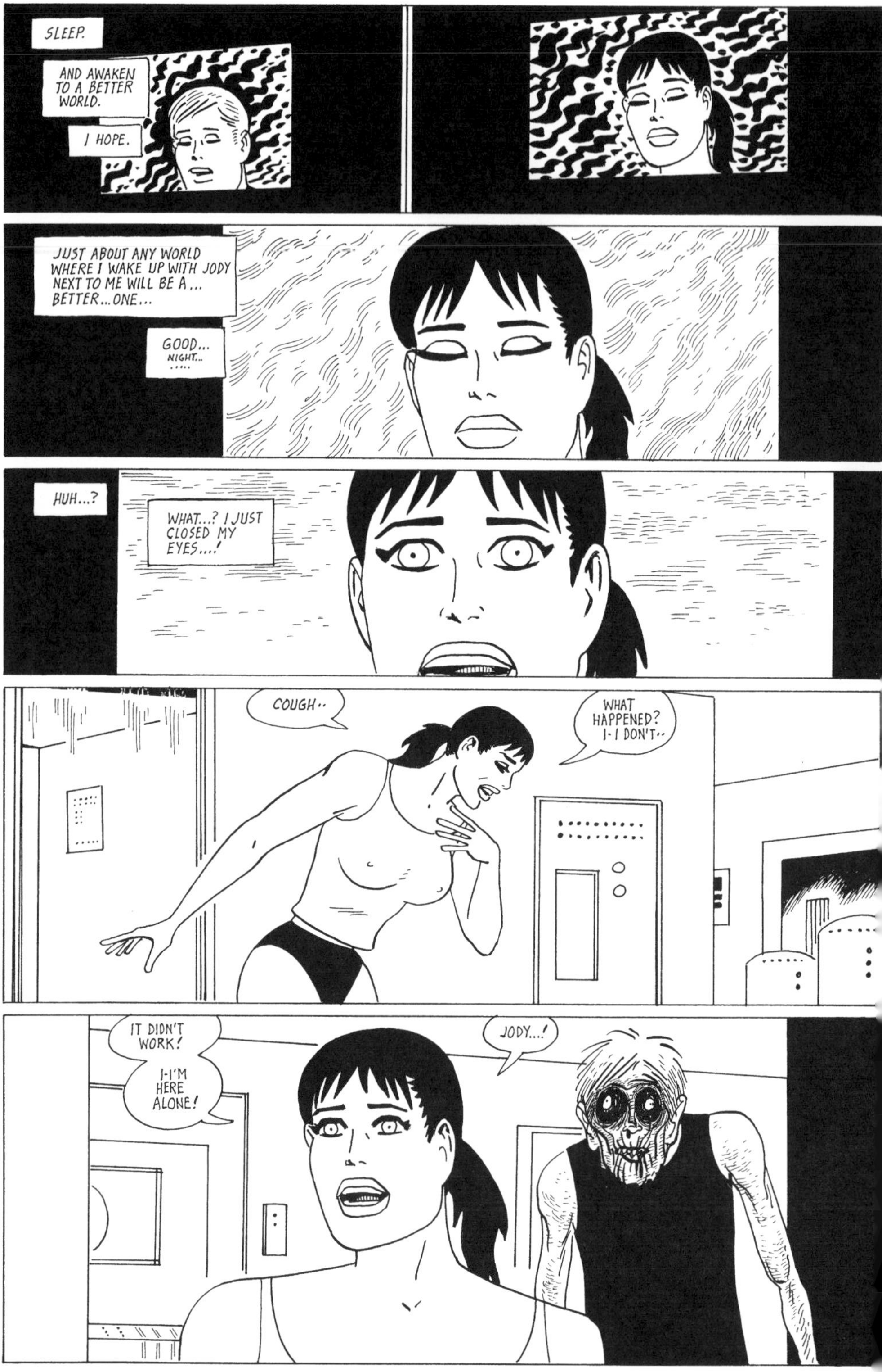
SLEEP.
AND AWAKEN TO A BETTER WORLD.
I HOPE.
JUST ABOUT ANY WORLD WHERE I WAKE UP WITH JODY NEXT TO ME WILL BE A... BETTER...ONE...
GOOD... NIGHT.. .....
HUH...?
WHAT...? I JUST CLOSED MY EYES...!
COUGH..
WHAT HAPPENED? I-I DON'T..
IT DIDN'T WORK!
I-I'M HERE ALONE!
JODY...!

FATIMA THE BLOOD SPINNERS³

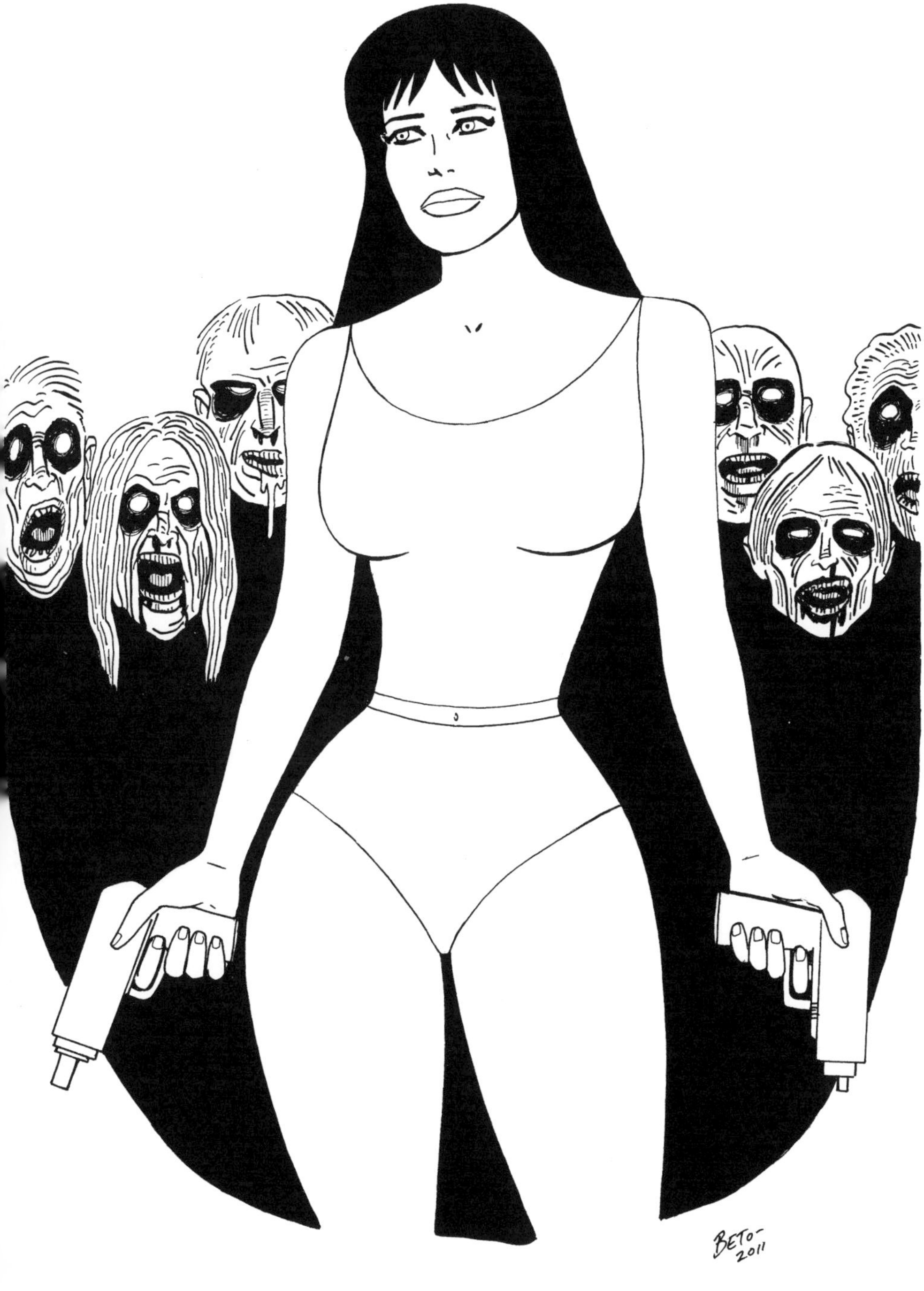
BETO-
2011

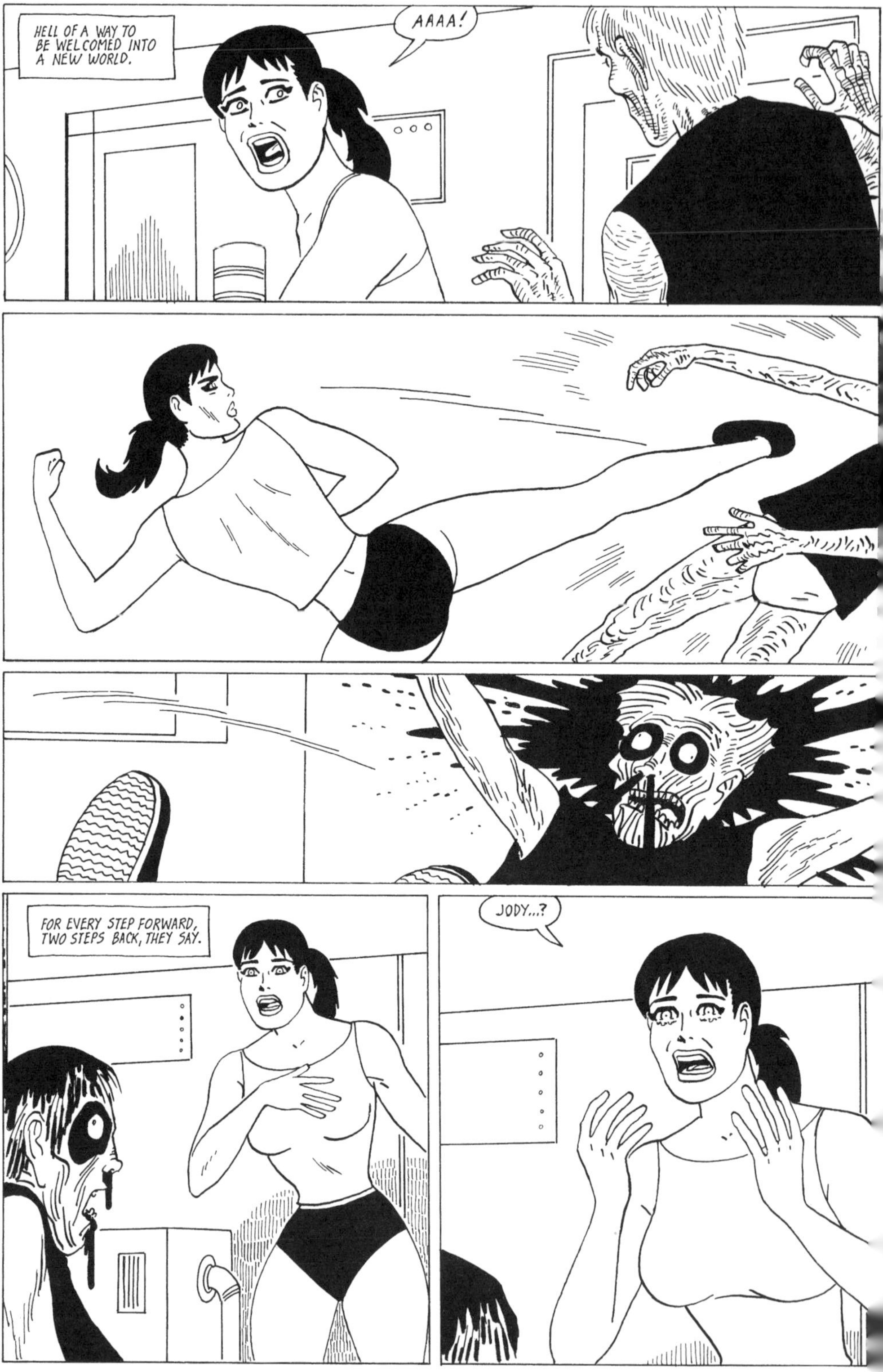
HELL OF A WAY TO BE WELCOMED INTO A NEW WORLD.
AAAA!
FOR EVERY STEP FORWARD, TWO STEPS BACK, THEY SAY.
JODY...?

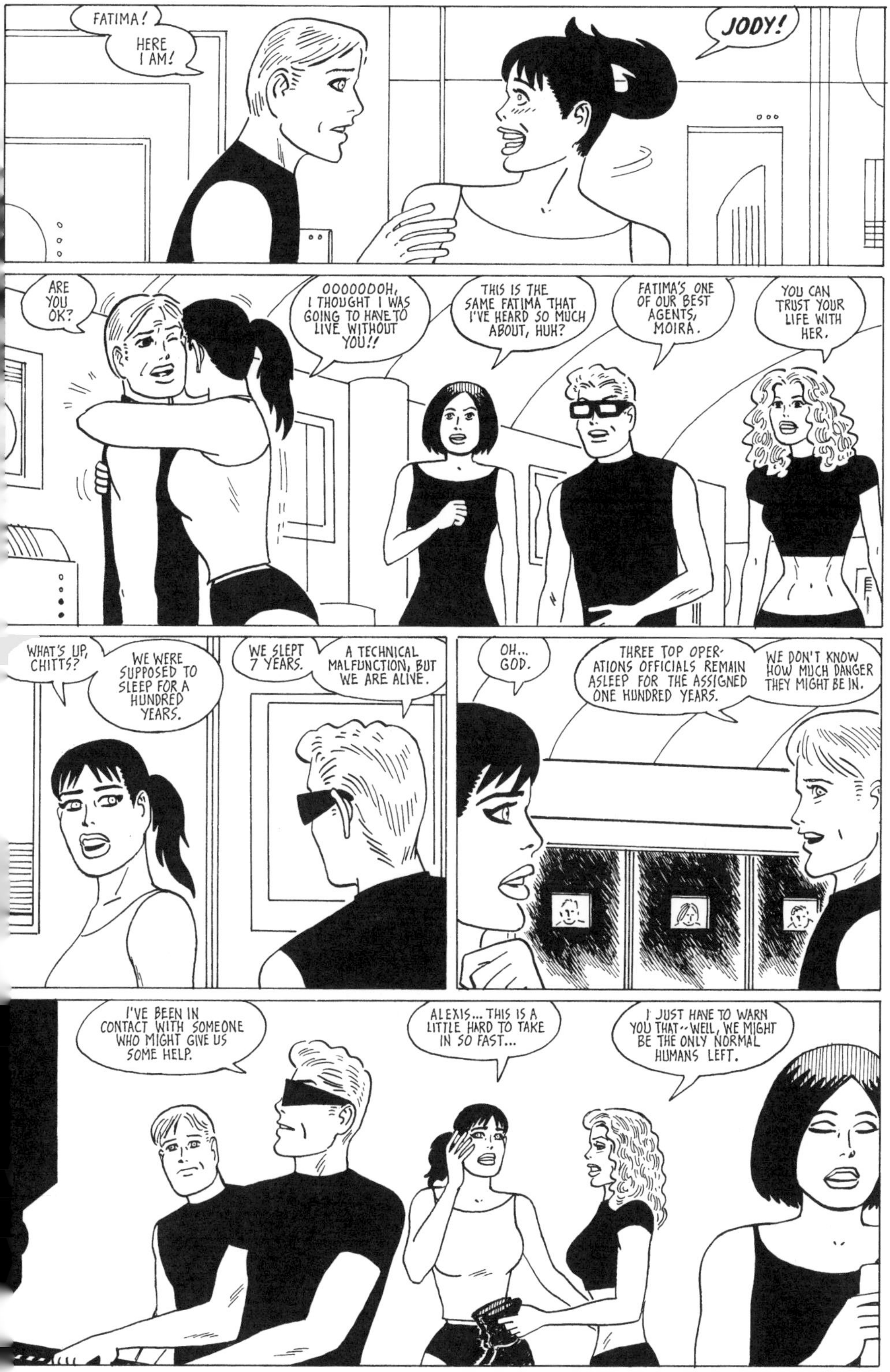
FATIMA!
HERE I AM!
JODY!
ARE YOU OK?
OOOOOOOH, I THOUGHT I WAS GOING TO HAVE TO LIVE WITHOUT YOU!!
THIS IS THE SAME FATIMA THAT I'VE HEARD SO MUCH ABOUT, HUH?
FATIMA'S ONE OF OUR BEST AGENTS, MOIRA.
YOU CAN TRUST YOUR LIFE WITH HER.
WHAT'S UP, CHITTS?
WE WERE SUPPOSED TO SLEEP FOR A HUNDRED YEARS.
WE SLEPT 7 YEARS.
A TECHNICAL MALFUNCTION, BUT WE ARE ALIVE.
OH... GOD.
THREE TOP OPERATIONS OFFICIALS REMAIN ASLEEP FOR THE ASSIGNED ONE HUNDRED YEARS.
WE DON'T KNOW HOW MUCH DANGER THEY MIGHT BE IN.
I'VE BEEN IN CONTACT WITH SOMEONE WHO MIGHT GIVE US SOME HELP.
ALEXIS... THIS IS A LITTLE HARD TO TAKE IN SO FAST...
I JUST HAVE TO WARN YOU THAT-- WELL, WE MIGHT BE THE ONLY NORMAL HUMANS LEFT.

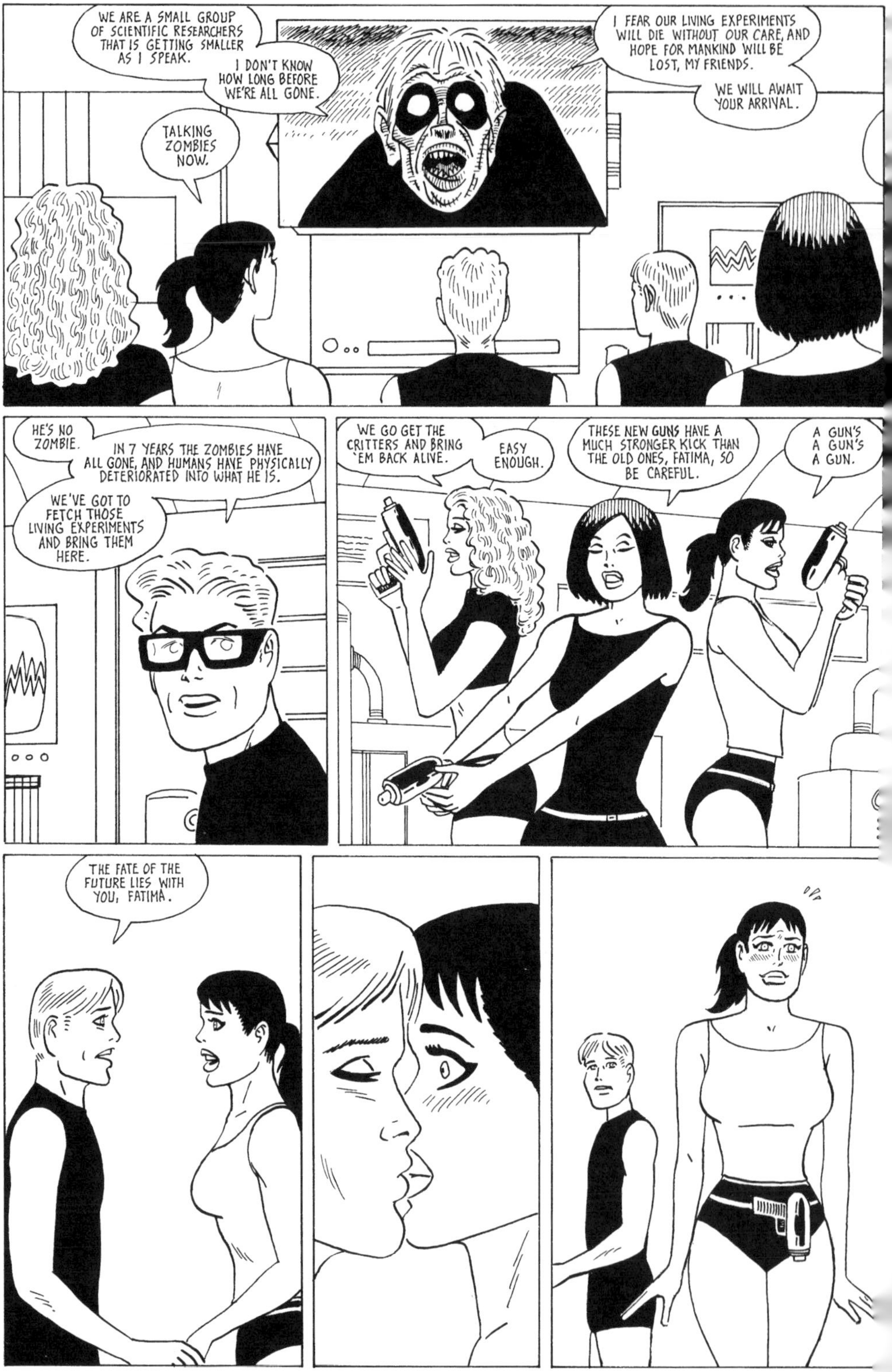
WE ARE A SMALL GROUP OF SCIENTIFIC RESEARCHERS THAT IS GETTING SMALLER AS I SPEAK.
I DON'T KNOW HOW LONG BEFORE WE'RE ALL GONE.
TALKING ZOMBIES NOW.
I FEAR OUR LIVING EXPERIMENTS WILL DIE WITHOUT OUR CARE, AND HOPE FOR MANKIND WILL BE LOST, MY FRIENDS.
WE WILL AWAIT YOUR ARRIVAL.
HE'S NO ZOMBIE.
IN 7 YEARS THE ZOMBIES HAVE ALL GONE, AND HUMANS HAVE PHYSICALLY DETERIORATED INTO WHAT HE IS.
WE'VE GOT TO FETCH THOSE LIVING EXPERIMENTS AND BRING THEM HERE.
WE GO GET THE CRITTERS AND BRING 'EM BACK ALIVE.
EASY ENOUGH.
THESE NEW GUNS HAVE A MUCH STRONGER KICK THAN THE OLD ONES, FATIMA, SO BE CAREFUL.
A GUN'S A GUN'S A GUN.
THE FATE OF THE FUTURE LIES WITH YOU, FATIMA.

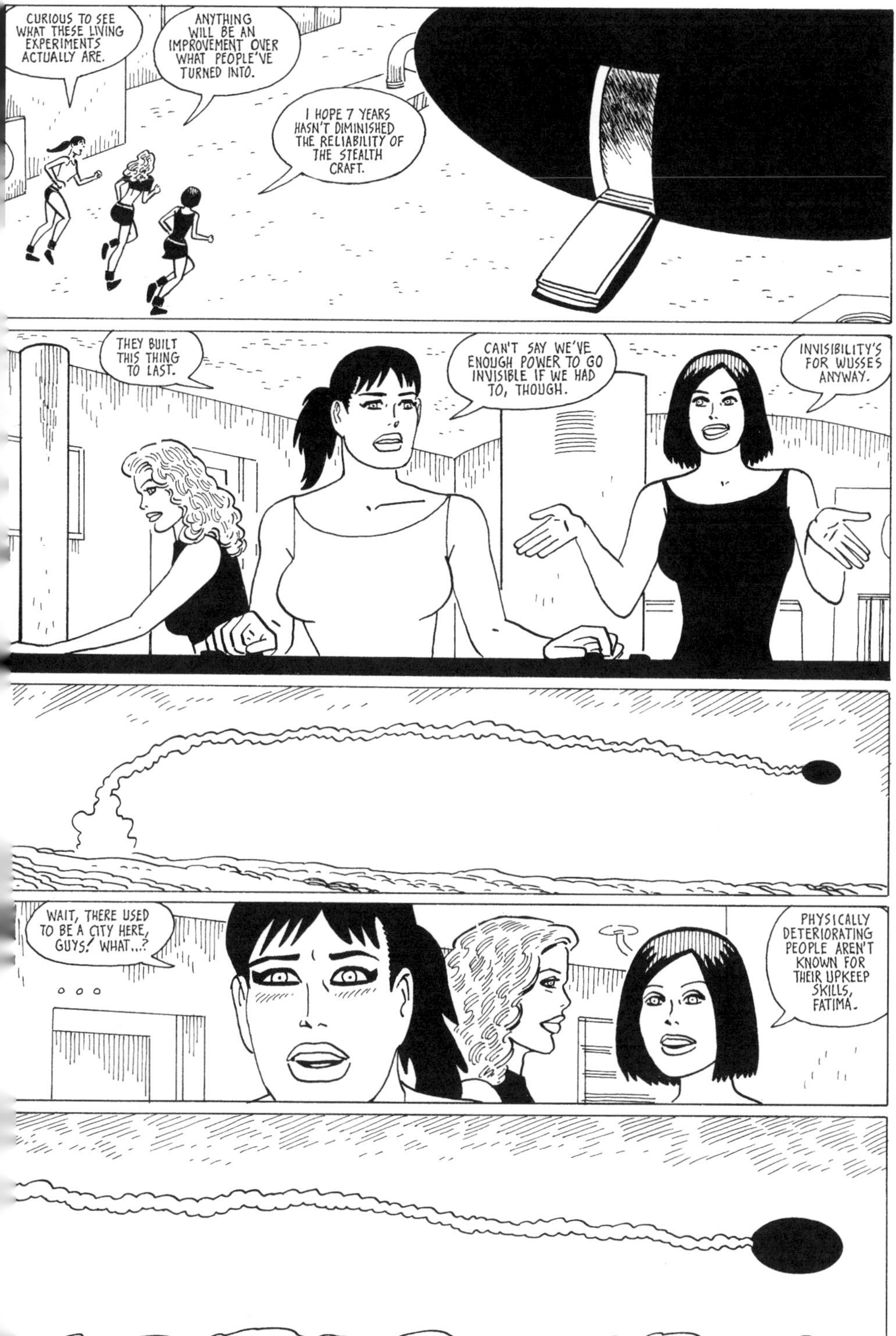
CURIOUS TO SEE WHAT THESE LIVING EXPERIMENTS ACTUALLY ARE.
ANYTHING WILL BE AN IMPROVEMENT OVER WHAT PEOPLE'VE TURNED INTO.
I HOPE 7 YEARS HASN'T DIMINISHED THE RELIABILITY OF THE STEALTH CRAFT.
THEY BUILT THIS THING TO LAST.
CAN'T SAY WE'VE ENOUGH POWER TO GO INVISIBLE IF WE HAD TO, THOUGH.
INVISIBILITY'S FOR WUSSES ANYWAY.
WAIT, THERE USED TO BE A CITY HERE, GUYS! WHAT...?
PHYSICALLY DETERIORATING PEOPLE AREN'T KNOWN FOR THEIR UPKEEP SKILLS, FATIMA.

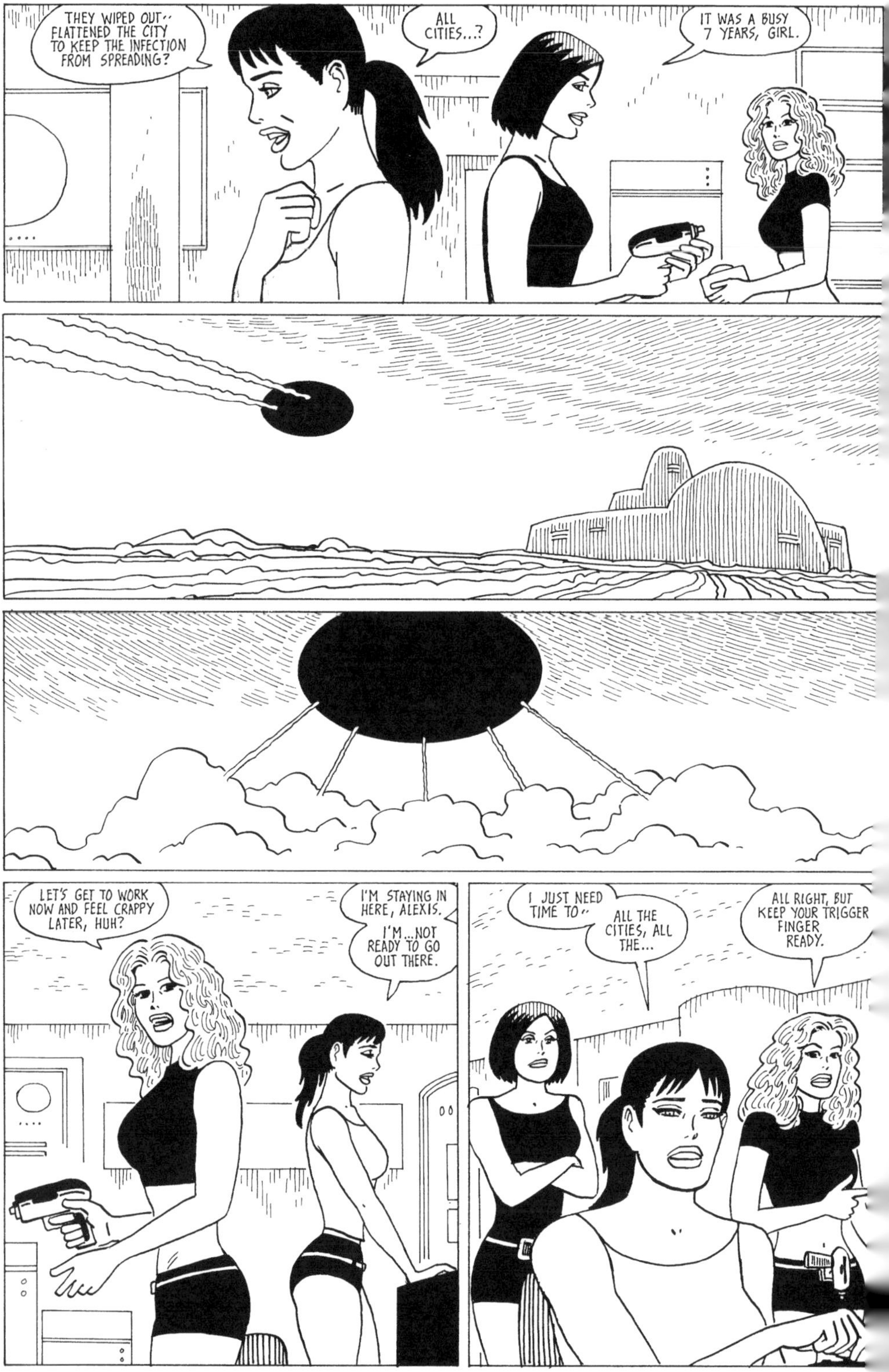
THEY WIPED OUT·· FLATTENED THE CITY TO KEEP THE INFECTION FROM SPREADING?
ALL CITIES...?
IT WAS A BUSY 7 YEARS, GIRL.
LET'S GET TO WORK NOW AND FEEL CRAPPY LATER, HUH?
I'M STAYING IN HERE, ALEXIS.
I'M...NOT READY TO GO OUT THERE.
I JUST NEED TIME TO··
ALL THE CITIES, ALL THE...
ALL RIGHT, BUT KEEP YOUR TRIGGER FINGER READY.

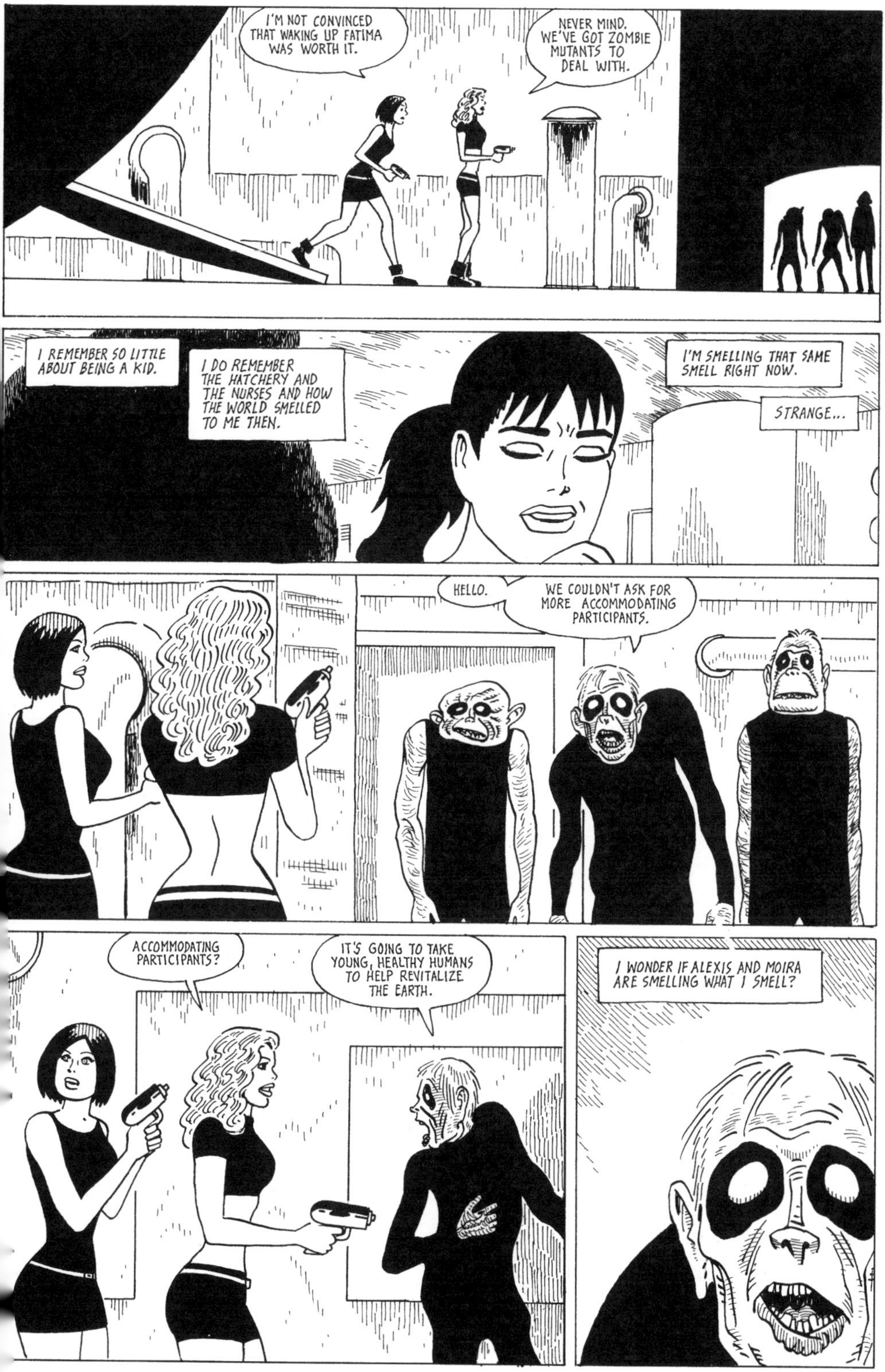

I'M NOT CONVINCED THAT WAKING UP FATIMA WAS WORTH IT.
NEVER MIND. WE'VE GOT ZOMBIE MUTANTS TO DEAL WITH.
I REMEMBER SO LITTLE ABOUT BEING A KID.
I DO REMEMBER THE HATCHERY AND THE NURSES AND HOW THE WORLD SMELLED TO ME THEN.
I'M SMELLING THAT SAME SMELL RIGHT NOW.
STRANGE...
HELLO.
WE COULDN'T ASK FOR MORE ACCOMMODATING PARTICIPANTS.
ACCOMMODATING PARTICIPANTS?
IT'S GOING TO TAKE YOUNG, HEALTHY HUMANS TO HELP REVITALIZE THE EARTH.
I WONDER IF ALEXIS AND MOIRA ARE SMELLING WHAT I SMELL?

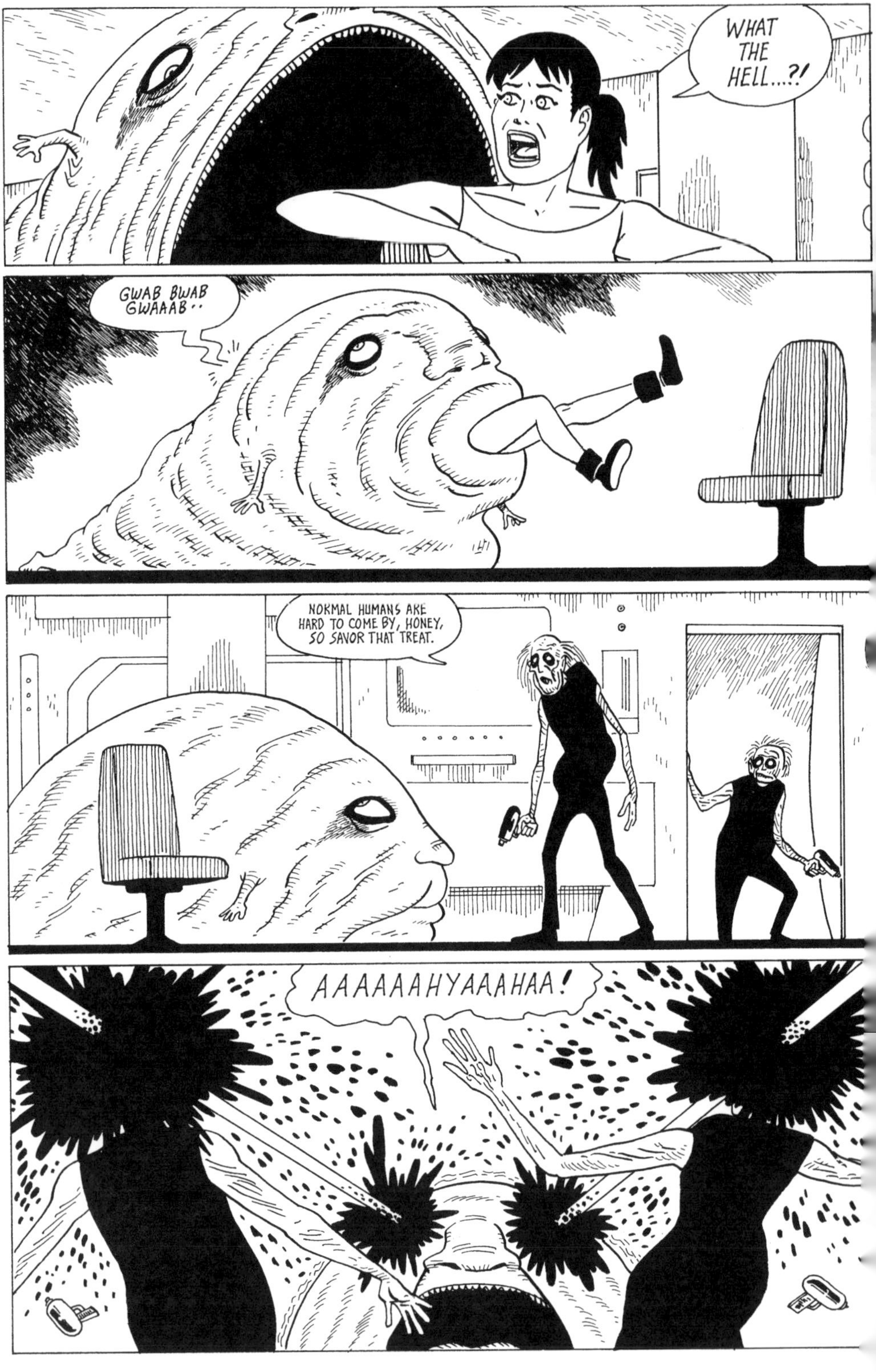
WHAT THE HELL...?!
GWAB BWAB GWAAAB..
NORMAL HUMANS ARE HARD TO COME BY, HONEY, SO SAVOR THAT TREAT.
AAAAAAHYAAAHAA!

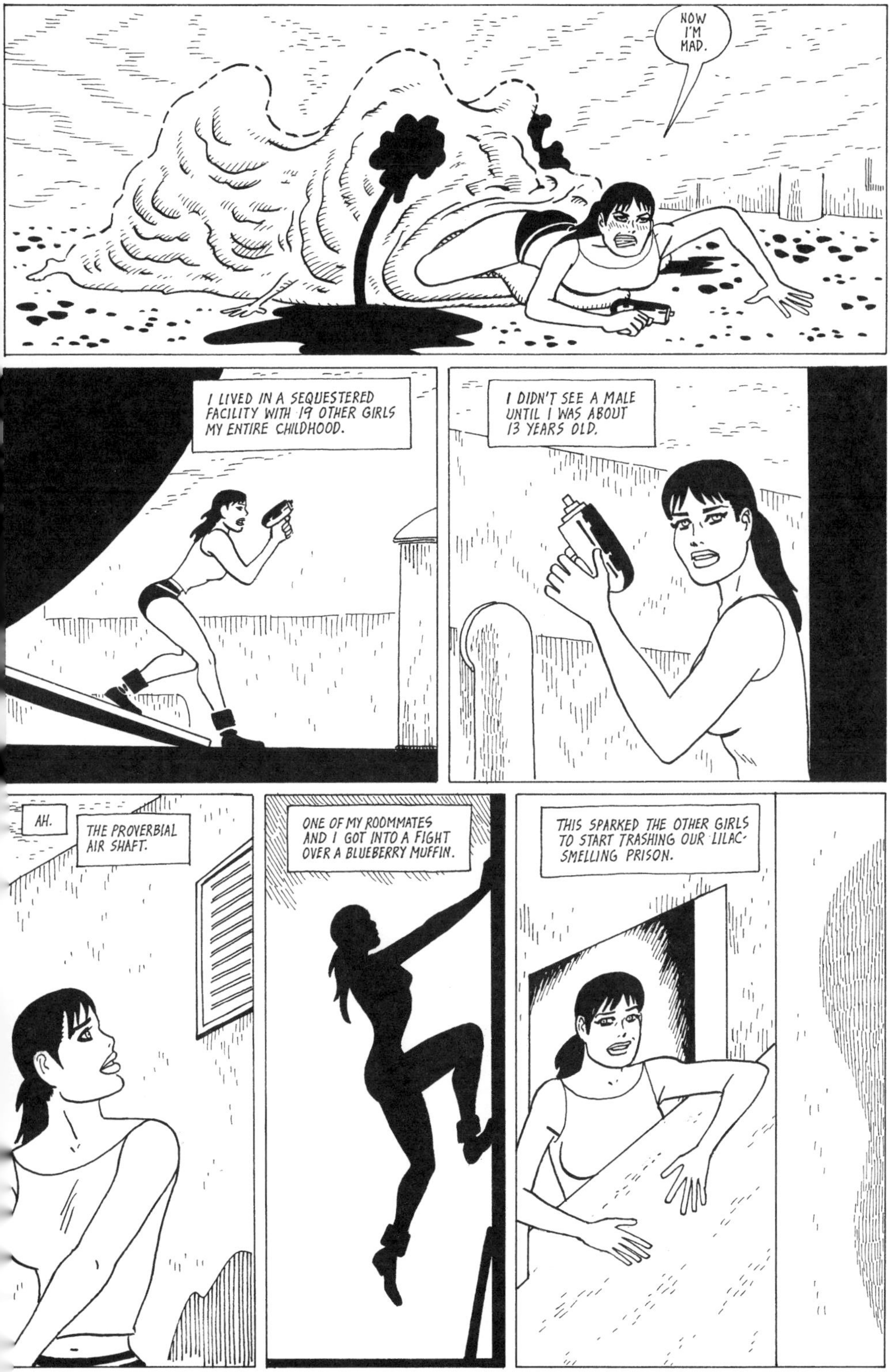

NOW I'M MAD.
I LIVED IN A SEQUESTERED FACILITY WITH 19 OTHER GIRLS MY ENTIRE CHILDHOOD.
I DIDN'T SEE A MALE UNTIL I WAS ABOUT 13 YEARS OLD.
AH.
THE PROVERBIAL AIR SHAFT.
ONE OF MY ROOMMATES AND I GOT INTO A FIGHT OVER A BLUEBERRY MUFFIN.
THIS SPARKED THE OTHER GIRLS TO START TRASHING OUR LILAC-SMELLING PRISON.

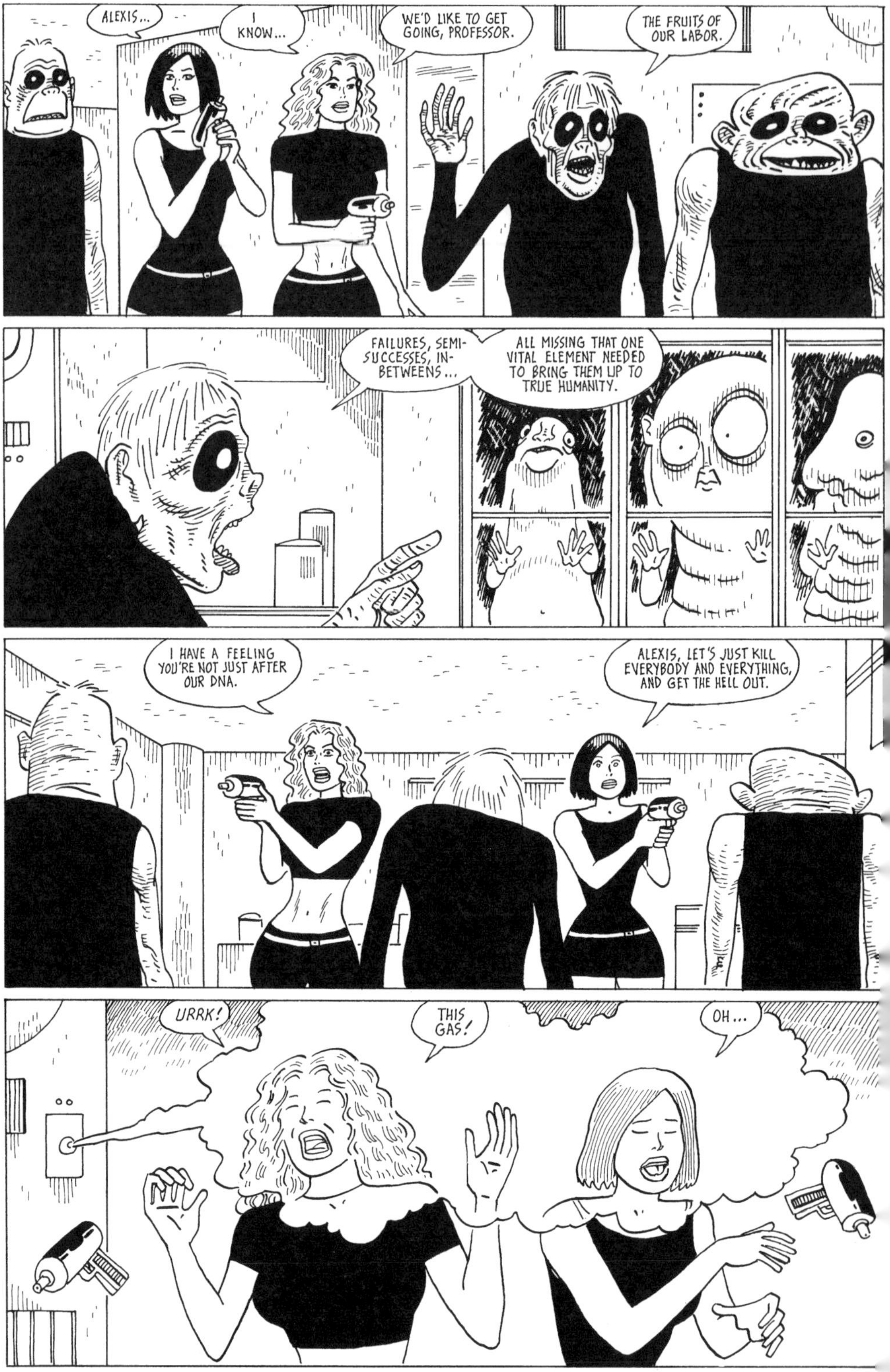

ALEXIS...
I KNOW...
WE'D LIKE TO GET GOING, PROFESSOR.
THE FRUITS OF OUR LABOR.
FAILURES, SEMI-SUCCESSES, IN-BETWEENS...
ALL MISSING THAT ONE VITAL ELEMENT NEEDED TO BRING THEM UP TO TRUE HUMANITY.
I HAVE A FEELING YOU'RE NOT JUST AFTER OUR DNA.
ALEXIS, LET'S JUST KILL EVERYBODY AND EVERYTHING, AND GET THE HELL OUT.
URRK!
THIS GAS!
OH...

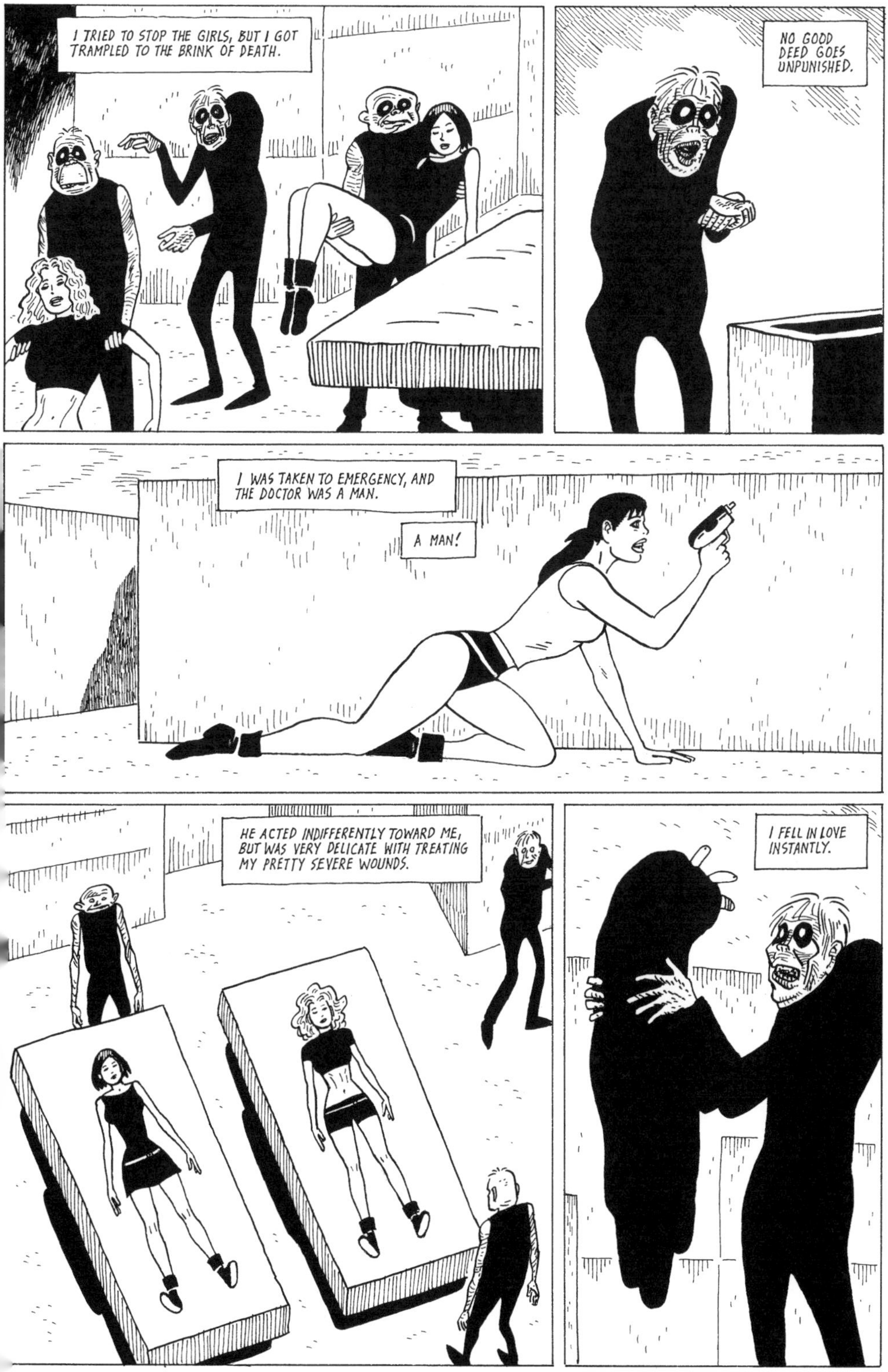
I TRIED TO STOP THE GIRLS, BUT I GOT TRAMPLED TO THE BRINK OF DEATH.
NO GOOD DEED GOES UNPUNISHED.
I WAS TAKEN TO EMERGENCY, AND THE DOCTOR WAS A MAN.
A MAN!
HE ACTED INDIFFERENTLY TOWARD ME, BUT WAS VERY DELICATE WITH TREATING MY PRETTY SEVERE WOUNDS.
I FELL IN LOVE INSTANTLY.

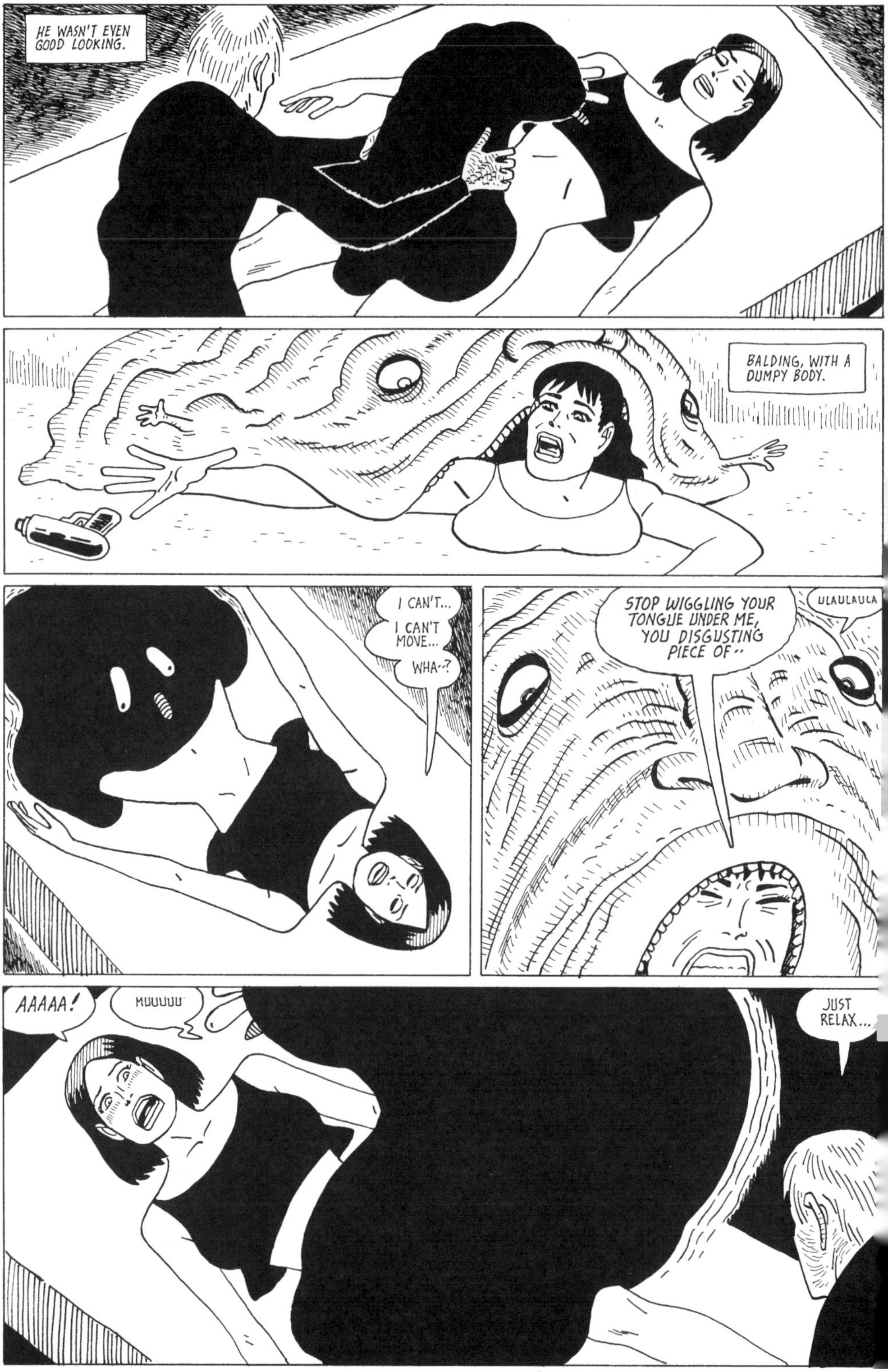
HE WASN'T EVEN GOOD LOOKING.
BALDING, WITH A DUMPY BODY.
I CAN'T...
I CAN'T MOVE...
WHA-?
STOP WIGGLING YOUR TONGUE UNDER ME, YOU DISGUSTING PIECE OF--
ULAULAULA
AAAAA!
MUUUUU
JUST RELAX...

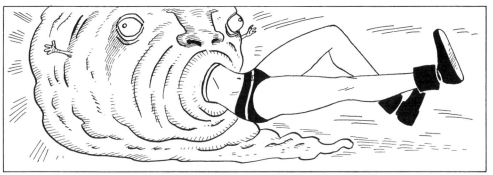

MUUUU

MUUU

MUUU

BUT TO MY EYES, HE WAS APOLLO.

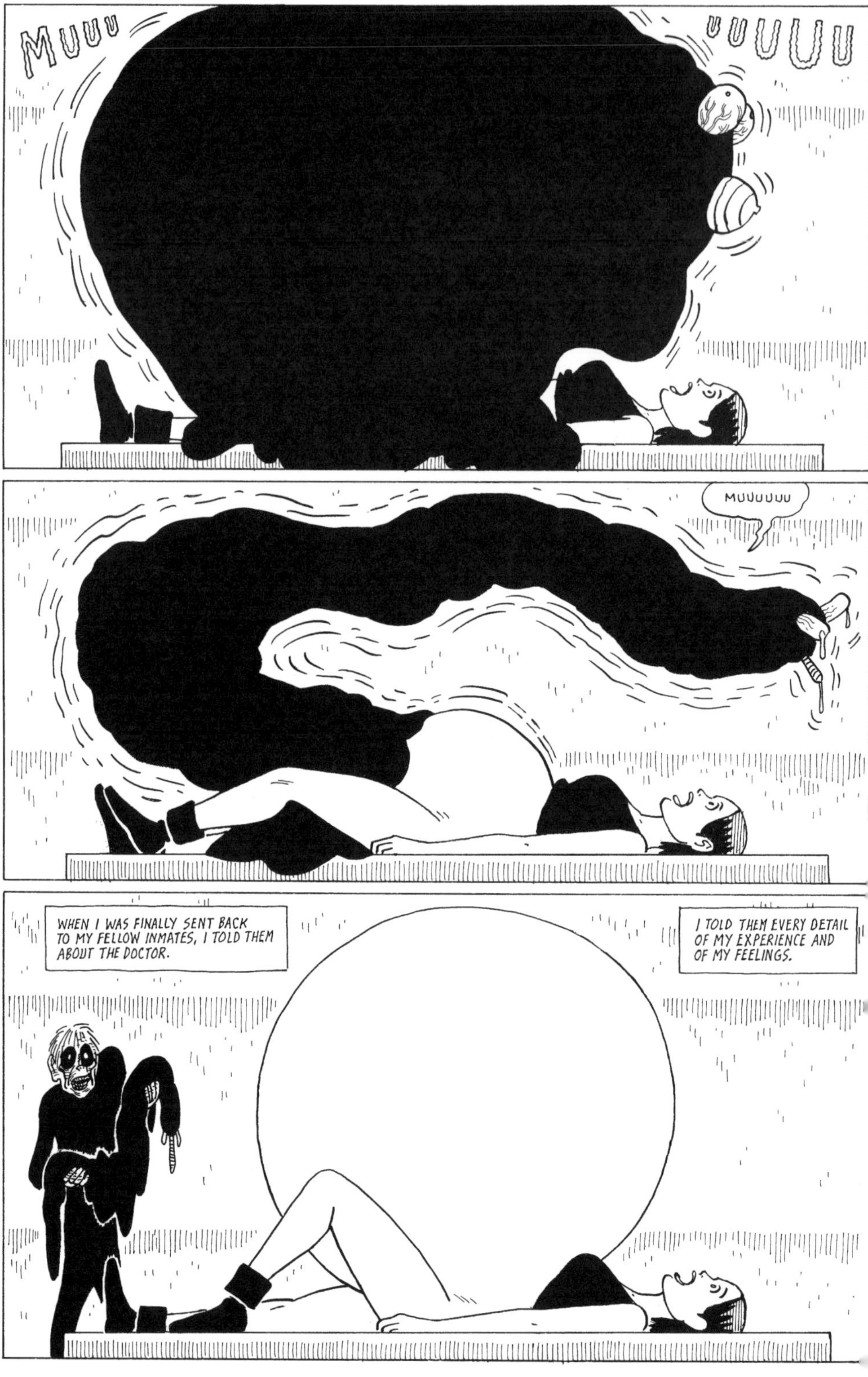
MUUU
UUUUU
MUUUUUU
WHEN I WAS FINALLY SENT BACK TO MY FELLOW INMATES, I TOLD THEM ABOUT THE DOCTOR.
I TOLD THEM EVERY DETAIL OF MY EXPERIENCE AND OF MY FEELINGS.

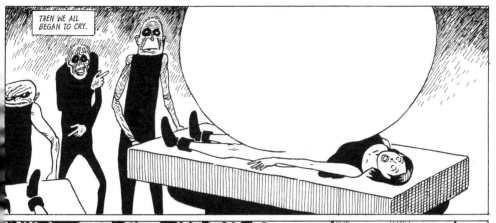

THEN WE ALL BEGAN TO CRY.

ALL TWENTY OF US, CRYING UNCONTROLLABLY.

MOIRA...

MUUUUU

WHAT... HAPPENED TO MOIRA ...?

AND THEN WE STOPPED.

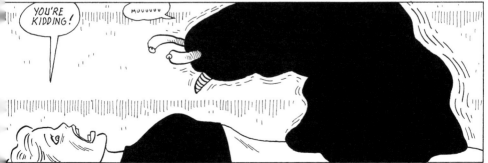

YOU'RE KIDDING!

MUUUUU

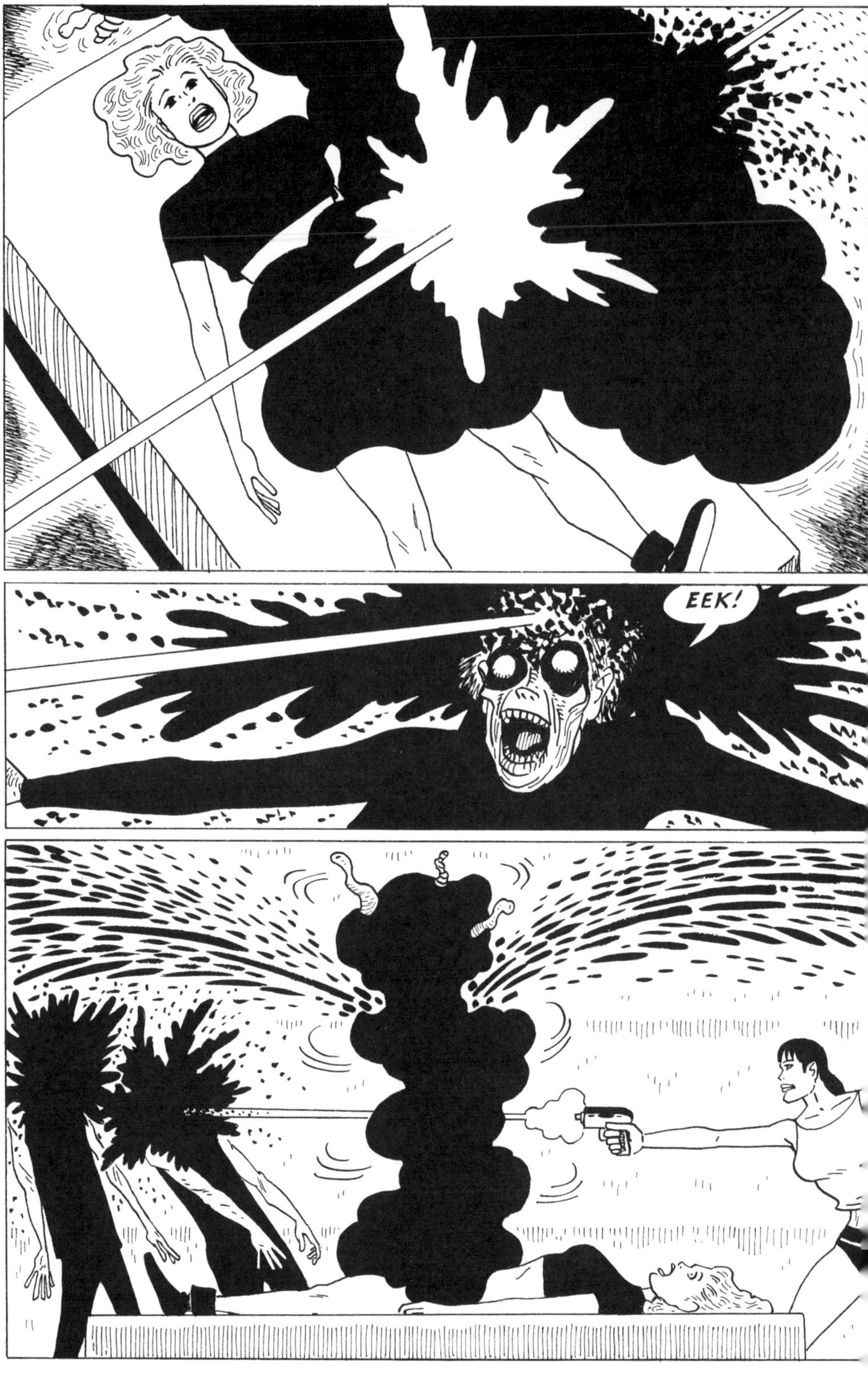
EEK!

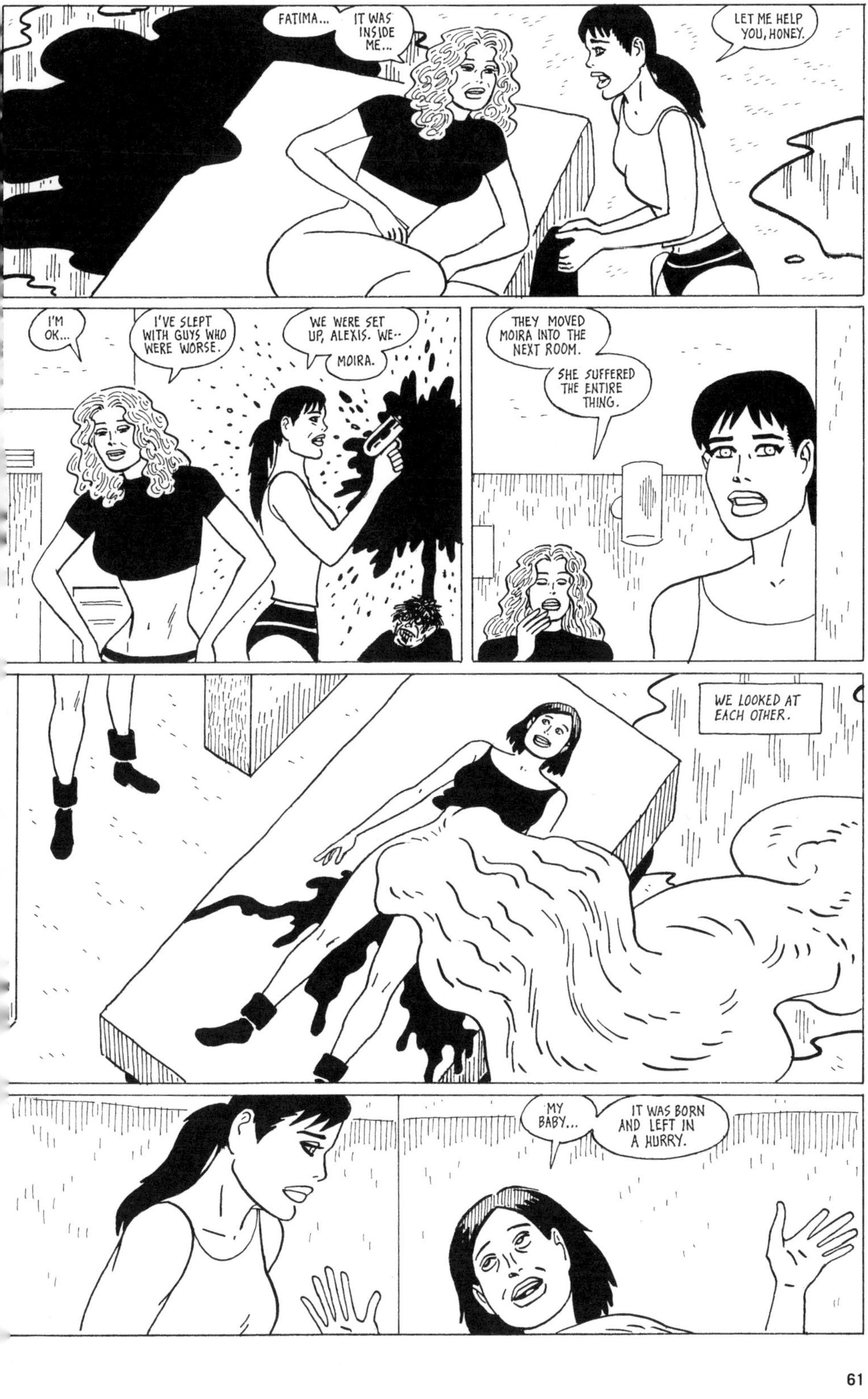
FATIMA...
IT WAS INSIDE ME...
LET ME HELP YOU, HONEY.
I'M OK...
I'VE SLEPT WITH GUYS WHO WERE WORSE.
WE WERE SET UP, ALEXIS. WE--
MOIRA.
THEY MOVED MOIRA INTO THE NEXT ROOM.
SHE SUFFERED THE ENTIRE THING.
WE LOOKED AT EACH OTHER.
MY BABY...
IT WAS BORN AND LEFT IN A HURRY.

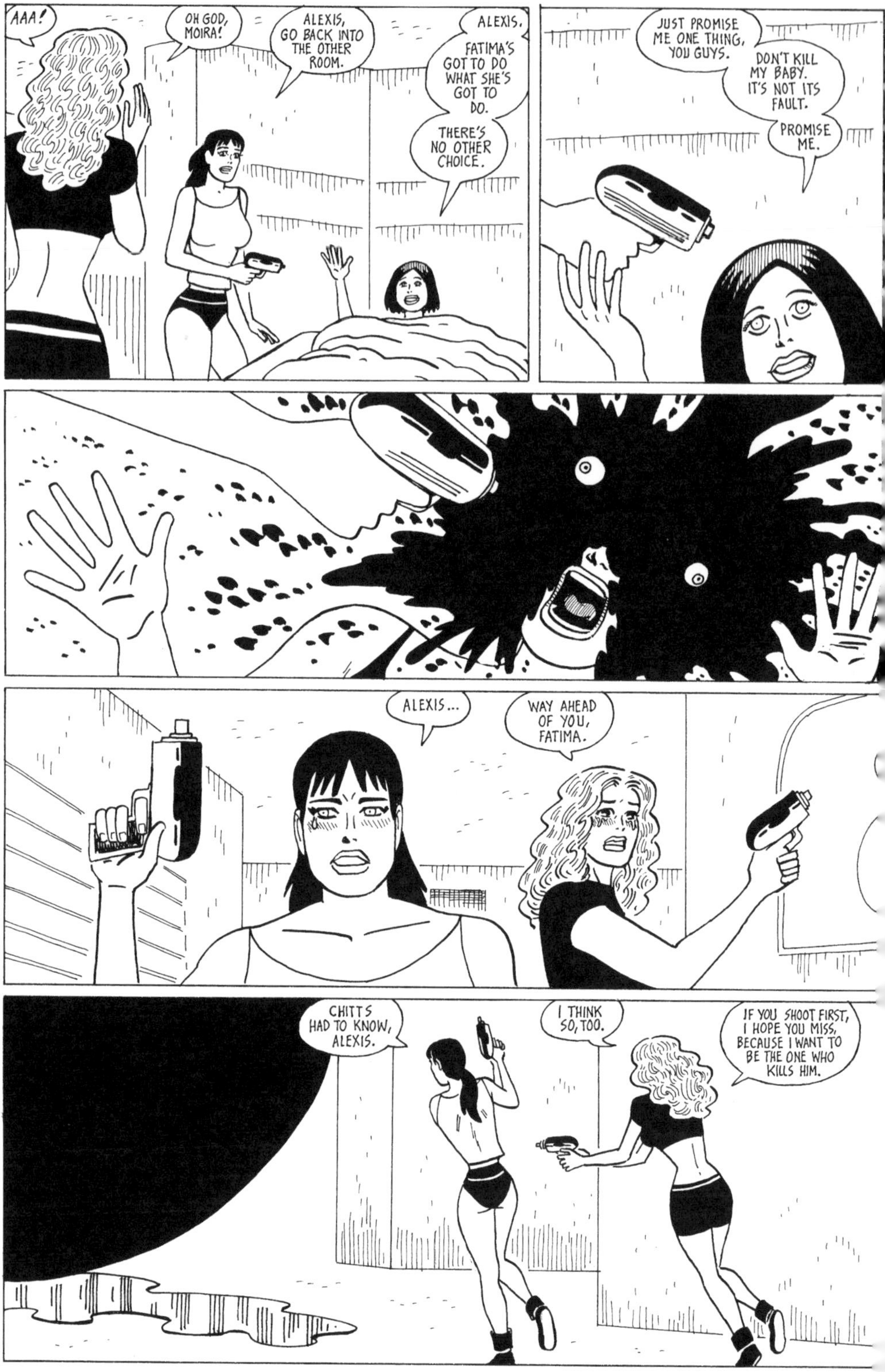
AAA!
OH GOD, MOIRA!
ALEXIS, GO BACK INTO THE OTHER ROOM.
ALEXIS.
FATIMA'S GOT TO DO WHAT SHE'S GOT TO DO.
THERE'S NO OTHER CHOICE.
JUST PROMISE ME ONE THING, YOU GUYS.
DON'T KILL MY BABY. IT'S NOT ITS FAULT.
PROMISE ME.
ALEXIS...
WAY AHEAD OF YOU, FATIMA.
CHITTS HAD TO KNOW, ALEXIS.
I THINK SO, TOO.
IF YOU SHOOT FIRST, I HOPE YOU MISS, BECAUSE I WANT TO BE THE ONE WHO KILLS HIM.

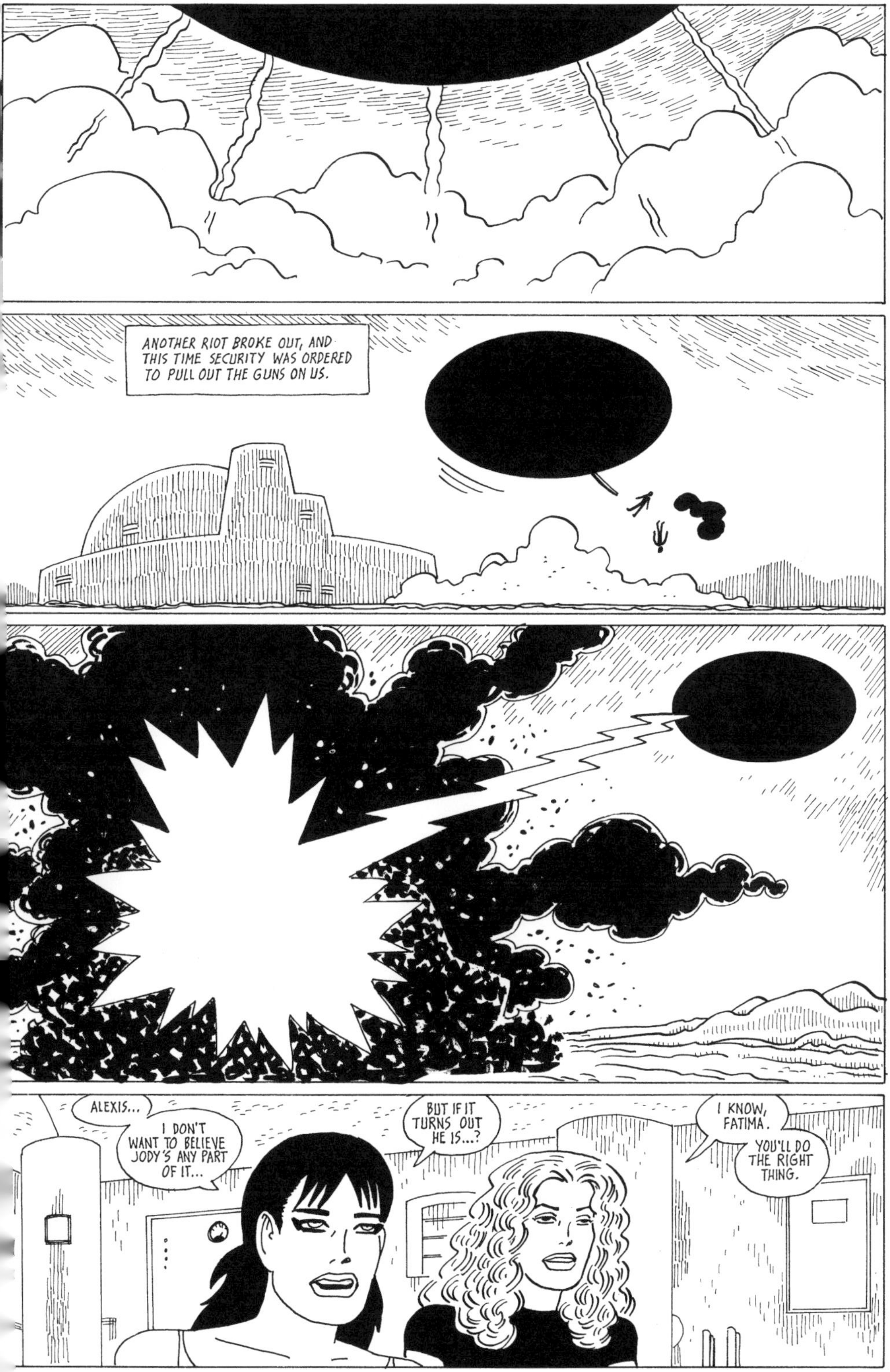
ANOTHER RIOT BROKE OUT, AND THIS TIME SECURITY WAS ORDERED TO PULL OUT THE GUNS ON US.
ALEXIS...
I DON'T WANT TO BELIEVE JODY'S ANY PART OF IT...
BUT IF IT TURNS OUT HE IS...?
I KNOW, FATIMA.
YOU'LL DO THE RIGHT THING.

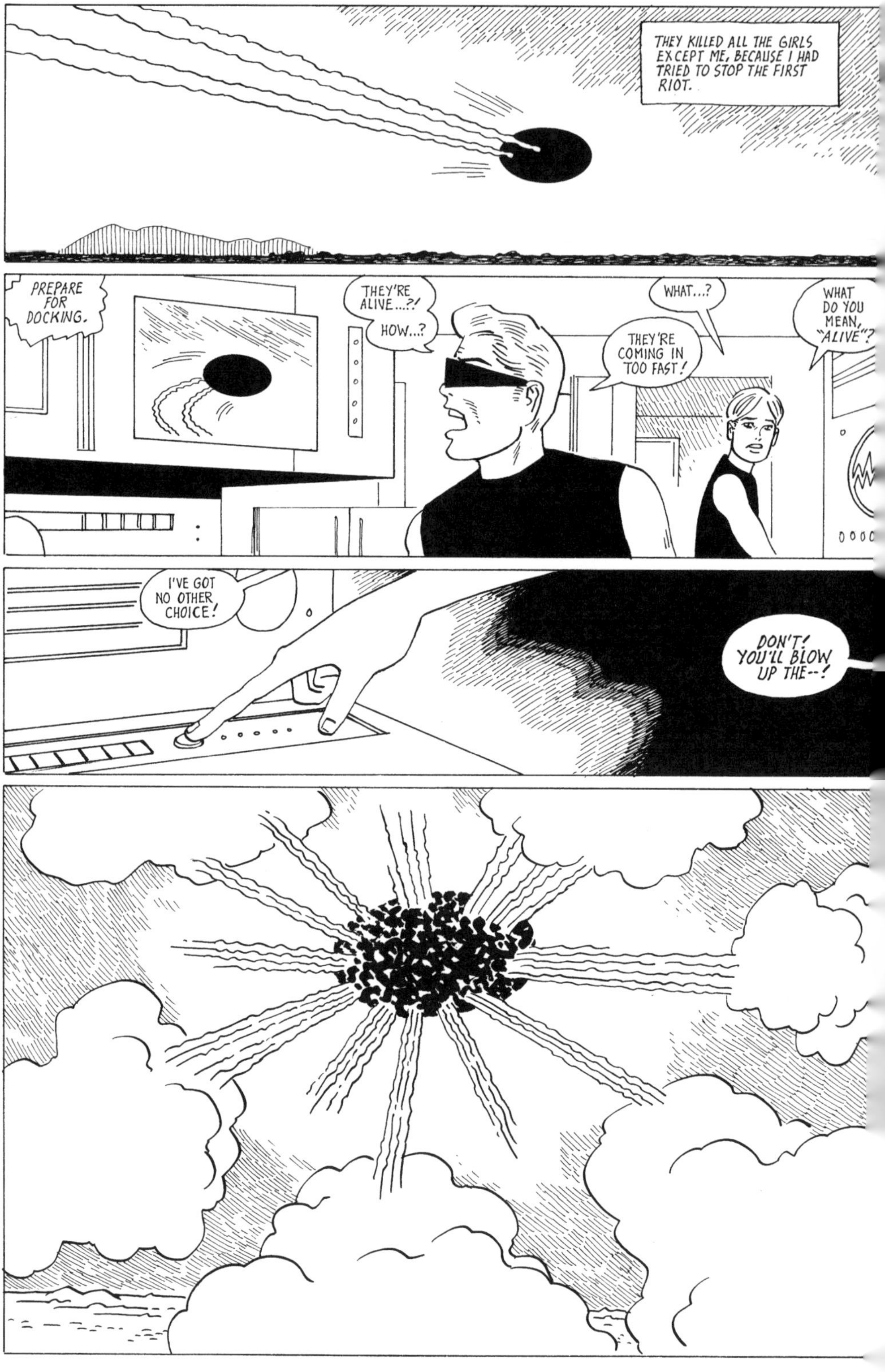
THEY KILLED ALL THE GIRLS EXCEPT ME, BECAUSE I HAD TRIED TO STOP THE FIRST RIOT.
PREPARE FOR DOCKING.
THEY'RE ALIVE...?!
HOW...?
WHAT...?
THEY'RE COMING IN TOO FAST!
WHAT DO YOU MEAN, "ALIVE"?
I'VE GOT NO OTHER CHOICE!
DON'T! YOU'LL BLOW UP THE--!

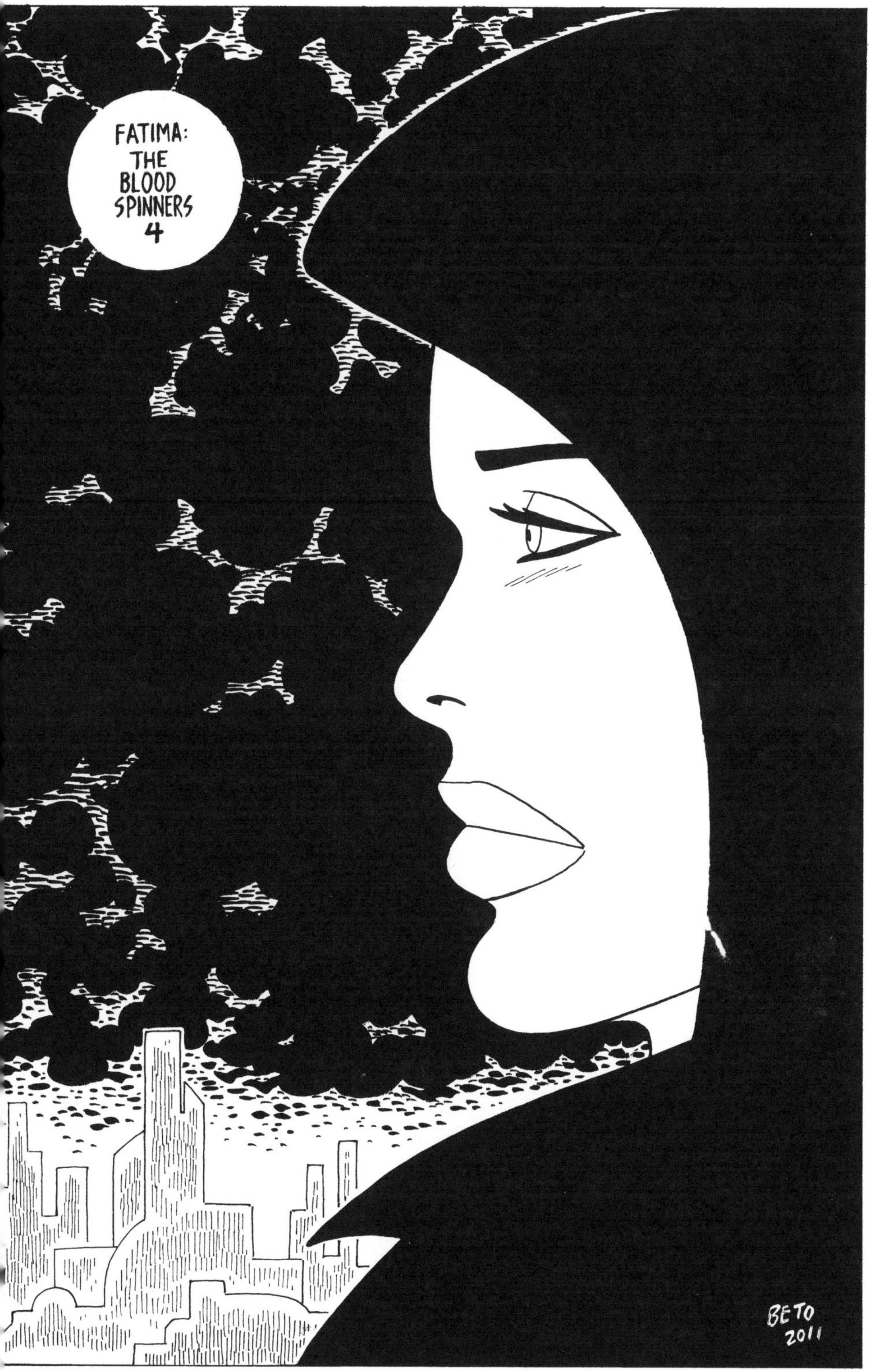
FATIMA:
THE
BLOOD
SPINNERS
4
BETO
2011

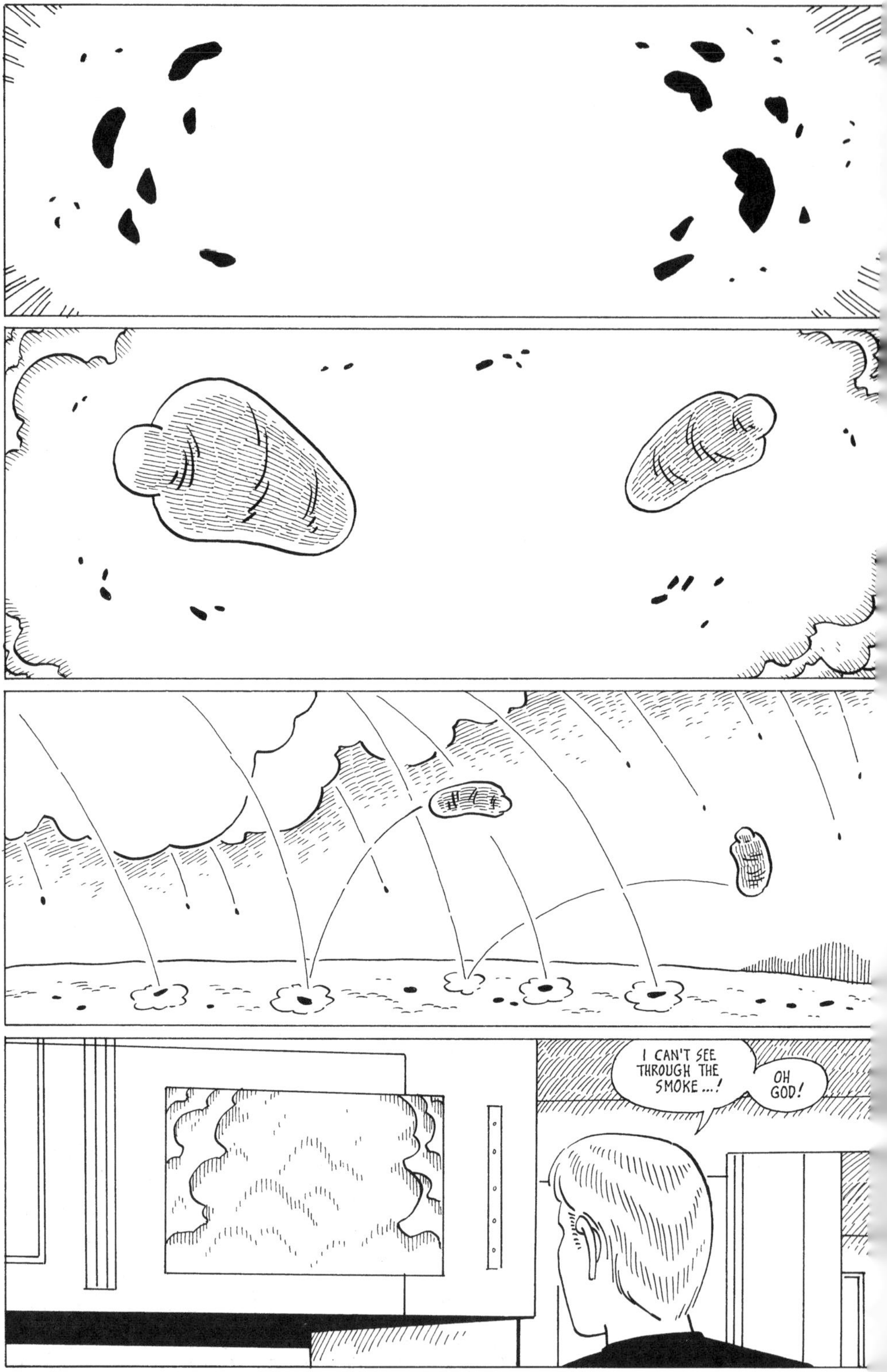
I CAN'T SEE THROUGH THE SMOKE...!
OH GOD!

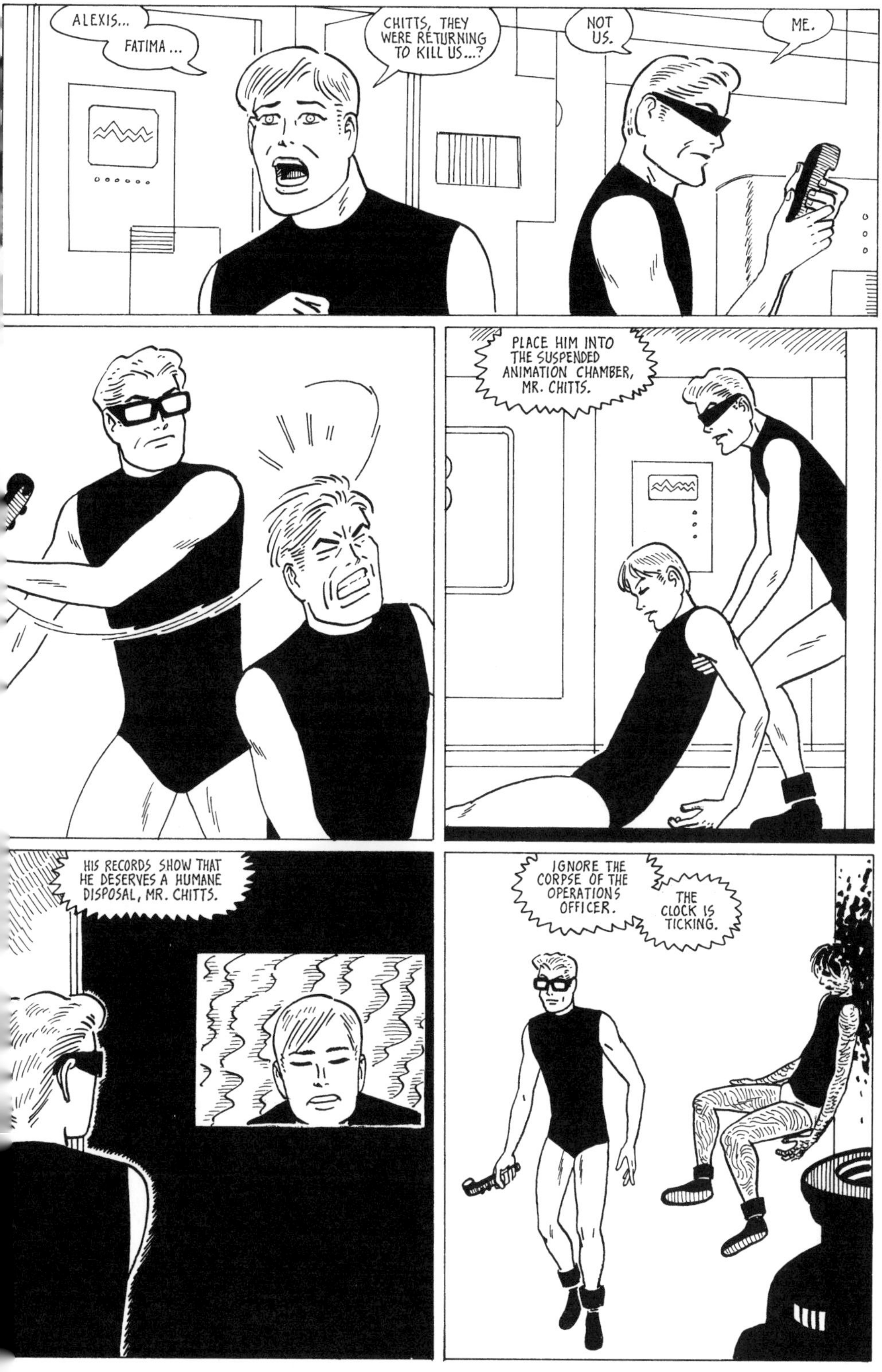
ALEXIS...
FATIMA ...
CHITTS, THEY WERE RETURNING TO KILL US...?
NOT US.
ME.
PLACE HIM INTO THE SUSPENDED ANIMATION CHAMBER, MR. CHITTS.
HIS RECORDS SHOW THAT HE DESERVES A HUMANE DISPOSAL, MR. CHITTS.
IGNORE THE CORPSE OF THE OPERATIONS OFFICER.
THE CLOCK IS TICKING.

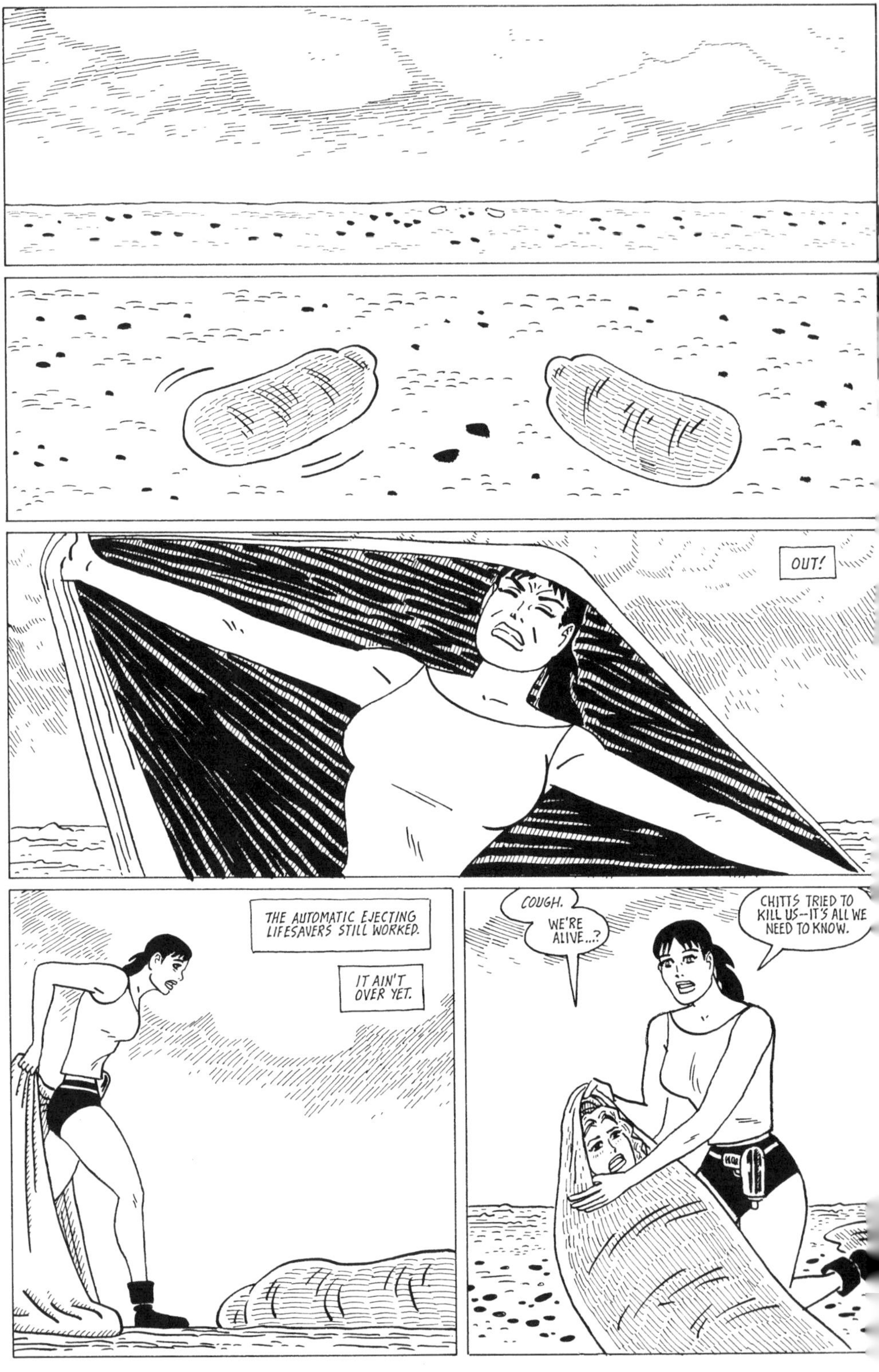
OUT!
THE AUTOMATIC EJECTING LIFESAVERS STILL WORKED.
IT AIN'T OVER YET.
COUGH.
WE'RE ALIVE...?
CHITTS TRIED TO KILL US--IT'S ALL WE NEED TO KNOW.

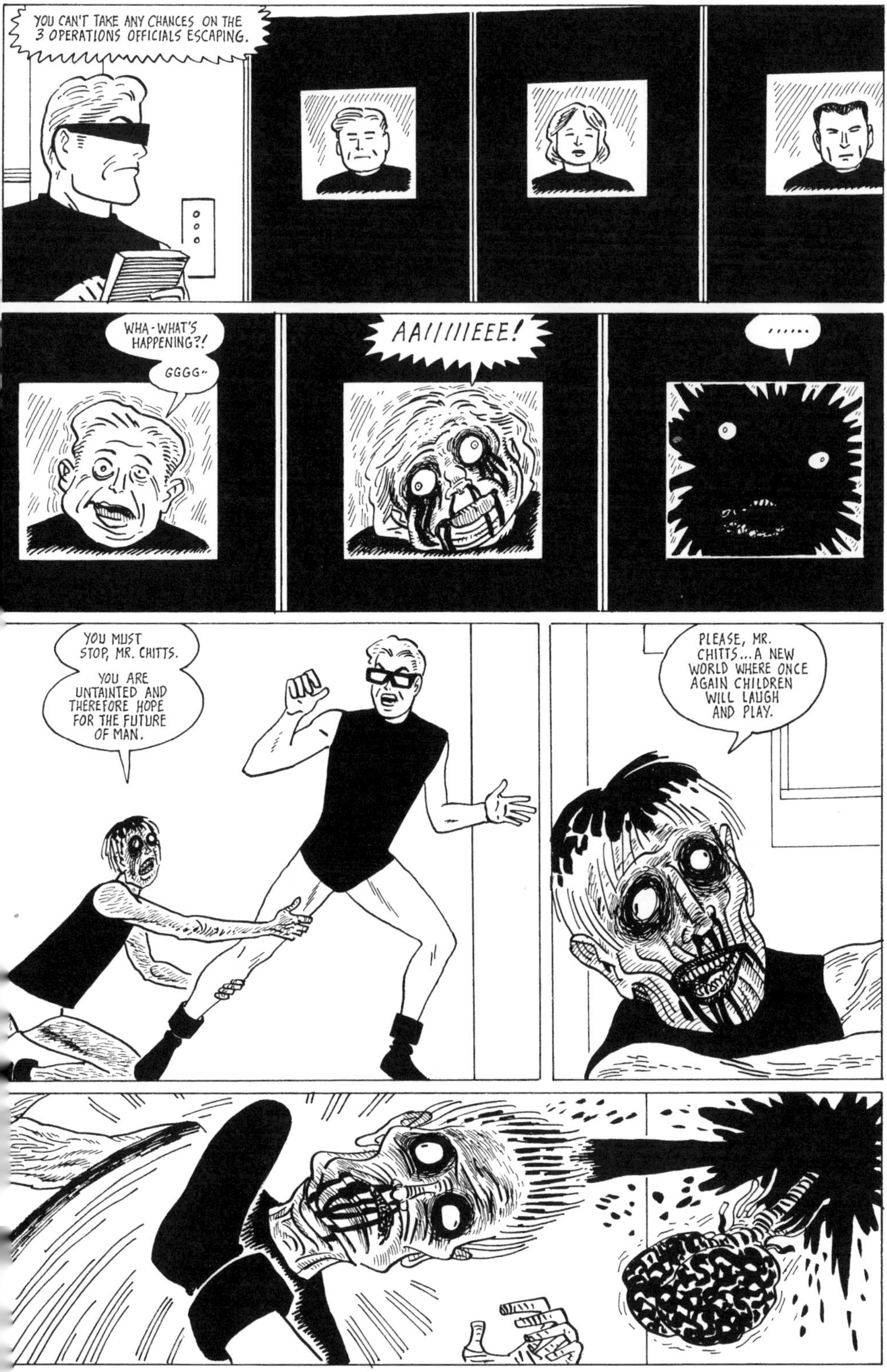
YOU CAN'T TAKE ANY CHANCES ON THE 3 OPERATIONS OFFICIALS ESCAPING.
WHA-WHAT'S HAPPENING?!
GGGG"
AAIIIIIEEE!
......
YOU MUST STOP, MR. CHITTS.
YOU ARE UNTAINTED AND THEREFORE HOPE FOR THE FUTURE OF MAN.
PLEASE, MR. CHITTS... A NEW WORLD WHERE ONCE AGAIN CHILDREN WILL LAUGH AND PLAY.

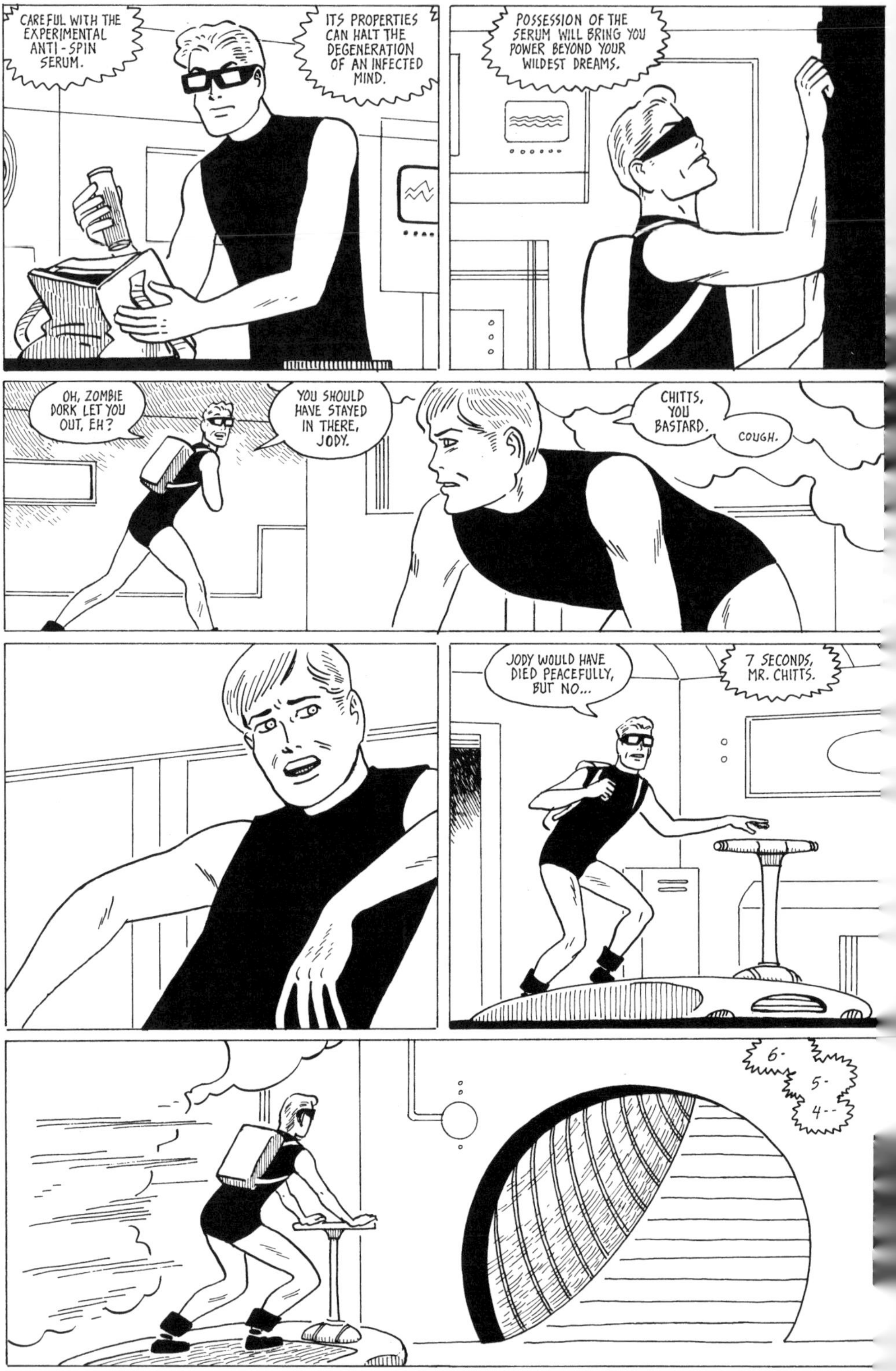
CAREFUL WITH THE EXPERIMENTAL ANTI-SPIN SERUM.
ITS PROPERTIES CAN HALT THE DEGENERATION OF AN INFECTED MIND.
POSSESSION OF THE SERUM WILL BRING YOU POWER BEYOND YOUR WILDEST DREAMS.
OH, ZOMBIE DORK LET YOU OUT, EH?
YOU SHOULD HAVE STAYED IN THERE, JODY.
CHITTS, YOU BASTARD.
COUGH.
JODY WOULD HAVE DIED PEACEFULLY, BUT NO...
7 SECONDS, MR. CHITTS.
6-
5-
4--

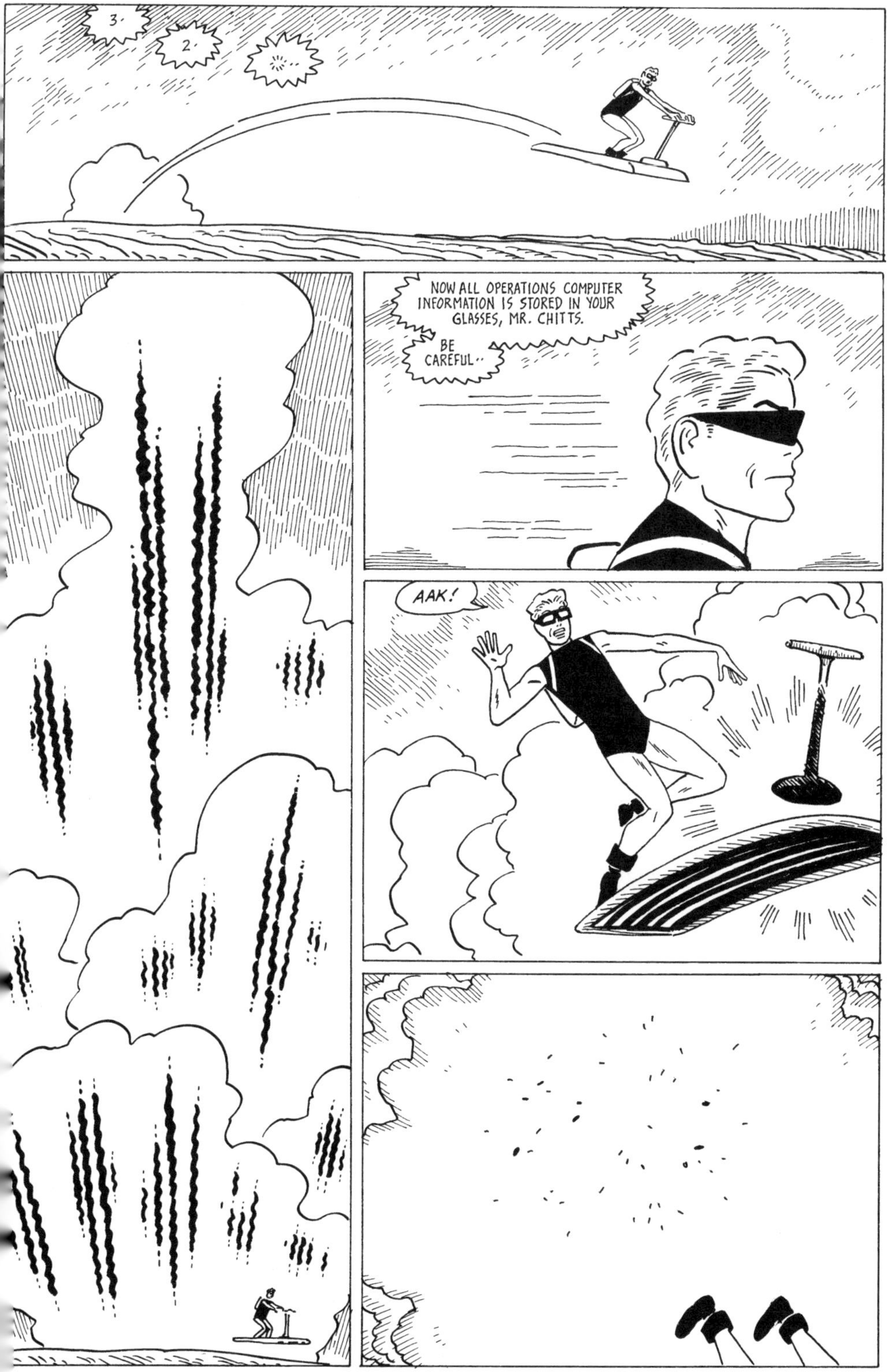
3·
2·
NOW ALL OPERATIONS COMPUTER INFORMATION IS STORED IN YOUR GLASSES, MR. CHITTS.
BE CAREFUL··
AAK!

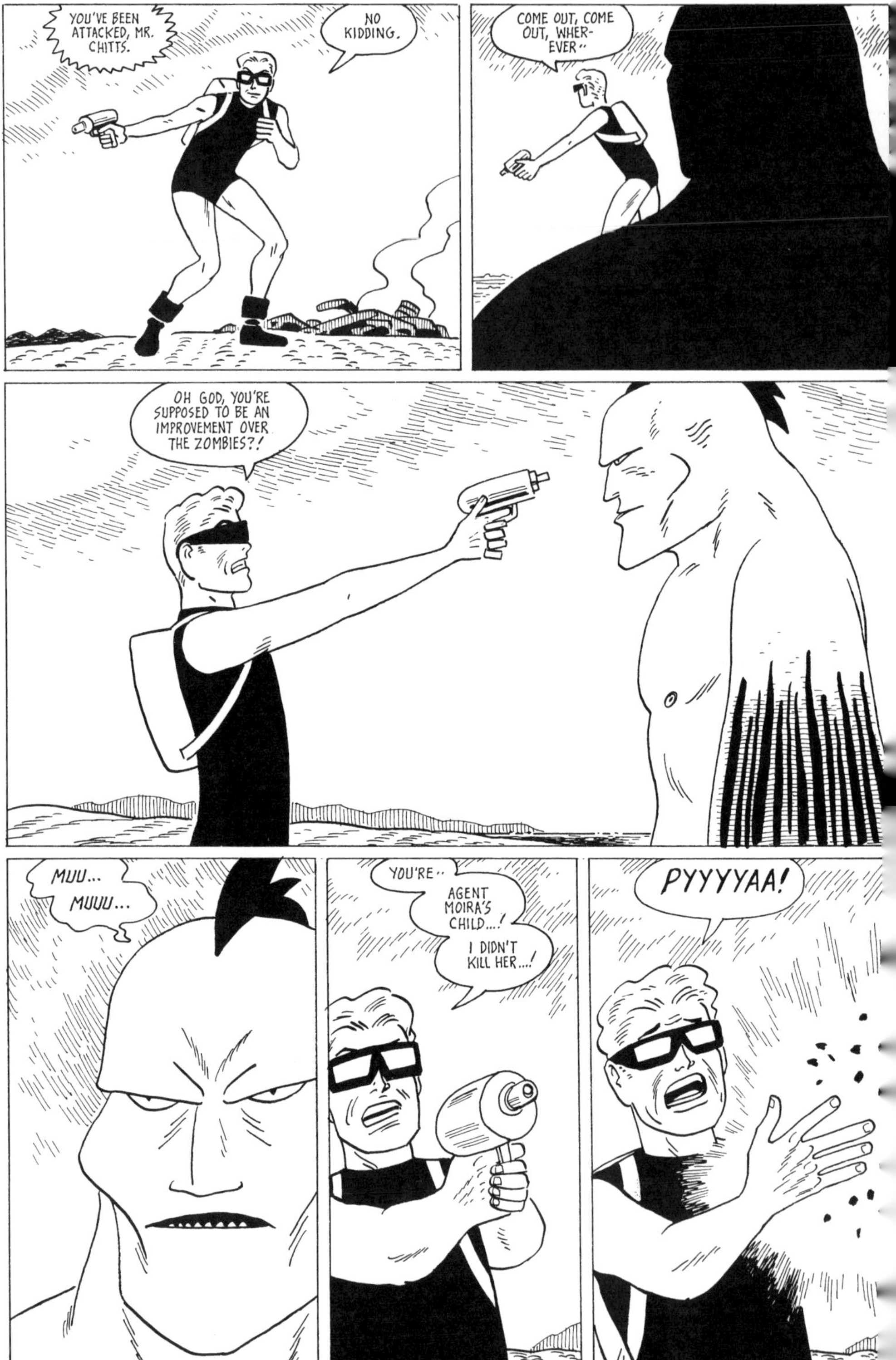

YOU'VE BEEN ATTACKED, MR. CHITTS.
NO KIDDING.
COME OUT, COME OUT, WHER- EVER..
OH GOD, YOU'RE SUPPOSED TO BE AN IMPROVEMENT OVER THE ZOMBIES?!
MUU... MUUU...
YOU'RE..
AGENT MOIRA'S CHILD....!
I DIDN'T KILL HER....!
PYYYYAA!

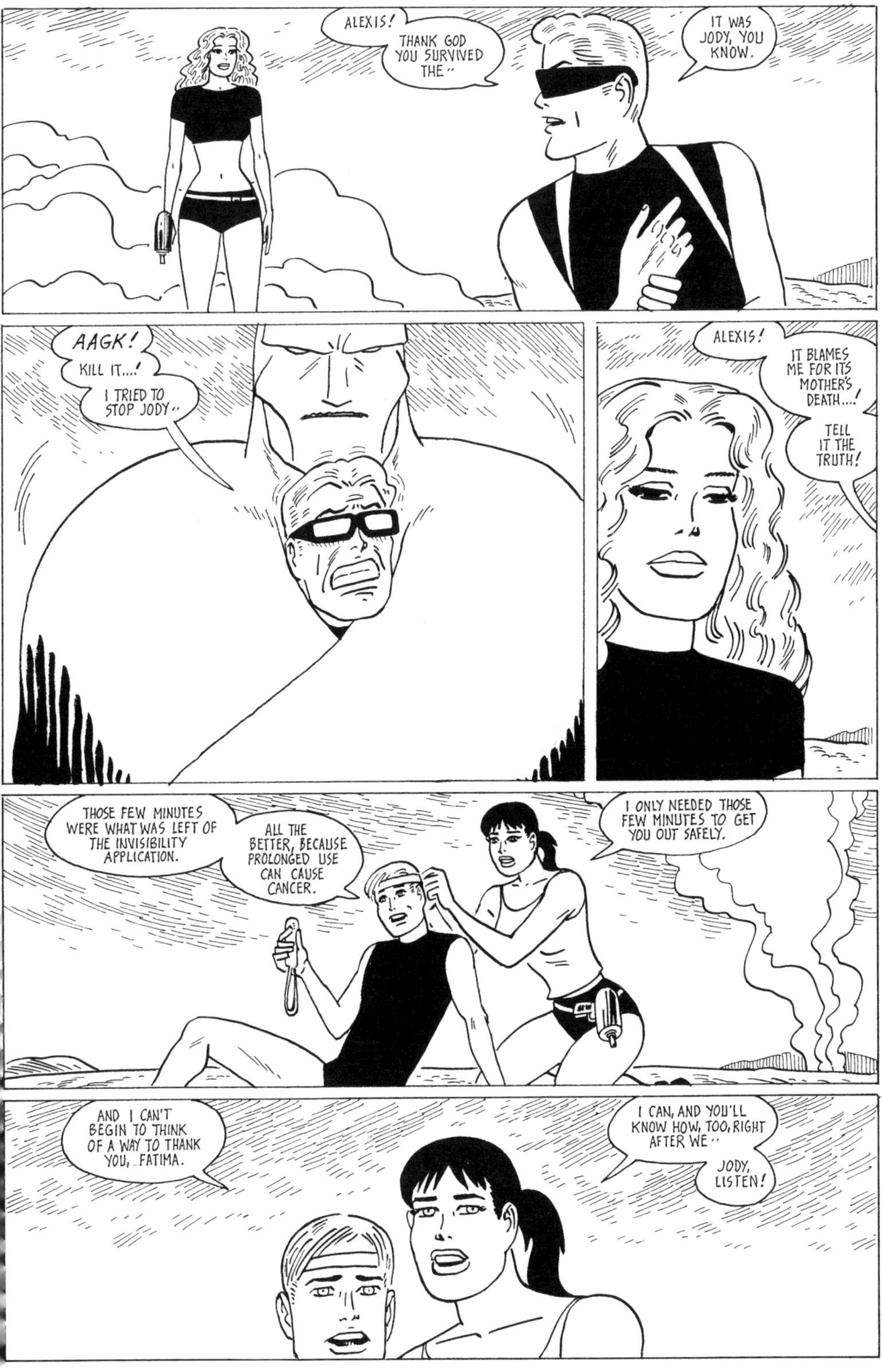
ALEXIS!
THANK GOD YOU SURVIVED THE··
IT WAS JODY, YOU KNOW.
AAGK!
KILL IT...!
I TRIED TO STOP JODY··
ALEXIS!
IT BLAMES ME FOR ITS MOTHER'S DEATH...!
TELL IT THE TRUTH!
THOSE FEW MINUTES WERE WHAT WAS LEFT OF THE INVISIBILITY APPLICATION.
ALL THE BETTER, BECAUSE PROLONGED USE CAN CAUSE CANCER.
I ONLY NEEDED THOSE FEW MINUTES TO GET YOU OUT SAFELY.
AND I CAN'T BEGIN TO THINK OF A WAY TO THANK YOU, FATIMA.
I CAN, AND YOU'LL KNOW HOW, TOO, RIGHT AFTER WE··
JODY, LISTEN!

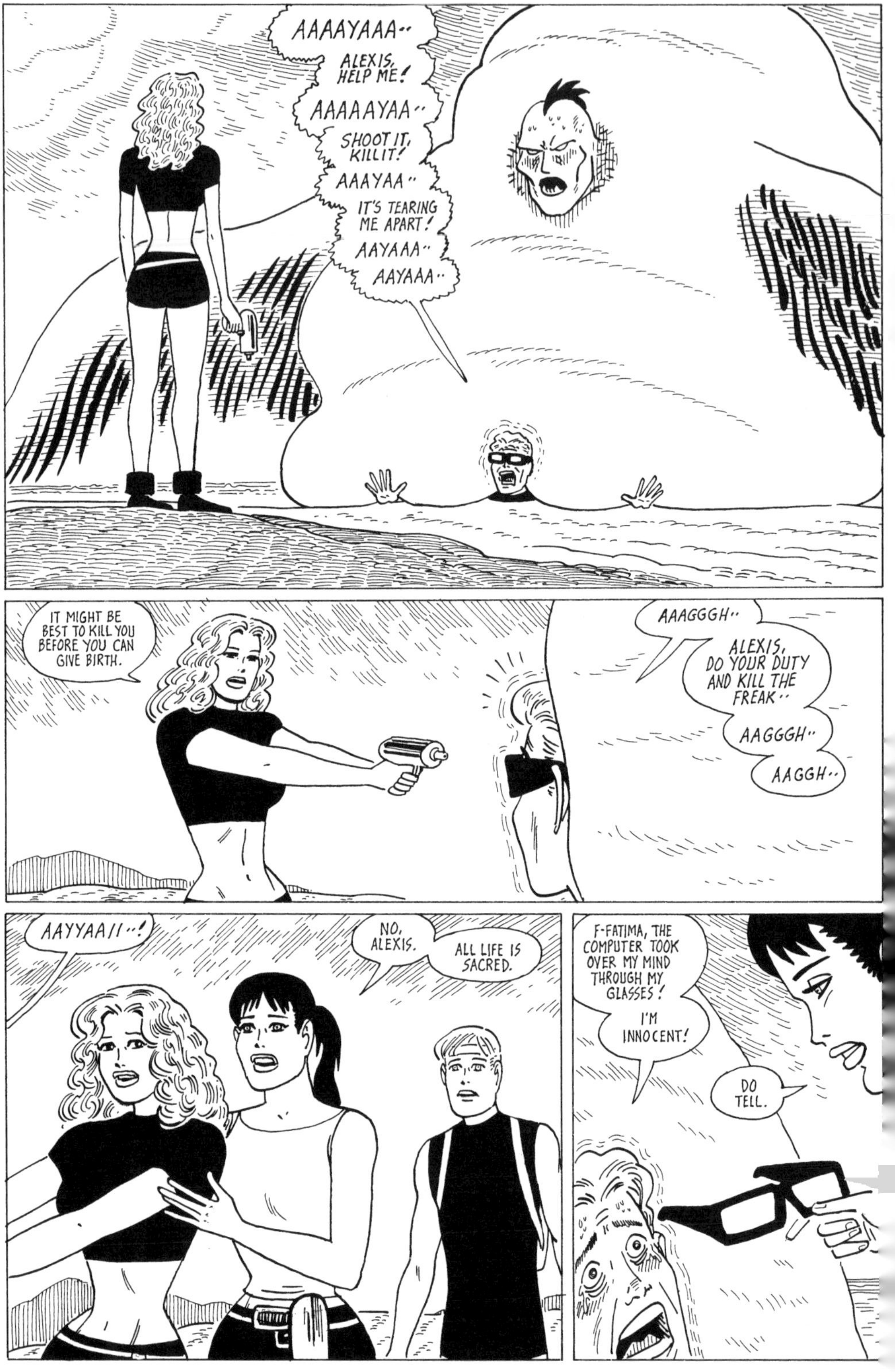
AAAAYAAA..
ALEXIS, HELP ME!
AAAAAYAA..
SHOOT IT, KILL IT!
AAAYAA..
IT'S TEARING ME APART!
AAYAAA..
AAYAAA..
IT MIGHT BE BEST TO KILL YOU BEFORE YOU CAN GIVE BIRTH.
AAAGGGH..
ALEXIS, DO YOUR DUTY AND KILL THE FREAK..
AAGGGH..
AAGGH..
AAYYAAII..!
NO, ALEXIS.
ALL LIFE IS SACRED.
F-FATIMA, THE COMPUTER TOOK OVER MY MIND THROUGH MY GLASSES!
I'M INNOCENT!
DO TELL.

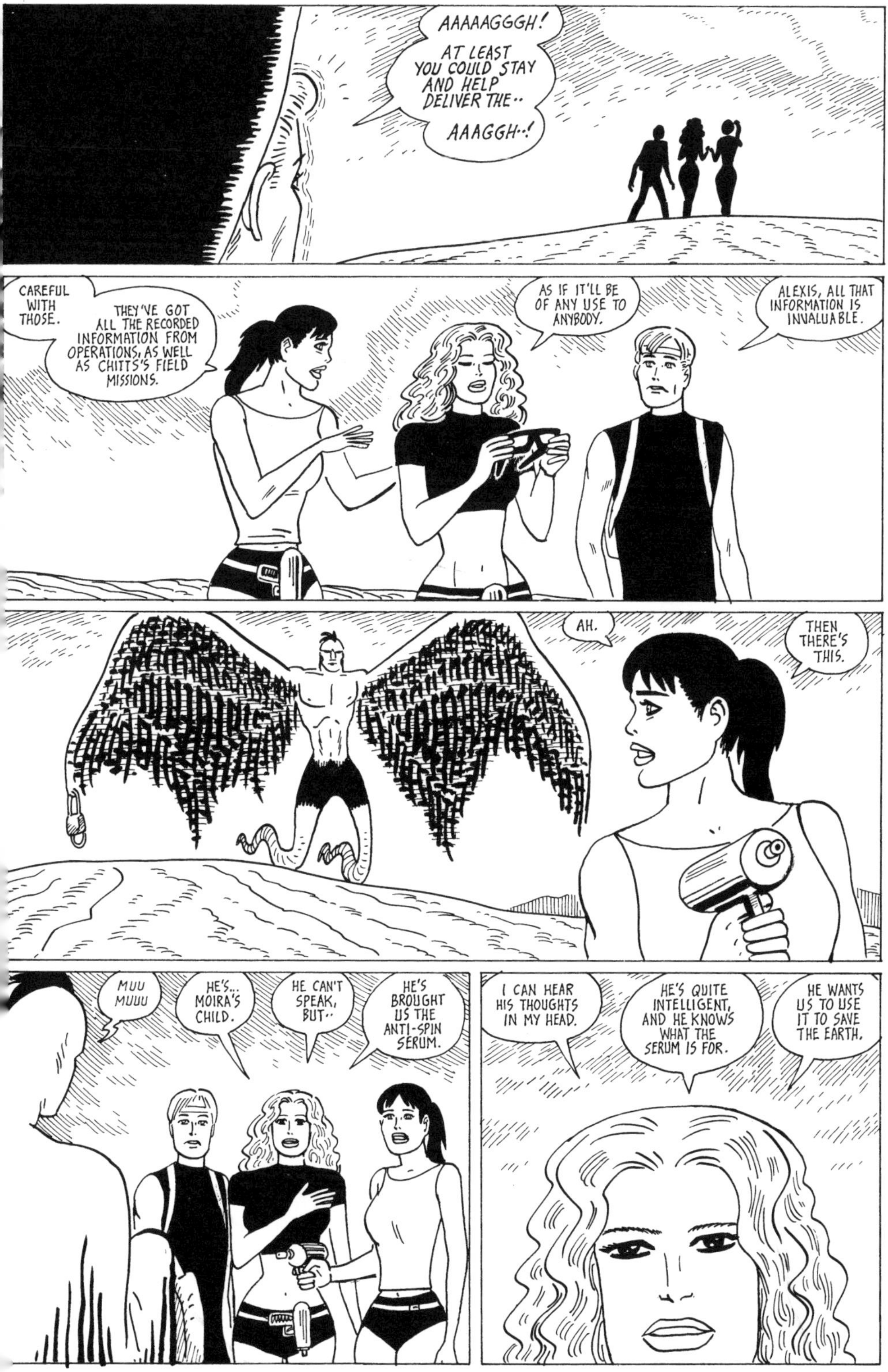
AAAAAGGGH!
AT LEAST YOU COULD STAY AND HELP DELIVER THE··
AAAGGH··!
CAREFUL WITH THOSE.
THEY'VE GOT ALL THE RECORDED INFORMATION FROM OPERATIONS, AS WELL AS CHITTS'S FIELD MISSIONS.
AS IF IT'LL BE OF ANY USE TO ANYBODY.
ALEXIS, ALL THAT INFORMATION IS INVALUABLE.
AH.
THEN THERE'S THIS.
MUU MUUU
HE'S... MOIRA'S CHILD.
HE CAN'T SPEAK, BUT··
HE'S BROUGHT US THE ANTI-SPIN SERUM.
I CAN HEAR HIS THOUGHTS IN MY HEAD.
HE'S QUITE INTELLIGENT, AND HE KNOWS WHAT THE SERUM IS FOR.
HE WANTS US TO USE IT TO SAVE THE EARTH.

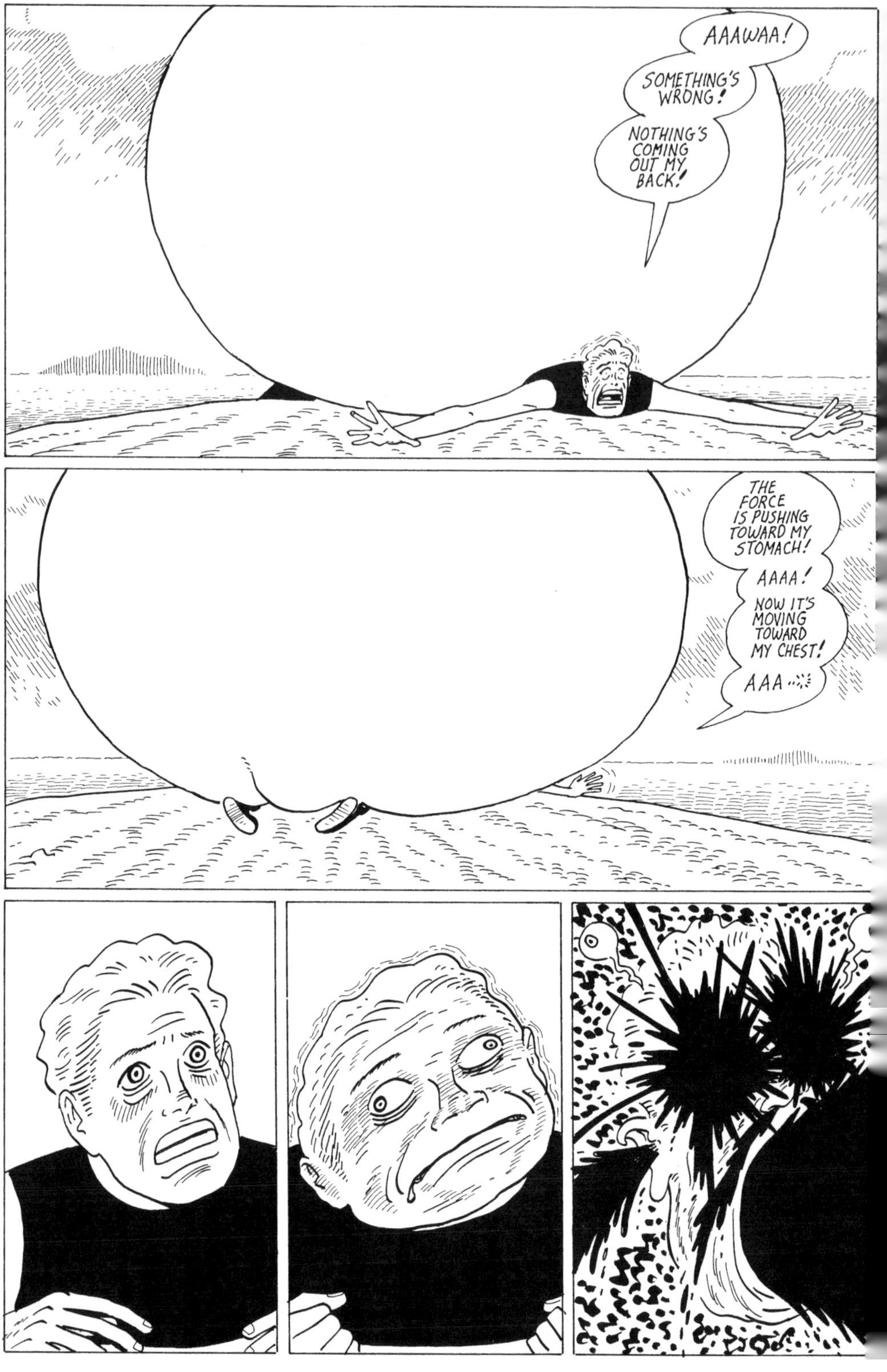
AAAWAA!
SOMETHING'S WRONG!
NOTHING'S COMING OUT MY BACK!
THE FORCE IS PUSHING TOWARD MY STOMACH!
AAAA!
NOW IT'S MOVING TOWARD MY CHEST!
AAA...

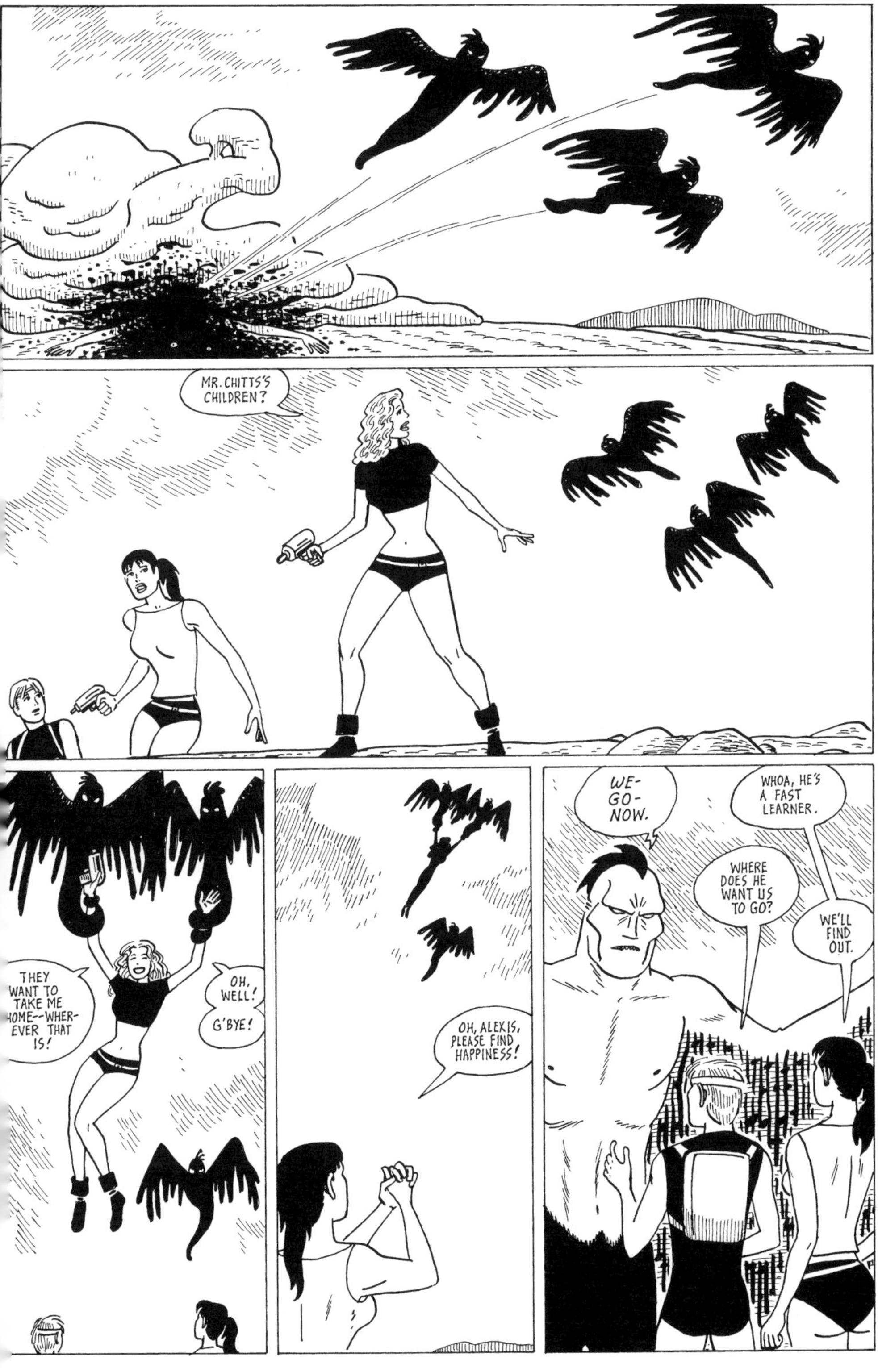
MR. CHITTS'S CHILDREN?
THEY WANT TO TAKE ME HOME--WHEREVER THAT IS!
OH, WELL!
G'BYE!
OH, ALEXIS, PLEASE FIND HAPPINESS!
WE- GO- NOW.
WHOA, HE'S A FAST LEARNER.
WHERE DOES HE WANT US TO GO?
WE'LL FIND OUT.

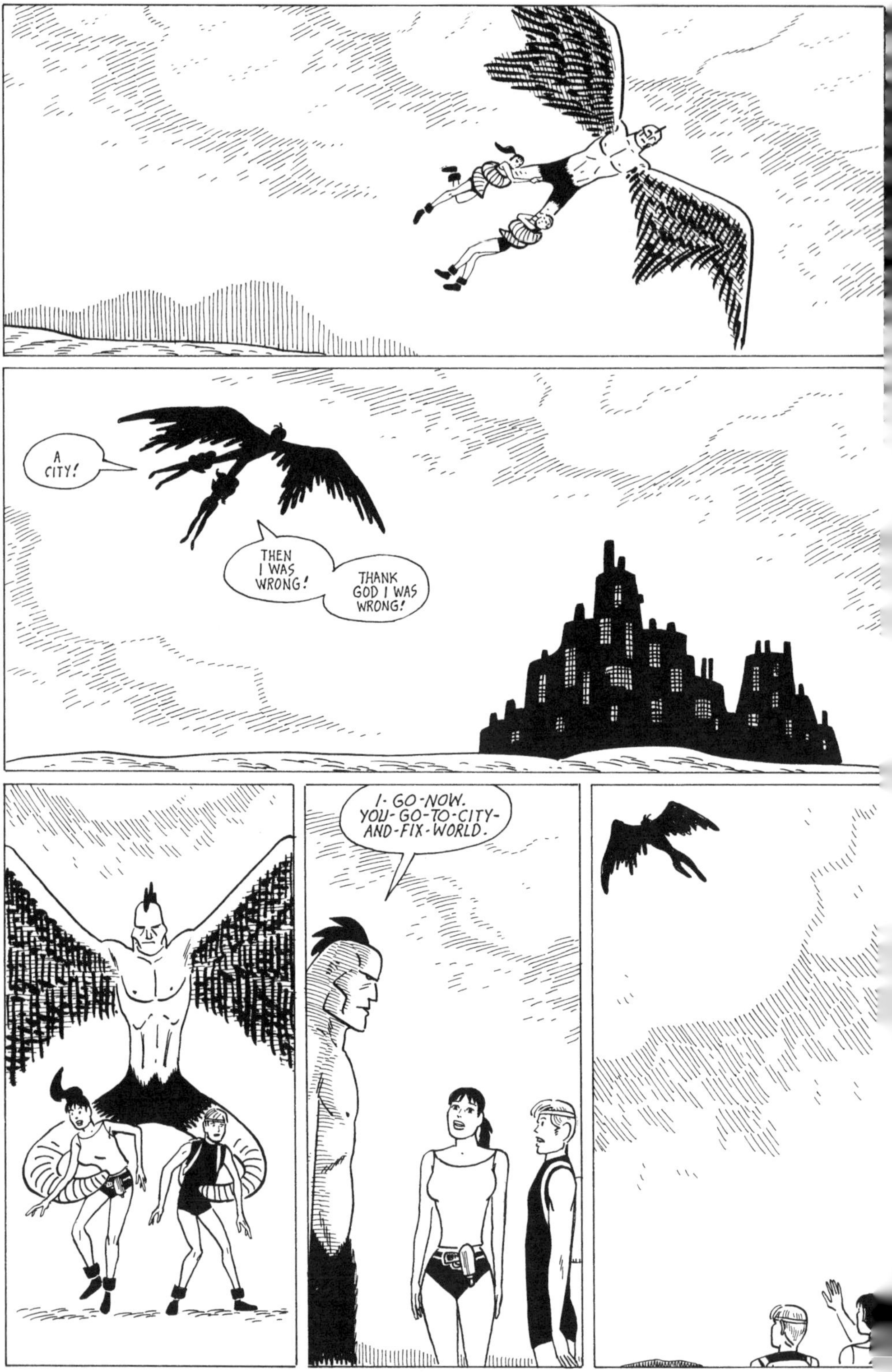
A CITY!
THEN I WAS WRONG!
THANK GOD I WAS WRONG!
I-GO-NOW. YOU-GO-TO-CITY-AND-FIX-WORLD.

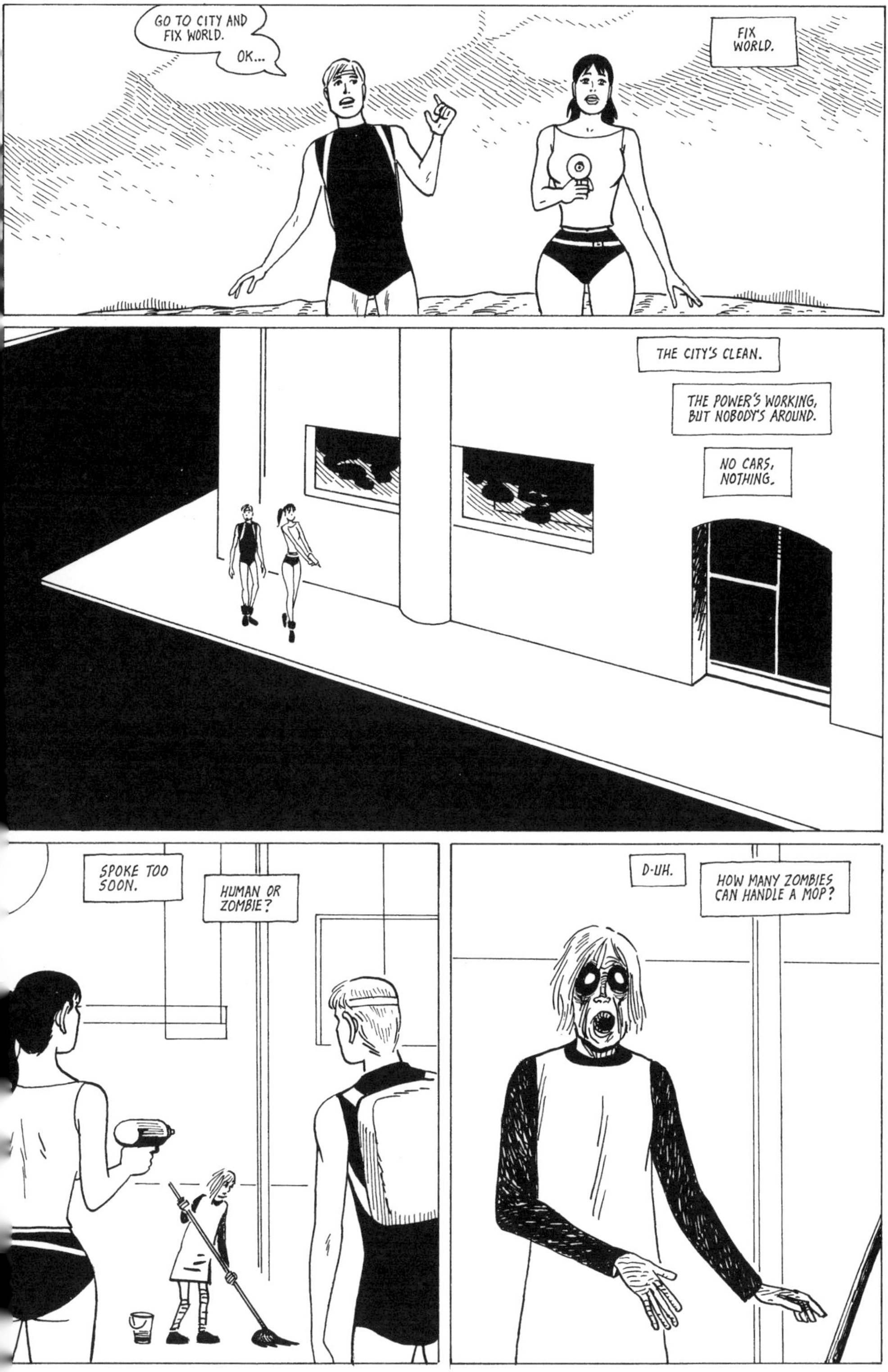
GO TO CITY AND FIX WORLD.
OK...
FIX WORLD.
THE CITY'S CLEAN.
THE POWER'S WORKING, BUT NOBODY'S AROUND.
NO CARS, NOTHING.
SPOKE TOO SOON.
HUMAN OR ZOMBIE?
D-UH.
HOW MANY ZOMBIES CAN HANDLE A MOP?

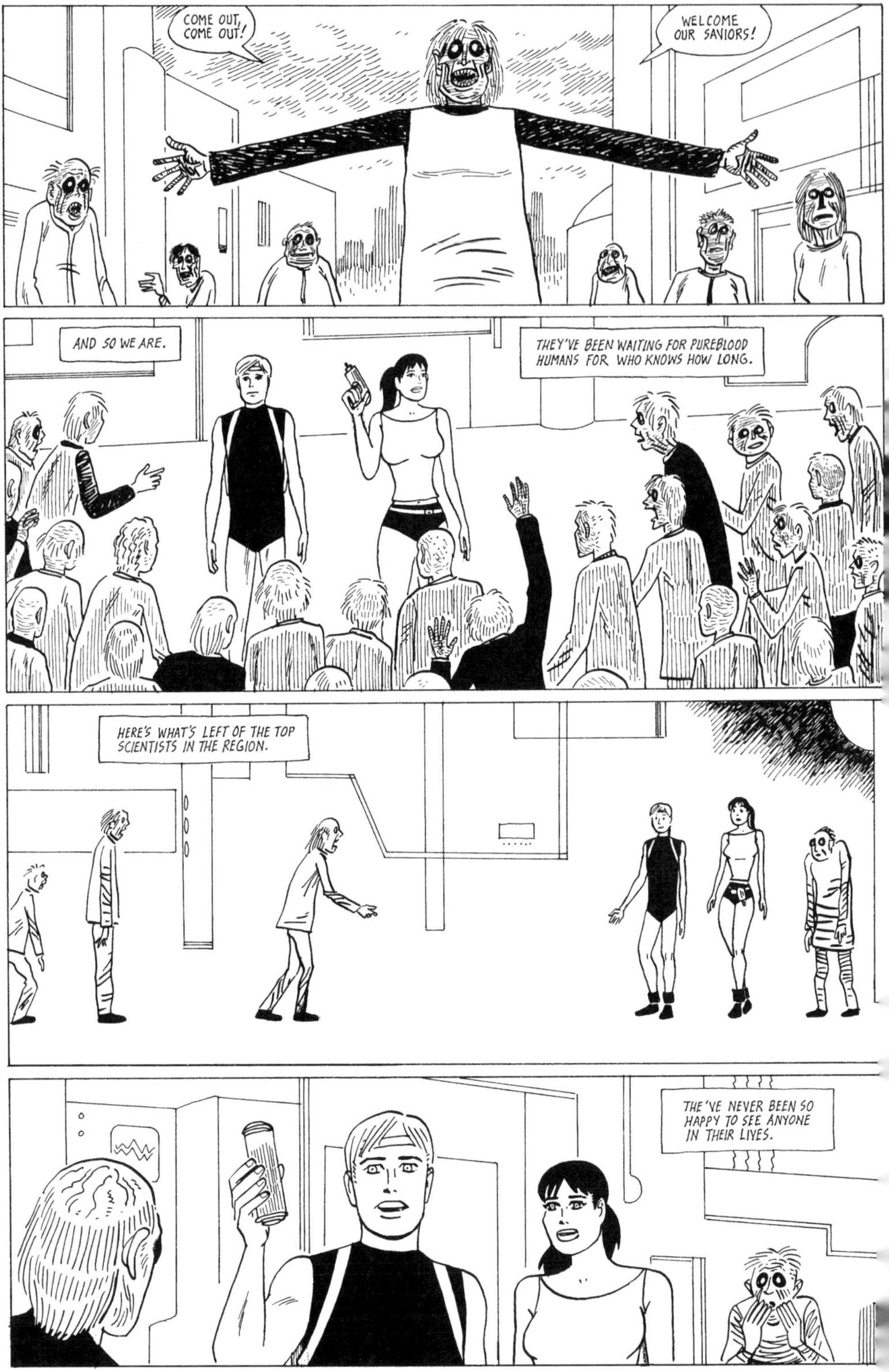
COME OUT, COME OUT!
WELCOME OUR SAVIORS!
AND SO WE ARE.
THEY'VE BEEN WAITING FOR PUREBLOOD HUMANS FOR WHO KNOWS HOW LONG.
HERE'S WHAT'S LEFT OF THE TOP SCIENTISTS IN THE REGION.
THE'VE NEVER BEEN SO HAPPY TO SEE ANYONE IN THEIR LIVES.

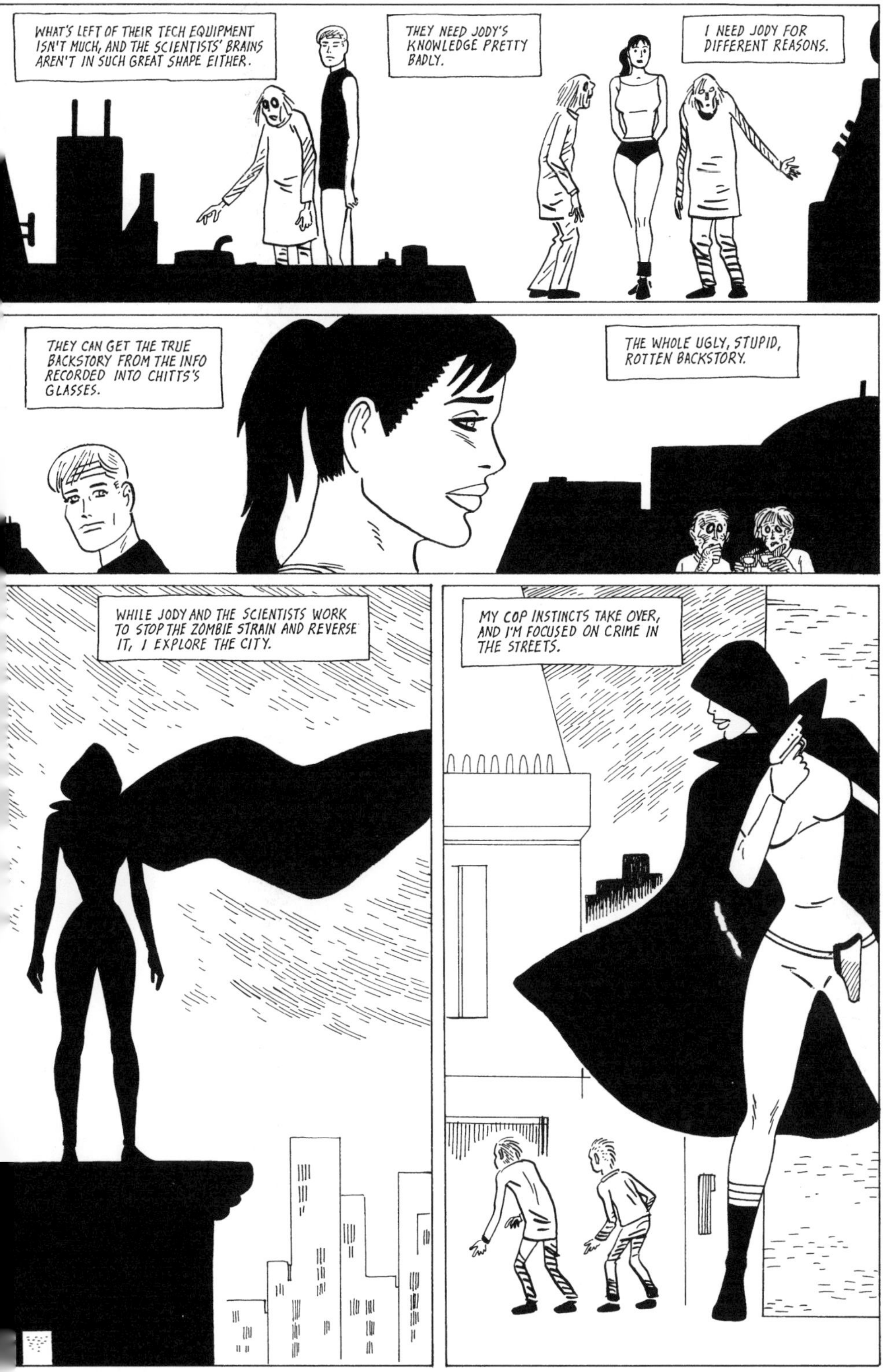
WHAT'S LEFT OF THEIR TECH EQUIPMENT ISN'T MUCH, AND THE SCIENTISTS' BRAINS AREN'T IN SUCH GREAT SHAPE EITHER.
THEY NEED JODY'S KNOWLEDGE PRETTY BADLY.
I NEED JODY FOR DIFFERENT REASONS.
THEY CAN GET THE TRUE BACKSTORY FROM THE INFO RECORDED INTO CHITTS'S GLASSES.
THE WHOLE UGLY, STUPID, ROTTEN BACKSTORY.
WHILE JODY AND THE SCIENTISTS WORK TO STOP THE ZOMBIE STRAIN AND REVERSE IT, I EXPLORE THE CITY.
MY COP INSTINCTS TAKE OVER, AND I'M FOCUSED ON CRIME IN THE STREETS.

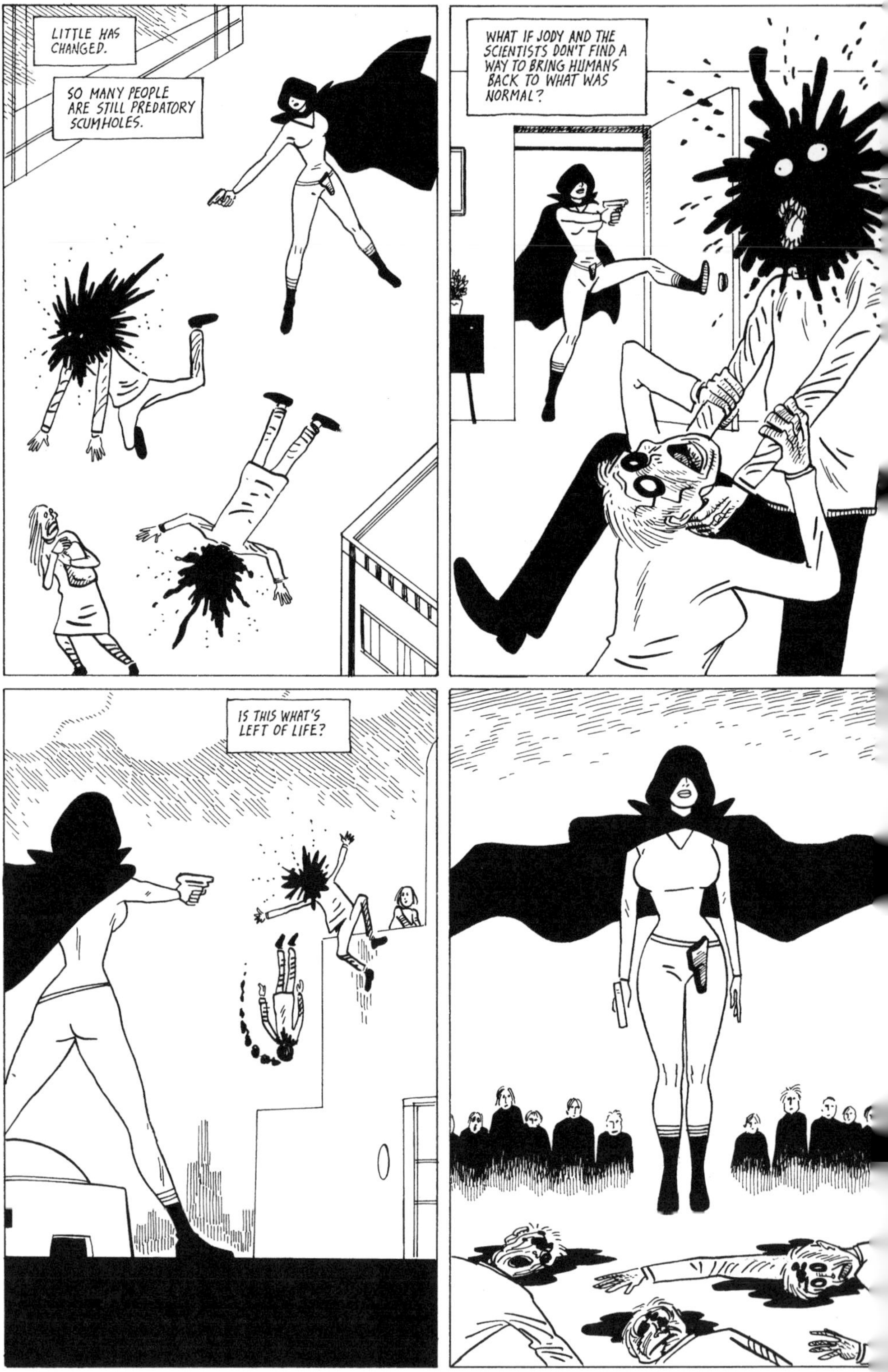
LITTLE HAS CHANGED.
SO MANY PEOPLE ARE STILL PREDATORY SCUMHOLES.
WHAT IF JODY AND THE SCIENTISTS DON'T FIND A WAY TO BRING HUMANS BACK TO WHAT WAS NORMAL?
IS THIS WHAT'S LEFT OF LIFE?

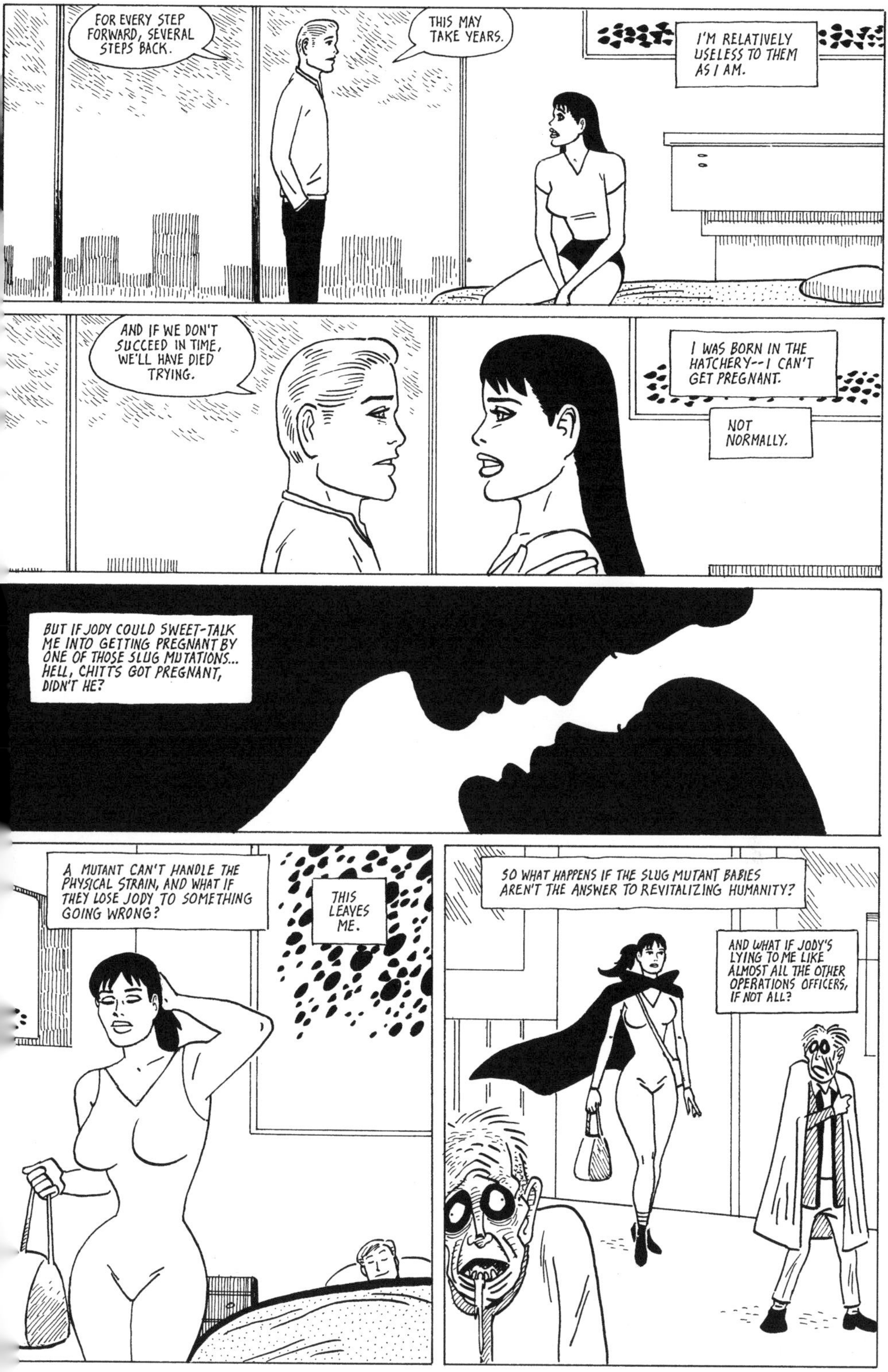
FOR EVERY STEP FORWARD, SEVERAL STEPS BACK.
THIS MAY TAKE YEARS.
I'M RELATIVELY USELESS TO THEM AS I AM.
AND IF WE DON'T SUCCEED IN TIME, WE'LL HAVE DIED TRYING.
I WAS BORN IN THE HATCHERY--I CAN'T GET PREGNANT.
NOT NORMALLY.
BUT IF JODY COULD SWEET-TALK ME INTO GETTING PREGNANT BY ONE OF THOSE SLUG MUTATIONS... HELL, CHITTS GOT PREGNANT, DIDN'T HE?
A MUTANT CAN'T HANDLE THE PHYSICAL STRAIN, AND WHAT IF THEY LOSE JODY TO SOMETHING GOING WRONG?
THIS LEAVES ME.
SO WHAT HAPPENS IF THE SLUG MUTANT BABIES AREN'T THE ANSWER TO REVITALIZING HUMANITY?
AND WHAT IF JODY'S LYING TO ME LIKE ALMOST ALL THE OTHER OPERATIONS OFFICERS, IF NOT ALL?

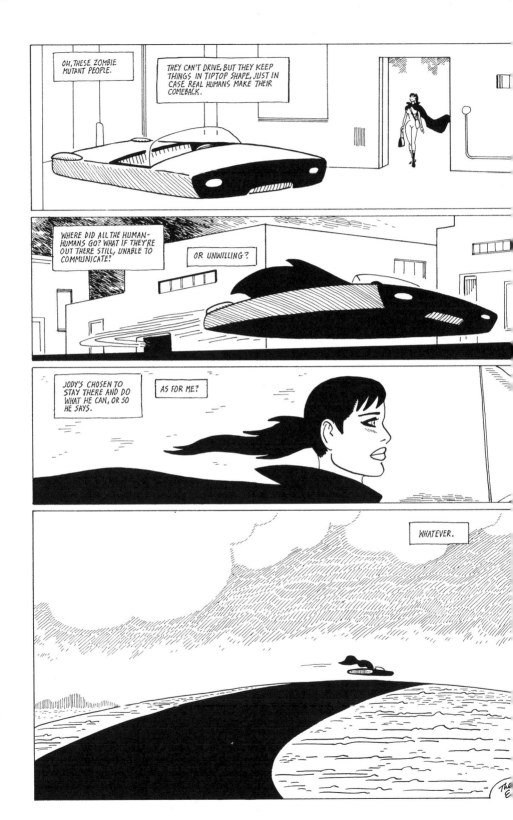

OH, THESE ZOMBIE MUTANT PEOPLE.

THEY CAN'T DRIVE, BUT THEY KEEP THINGS IN TIPTOP SHAPE, JUST IN CASE REAL HUMANS MAKE THEIR COMEBACK.

WHERE DID ALL THE HUMAN-HUMANS GO? WHAT IF THEY'RE OUT THERE STILL, UNABLE TO COMMUNICATE?

OR UNWILLING?

JODY'S CHOSEN TO STAY THERE AND DO WHAT HE CAN, OR SO HE SAYS.

AS FOR ME?

WHATEVER.

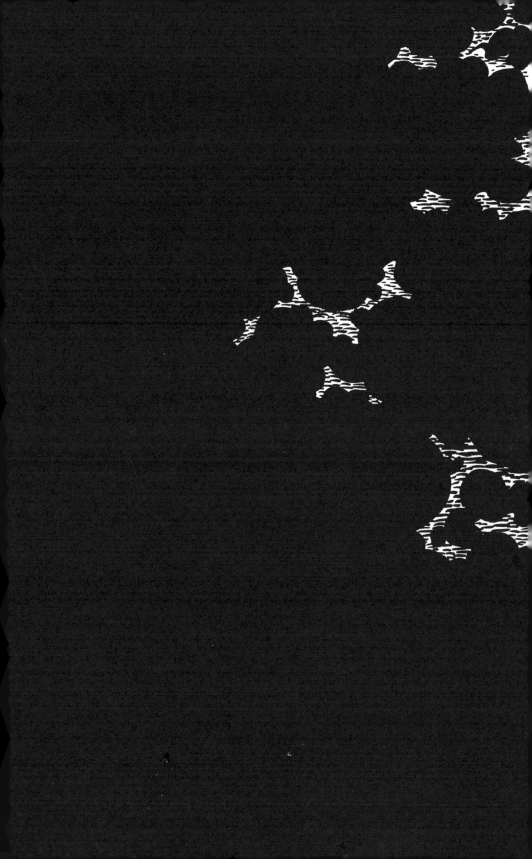

FATIMA COVER GALLERY

by Gilbert Hernandez

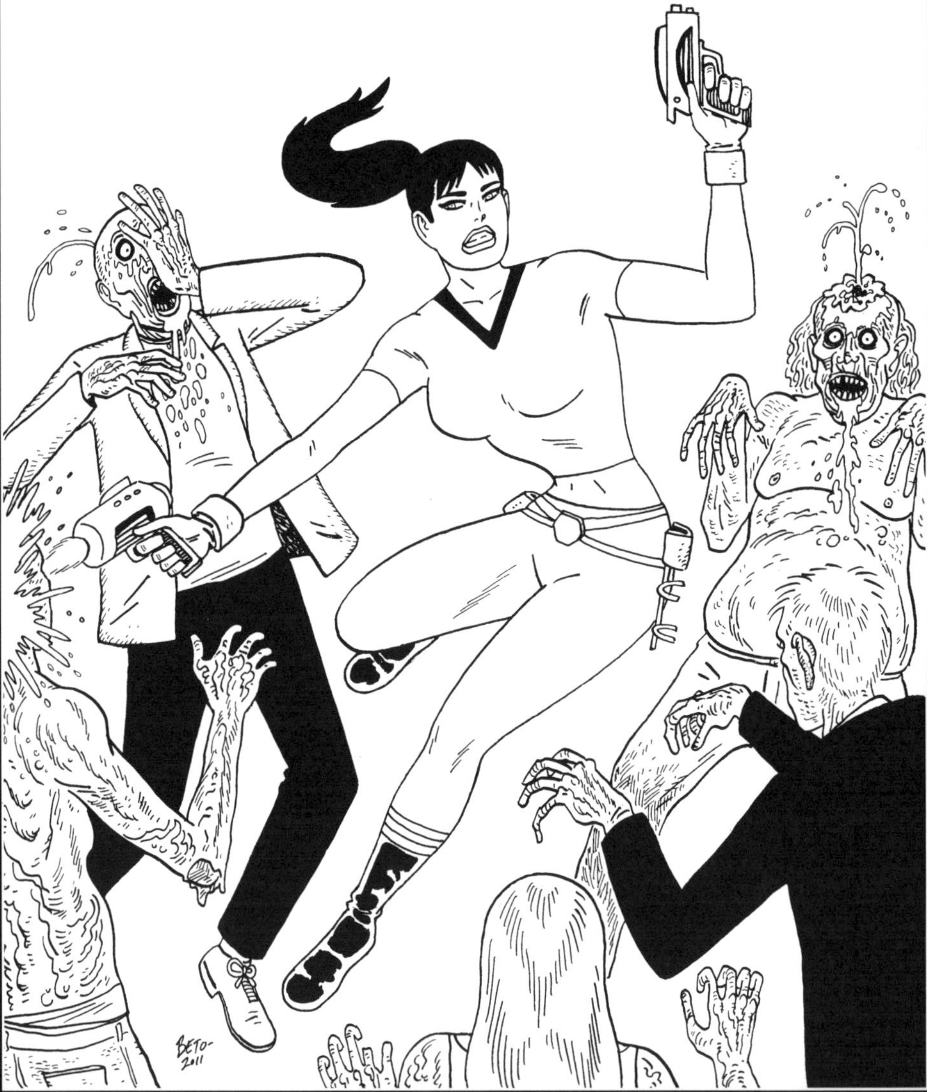
BETO-
2011

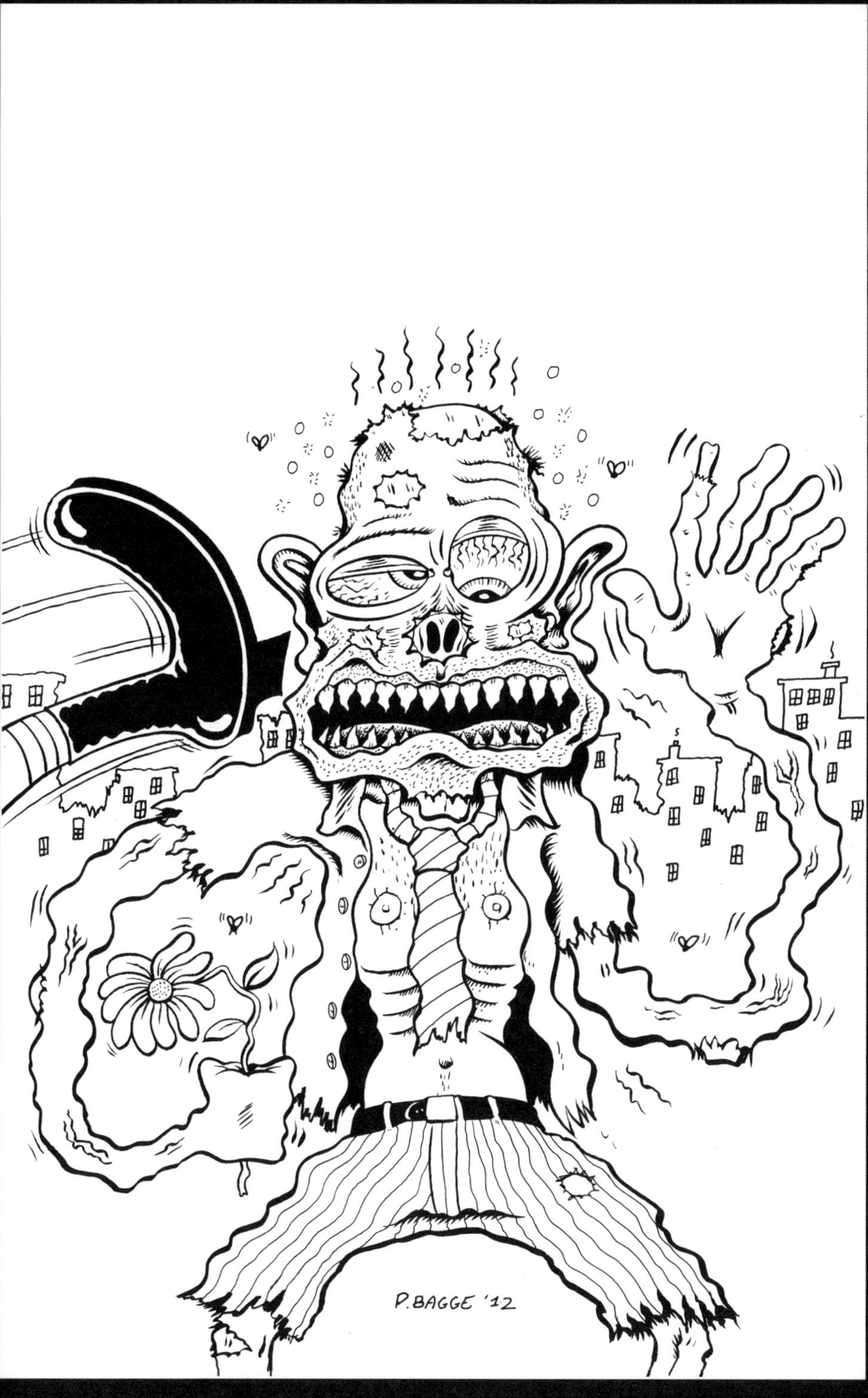
P. BAGGE '12

Alternate cover by Peter Bagge

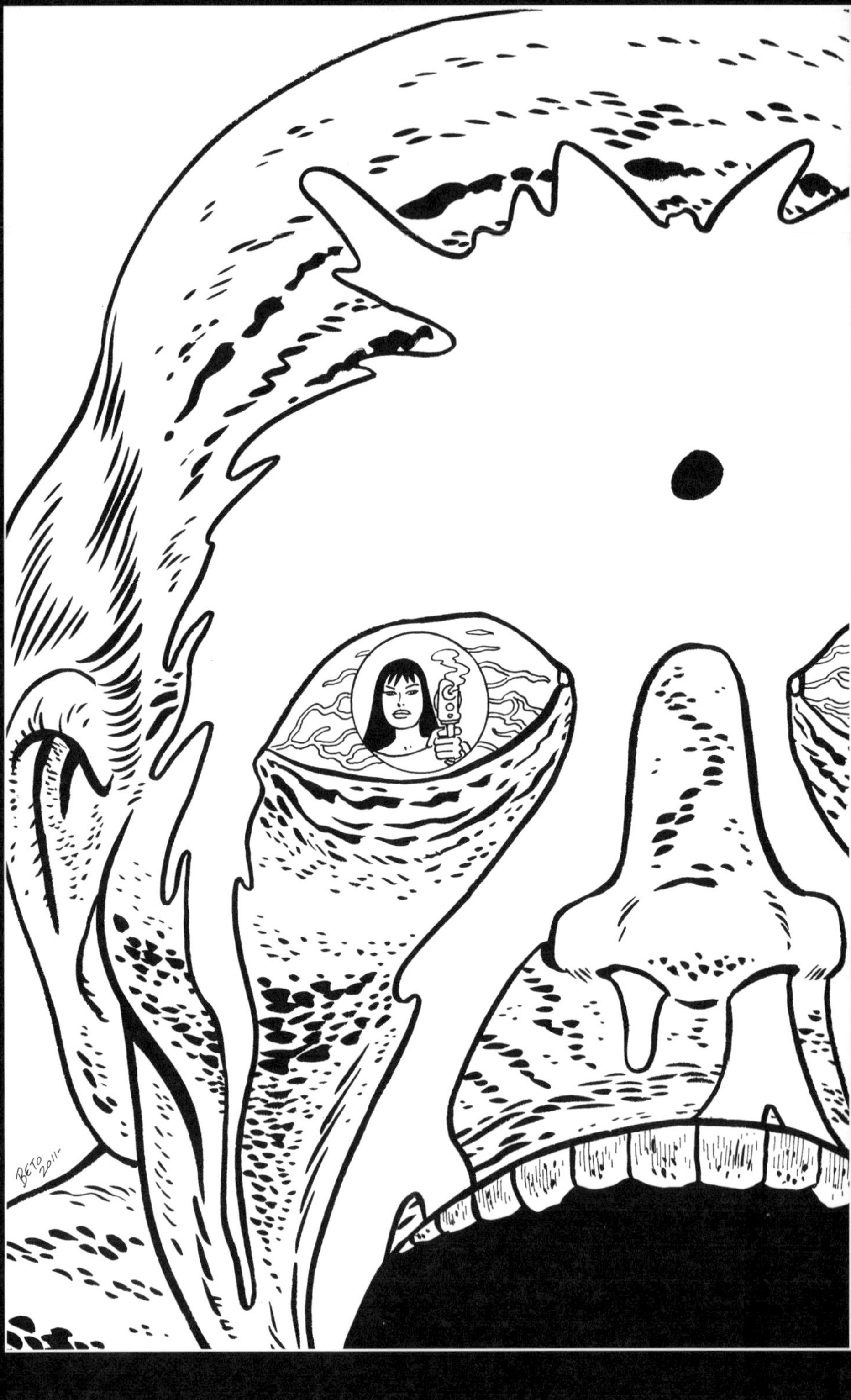
BETO 2011

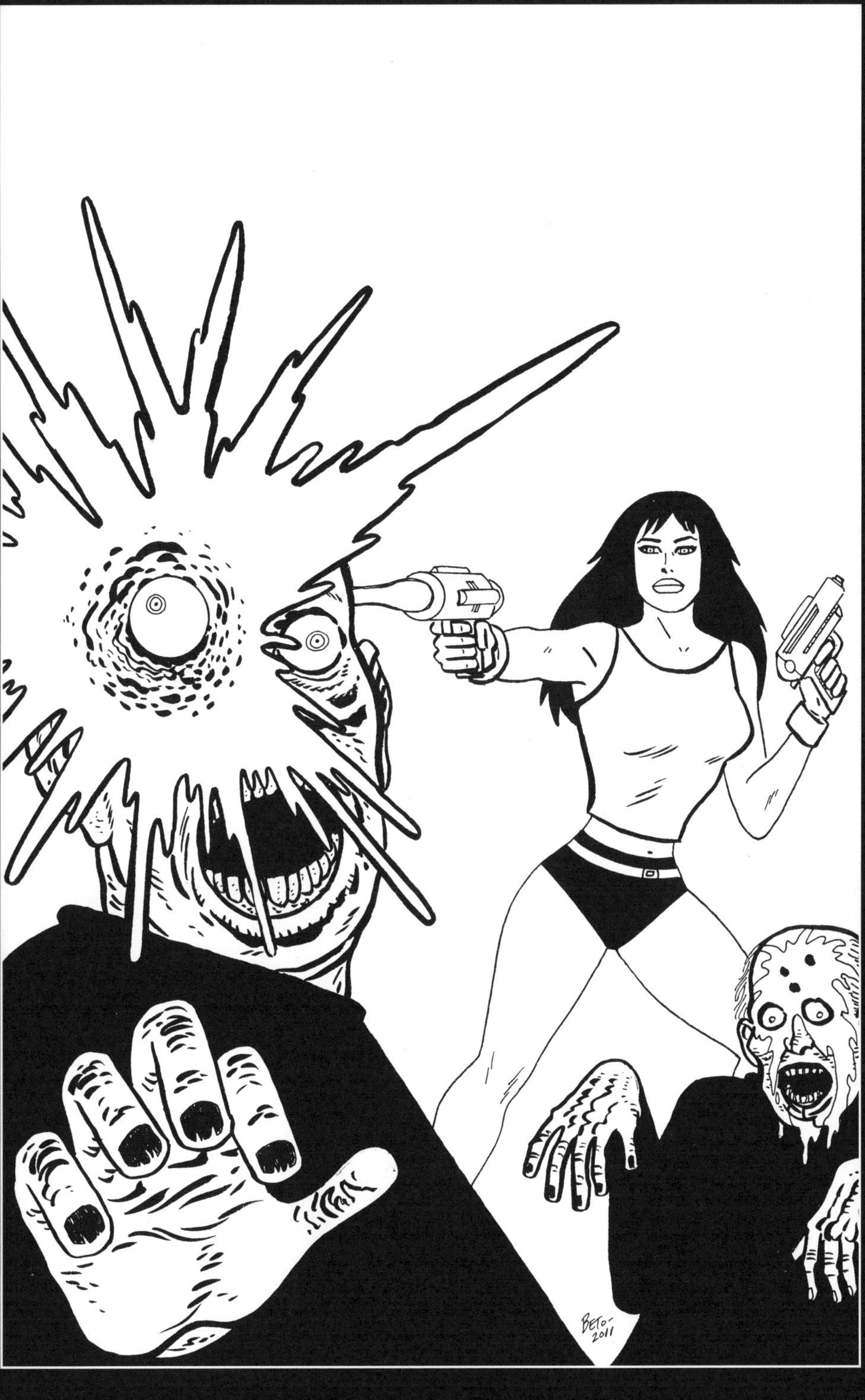
BETO-
2011

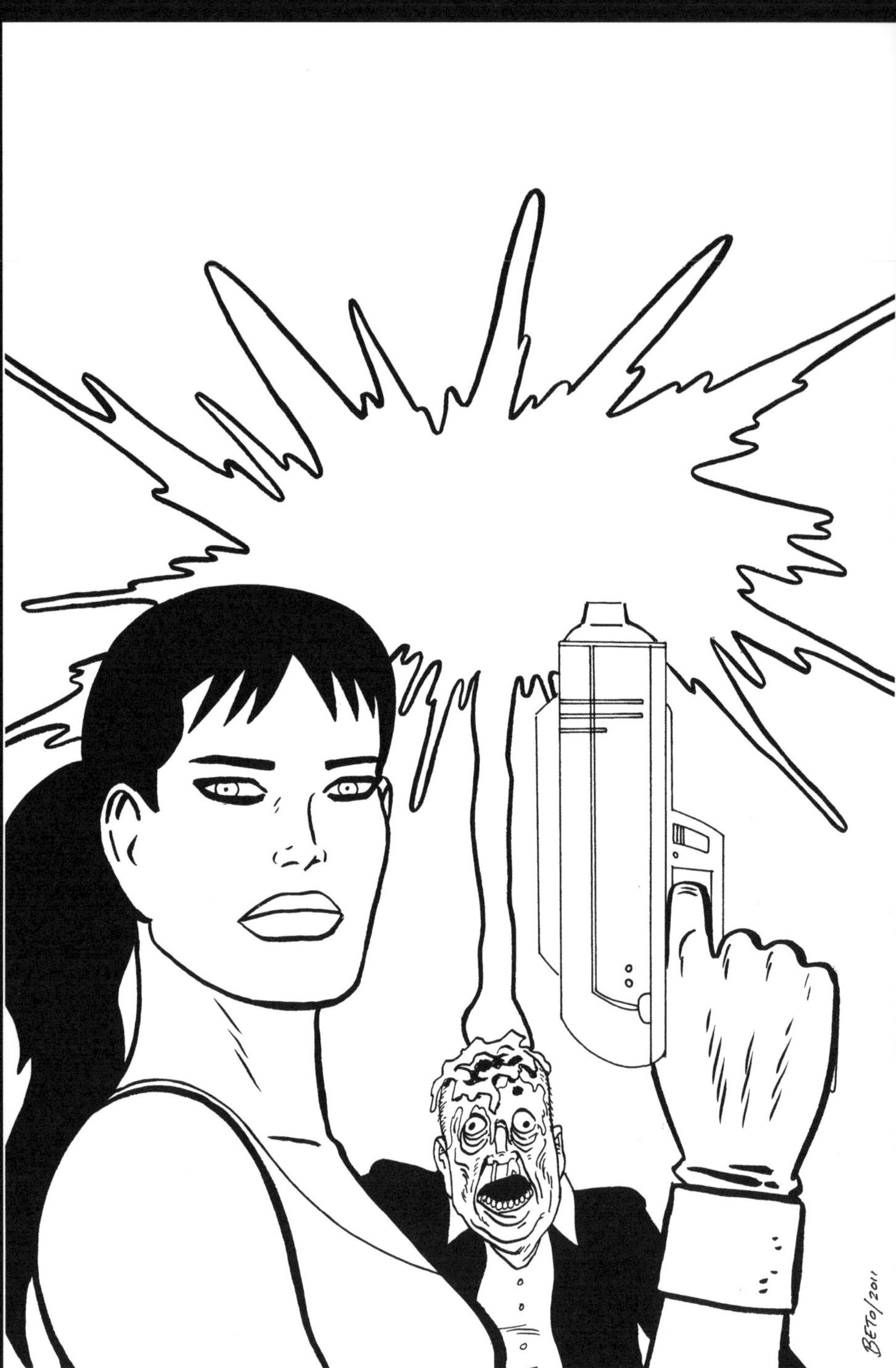
BETO/2011

FATIMA SKETCHBOOK

Some of the early designs and sketches for this series.

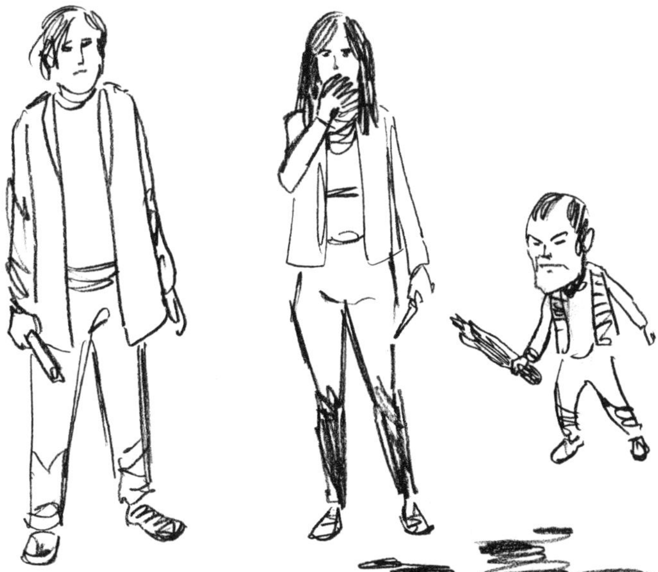

"A lot of times the crazy stuff I do comes from my unconscious."
—Gilbert Hernandez

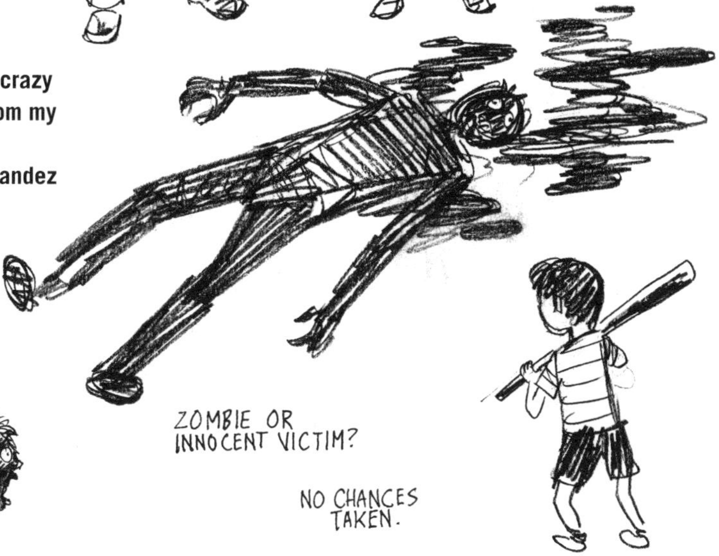
ZOMBIE OR
INNOCENT VICTIM?
NO CHANCES
TAKEN.

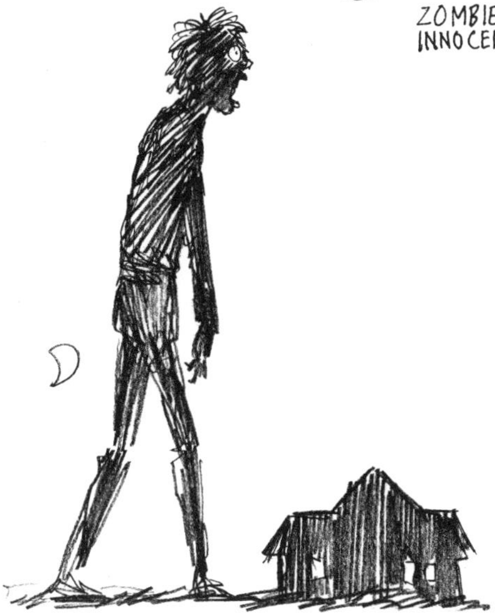
ZOMBIE ZEN

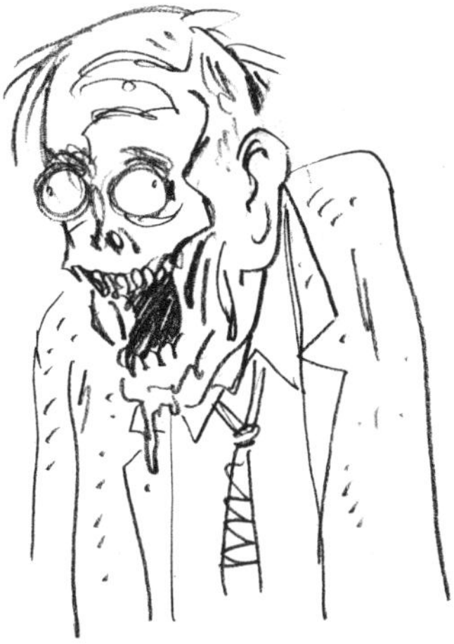

Cover color guide for this volume, reproduced here in black-and-white.

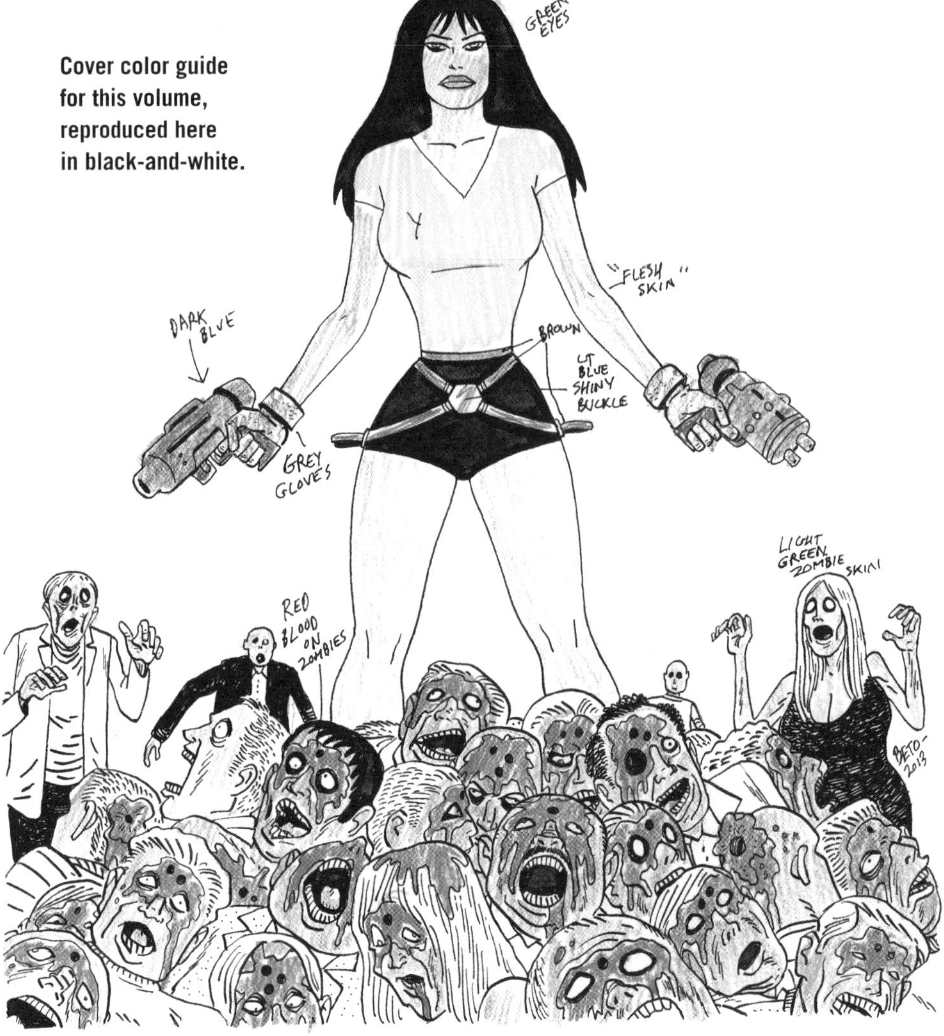
GREEN EYES
"FLESH SKIN"
DARK BLUE
BROWN
LT BLUE SHINY BUCKLE
GREY GLOVES
LIGHT GREEN ZOMBIE SKIN
RED BLOOD ON ZOMBIES
BETO-2013

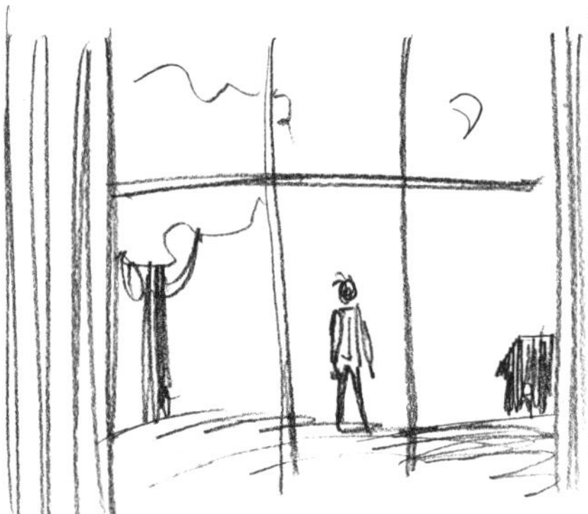

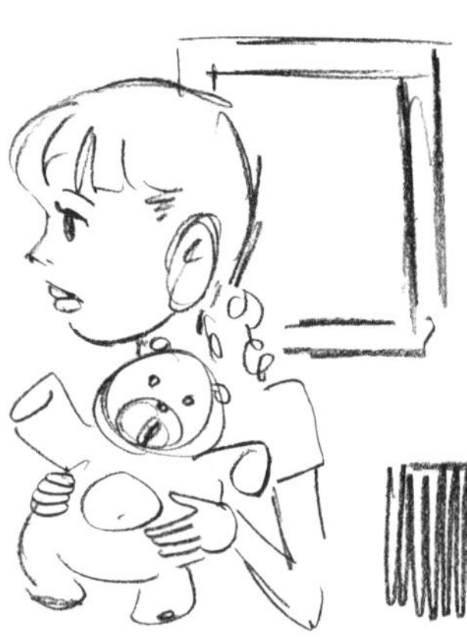

DADDY'S HOME

Pending reader interest, Fatima's story may not be done, as these four layout pages reveal What Happens Next . . .

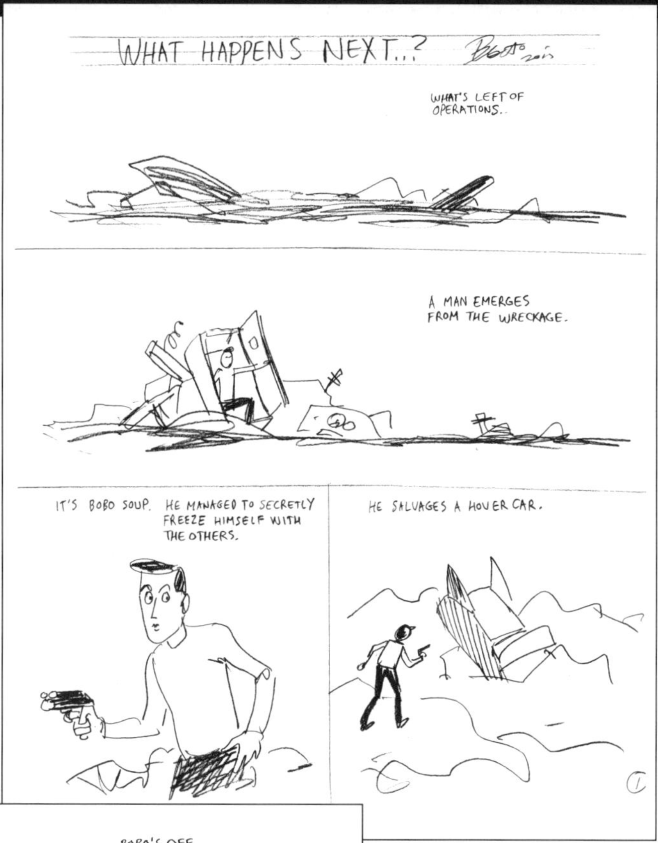

WHAT HAPPENS NEXT...?
WHAT'S LEFT OF OPERATIONS..
A MAN EMERGES FROM THE WRECKAGE.
IT'S BOBO SOUP. HE MANAGED TO SECRETLY FREEZE HIMSELF WITH THE OTHERS.
HE SALVAGES A HOVER CAR.
1

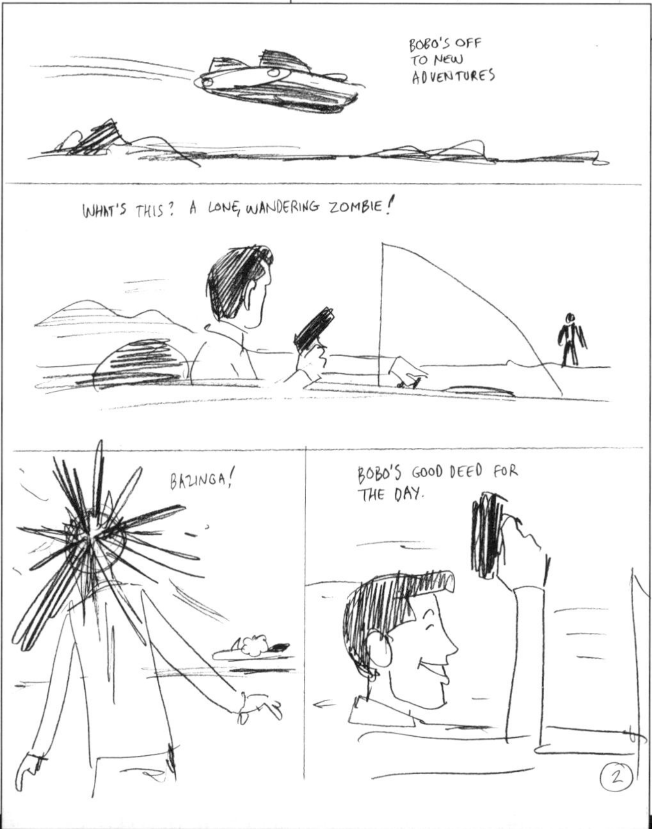

BOBO'S OFF TO NEW ADVENTURES
WHAT'S THIS? A LONE, WANDERING ZOMBIE!
BAZINGA!
BOBO'S GOOD DEED FOR THE DAY.
2

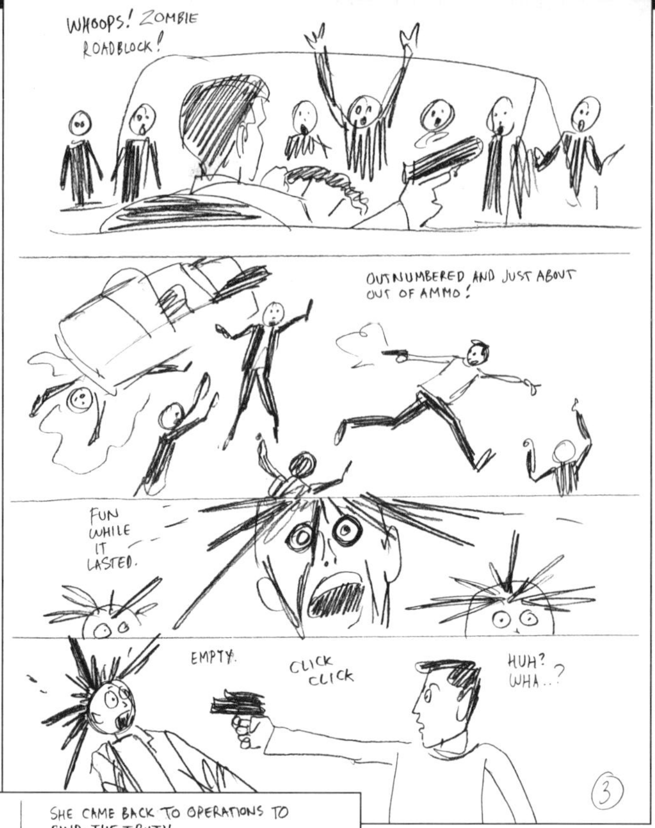
WHOOPS! ZOMBIE ROADBLOCK!
OUTNUMBERED AND JUST ABOUT OUT OF AMMO!
FUN WHILE IT LASTED.
EMPTY.
CLICK CLICK
HUH? WHA..?
3

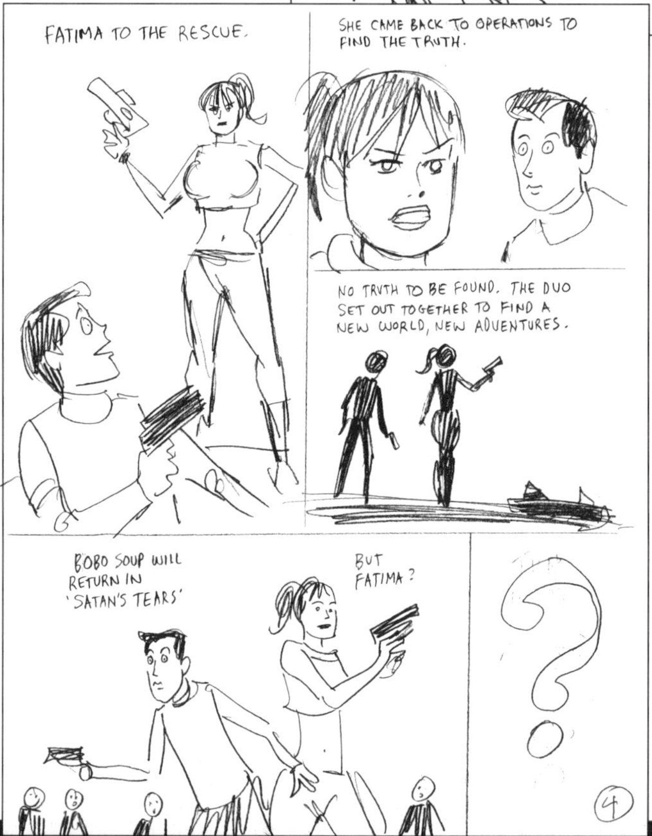
FATIMA TO THE RESCUE.
SHE CAME BACK TO OPERATIONS TO FIND THE TRUTH.
NO TRUTH TO BE FOUND. THE DUO SET OUT TOGETHER TO FIND A NEW WORLD, NEW ADVENTURES.
BOBO SOUP WILL RETURN IN 'SATAN'S TEARS'
BUT FATIMA?
?
4

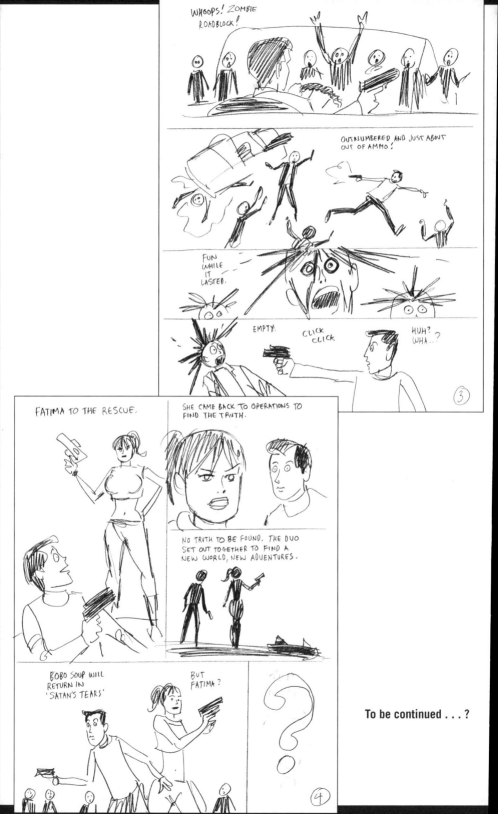

To be continued . . . ?

Gilbert "Beto" Hernandez was born and raised in Oxnard, California, and now lives in Nevada with his wife, Carol, and their daughter, Natalia. He grew up with his five brothers and one sister in a household where an interest in comic books and drawing was a family tradition. Early influences on his art include Jack Kirby, Steve Ditko, Hank Ketcham, and the artists of the Archie Comics line. Later, Gilbert would add underground comix and rock music—and still later, punk rock—to this formative mix.

In 1981, with his brothers Jaime and Mario, Gilbert self-published the first issue of their now legendary, groundbreaking comic *Love and Rockets*. After Los Bros. sent a copy to *The Comics Journal*, Fantagraphics Books began publishing the series in 1982. It quickly garnered a wider audience, as well as much critical acclaim, and went on to be recognized as a seminal work in the history of comics. Among Gilbert's many contributions to the title is his long-running masterpiece of magical realism, collected as *Palomar*.

Love and Rockets has continued in one form or another for over thirty years, while Gilbert has also produced a variety of original graphic novels and miniseries, including *Girl Crazy*, *Luba*, *Citizen Rex* (with brother Mario), and *Marble Season*, among many others.

The numerous accolades Gilbert has received for his work include a Kirby Award, an Inkpot Award, several Harvey Awards, a 2009 United States Artists Fellowship Award for Literature, and the 2013 PEN Center USA's Graphic Literature Award for Outstanding Body of Work,

GRAPHIC NOVELS BY GILBERT HERNANDEZ

available from Dark Horse Books®

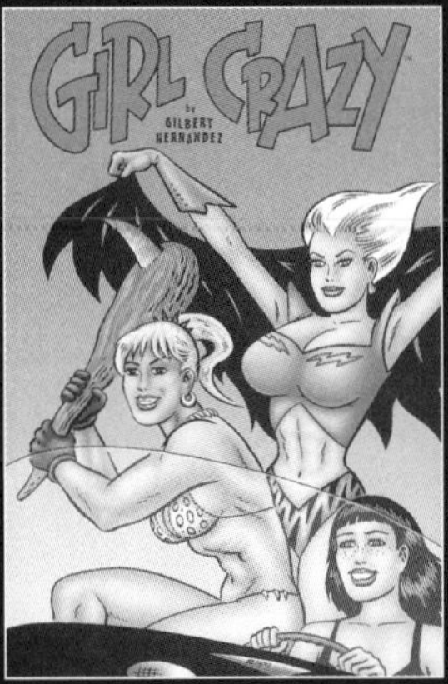
GIRL CRAZY
by GILBERT HERNANDEZ

ISBN 978-1-56971-264-1 $9.95

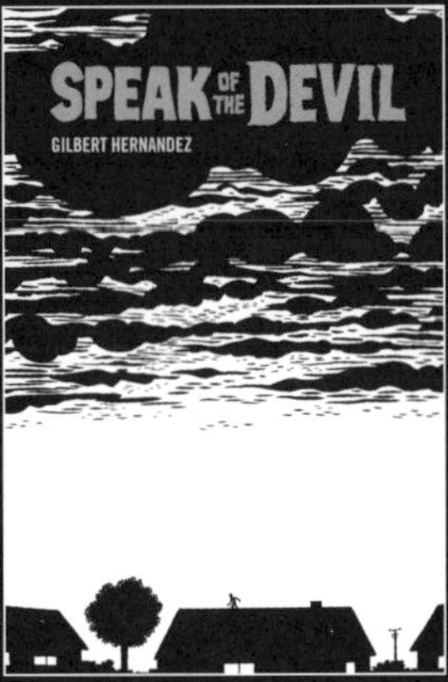
SPEAK OF THE DEVIL
GILBERT HERNANDEZ

ISBN 978-1-59582-193-5 $19.95

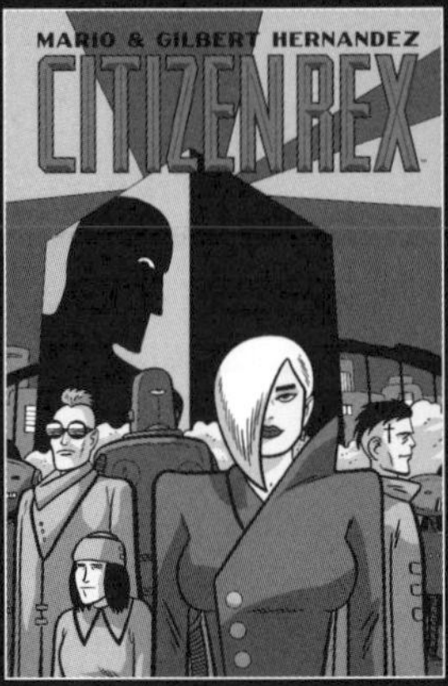
MARIO & GILBERT HERNANDEZ
CITIZEN REX

Written by Mario Hernandez
ISBN 978-1-59582-556-8 $19.99

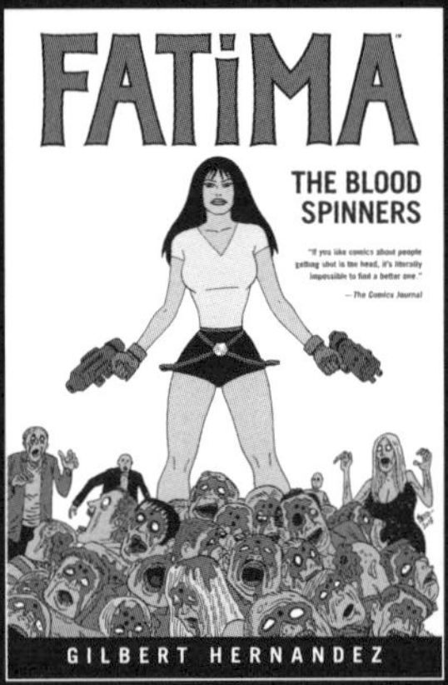
FATIMA
THE BLOOD SPINNERS
GILBERT HERNANDEZ

ISBN 978-1-61655-340-1 $19.99

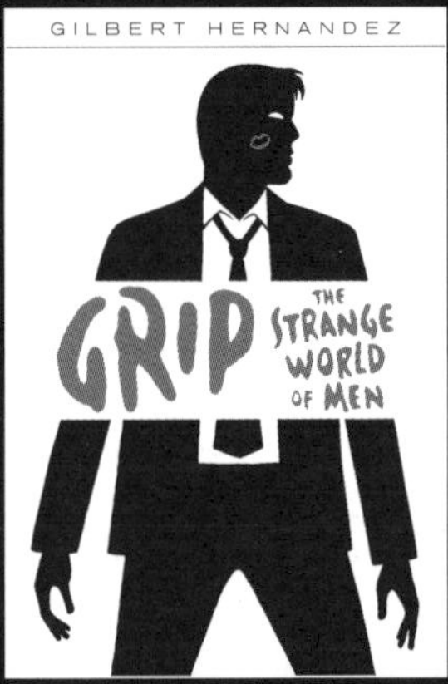
GILBERT HERNANDEZ
GRIP
THE STRANGE WORLD OF MEN

Coming in July 2014 $19.99

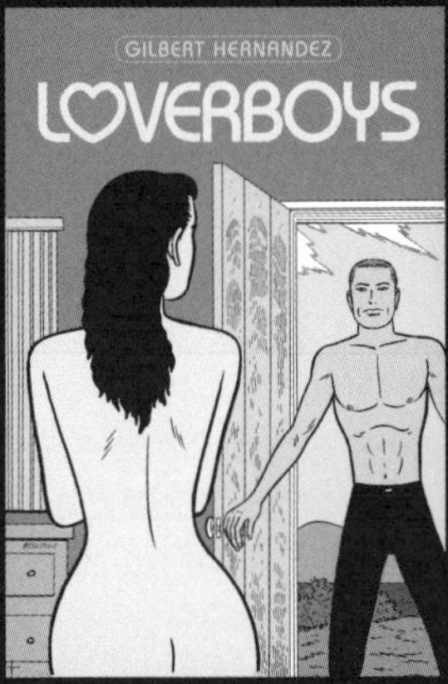
GILBERT HERNANDEZ
LOVERBOYS

Coming in October 2014 $19.99

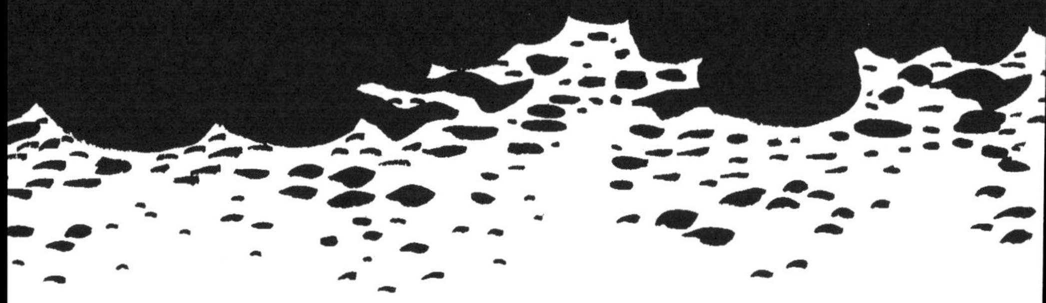

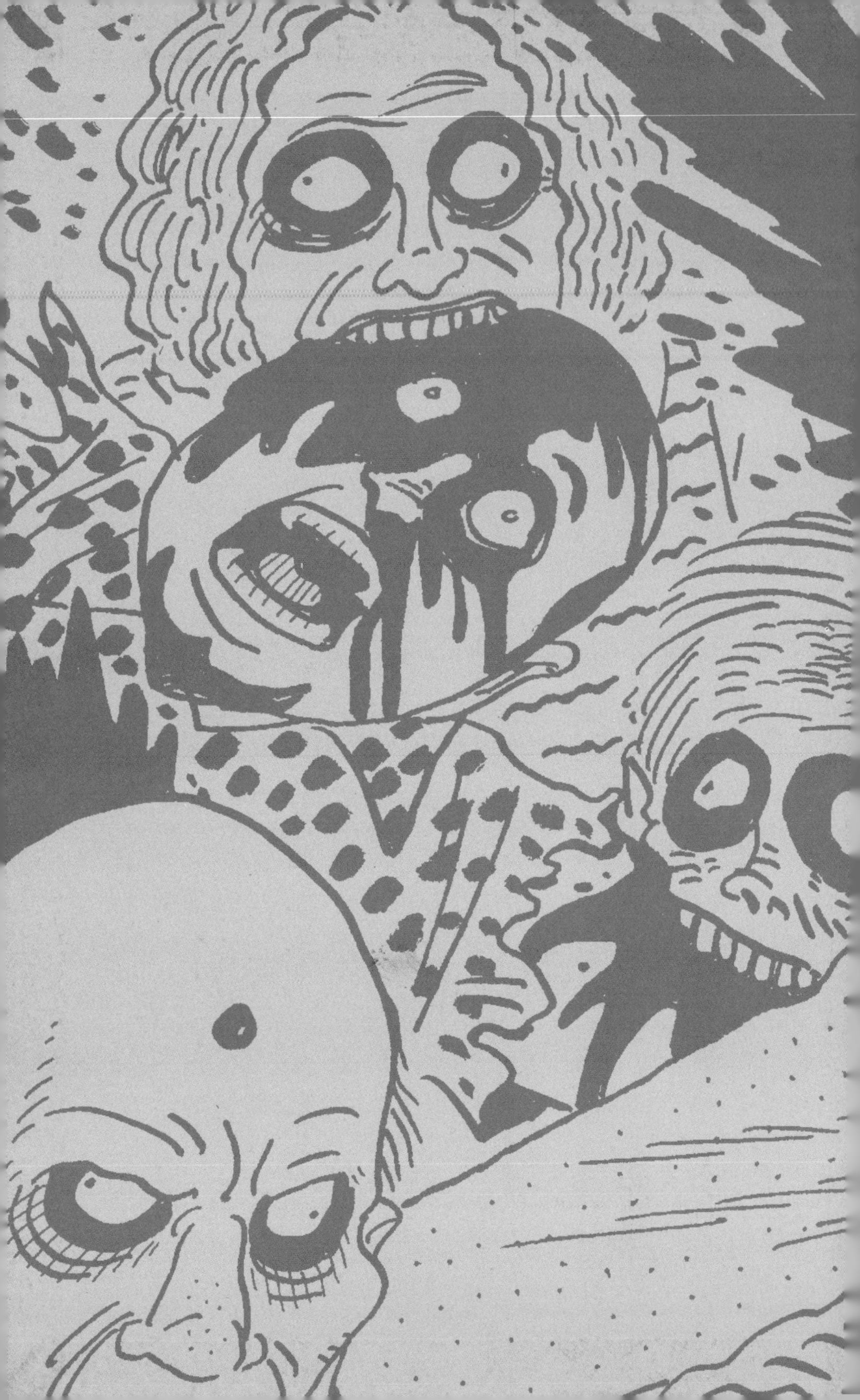